Mel Bay Presents

50 Tunes for Mandolin

Traditional, Old Time, Bluegrass & Celtic Solos

Volume 1

By Mark Geslison

Additional titles in this series:
99938BCD 50 Tunes for Fiddle • 99939BCD 50 Tunes for Banjo
99940BCD 50 Tunes for Bass • 99941BCD 50 Tunes for Guitar

CD contents

CD 1	CD 2	CD 3
1. Angus Campbell	1. Forked Deer	1. Red-haired Boy
2. Arkansas Traveler	2. Gardenia Waltz	2. Red Wing
3. Aura Lee	3. Grandfather's Clock	3. Sailor's Hornpipe/College Hornpipe
4. The Battle Cry of Freedom	4. Green Willis	4. Saint Anne's Reel
5. Beaumont Rag	5. Indian's Farewell Waltz	5. Sally Ann
6. Billy in the Lowground	6. Irish Washerwoman	6. Sally Goodin'
7. Blackberry Blossom	7. La Bastringue	7. Sally Johnson
8. Bonaparte's Retreat	8. Leather Britches	8. Salt Creek
9. Carthage Waltz	9. Liberty	9. Soldier's Joy
10. Cherokee Shuffle	10. Martin's Waltz	10. Swallowtail Jig
11. Cluck Old Hen	11. Mason's Apron	11. Temperance Reel
12. Cotton-eyed Joe	12. Mississippi Hornpipe	12. Tom and Jerry
13. Cotton Patch Rag	13. Mississippi Sawyer	13. Turkey in the Straw
14. Cripple Creek	14. Old Dan Tucker	14. Uncle Joe
15. Devil's Dream	15. Old Joe Clark	15. Under the Double Eagle
16. Down Yonder	16. President Garfield's Hornpipe	16. Whiskey Before Breakfast
17. Eighth of January	17. Pretty Peg	

1 2 3 4 5 6 7 8 9 0

© 2004 BY MEL BAY PUBLICATIONS, INC., PACIFIC, MO 63069.
ALL RIGHTS RESERVED. INTERNATIONAL COPYRIGHT SECURED. B.M.I. MADE AND PRINTED IN U.S.A.
No part of this publication may be reproduced in whole or in part, or stored in a retrieval system, or transmitted in any form
or by any means, electronic, mechanical, photocopy, recording, or otherwise, without written permission of the publisher.

Visit us on the Web at www.melbay.com — E-mail us at email@melbay.com

Table of Contents

About the Author	3
Foreword	4
Preface	5
Angus Campbell	7
Arkansas Traveler	8
Aura Lee	12
The Battle Cry of Freedom	14
Beaumont Rag	18
Billy in the Lowground	20
Blackberry Blossom	22
Bonaparte's Retreat	24
Carthage Waltz	28
Cherokee Shuffle	32
Cluck Old Hen	36
Cotton Eyed Joe	38
Cotton Patch Rag	42
Cripple Creek	44
Devil's Dream	48
Down Yonder	56
Eighth of January	58
Forked Deer	62
Gardenia Waltz	64
Grandfather's Clock	66
Green Willis	68
Indian's Farewell Waltz	69
Irish Washerwoman	70
La Bastringue	74
Leather Britches	78
Liberty	80
Martin's Waltz	84
Mason's Apron	88
Mississippi Hornpipe	90
Mississippi Sawyer	92
Old Dan Tucker	94
Old Joe Clark	96
President Garfield's Hornpipe	98
Pretty Peg	102
Red-haired Boy	104
Red Wing	106
Sailor's Hornpipe	109
College Hornpipe*	110
Saint Anne's Reel	112
Sally Ann	114
Sally Goodin'	120
Sally Johnson	122
Salt Creek	124
Soldier's Joy	128
Swallowtail Jig	132
Temperance Reel	134
Tom and Jerry	137
Turkey in the Straw	140
Uncle Joe	145
Under the Double Eagle	146
Whiskey Before Breakfast	150

*This tune is out of alphabetical order because it is the second tune of a medley.

Appendix	155

About the Author

Mark Geslison, the author and coordinator of this series, is a multi-instrumentalist who plays the mandolin, guitar, bass, percussion, banjo and dulcimer. He has performed traditional music for most of his life and has been an instrumental champion several times since the mid-1980s including: Western Regional Guitar Champion 1988, 1989; Western Regional Mandolin Champion 1988, 1989; Utah State Guitar Champion 1988, 1989, 1992; Utah State Mandolin Champion 1988, 1989, 1992, 1994 and 2002; and Utah State Banjo Champion 2001 (4-string).

Mark has been the director of the Folk Music Ensemble program at Brigham Young University since 1992. The Folk Music Ensemble program includes performing groups that focus on Bluegrass, Appalachian, Early American and Celtic music styles. His students perform approximately one hundred times per year in all parts of the world including the South Pacific, Asia, Europe and North and South America.

Mark is also the founder and director of the Institute of American Music (IAM). IAM is a non-profit, private school of music designed to teach traditional music in an ensemble setting to young people and families. This series originated within IAM where Mark noticed a need for ensemble arrangements.

Visit... **www.instituteofamericanmusic.com**

for additional products that will assist you with your study of the 50 Tunes series including:

• Curriculum books with scales, exercises, technique and graduation check-off.
• Rhythm tracks (guitar chords and metronome) for practicing all of the 50 Tunes at varying metronome speeds.
• Bluegrass and Celtic songbooks.
• Information on creating and maintaining ensembles, family bands and "communities" of music.
• Free downloads of mp3 audio tracks and pdf sheet music.

Foreword

This book contains just over 50 tunes from the United States, the British Isles and Canada. The companion CD set includes the recorded version these 50 tunes. The appendix at the back of this book contains instructions on tablature reading, picking exercises, chord diagrams and chord charts. These components are designed to help you learn the enclosed 50 tunes and to promote proficiency at performing these tunes. If you are a beginner it is recommended that you master the exercises and chords in the appendix before moving on to the tunes. If you consider yourself an intermediate to advanced player you should make sure that you understand the components of the appendix.

50 Tunes Volume 1 is not meant to be the ultimate beginning-to-advanced tool. Rather, it is intended to give a broad tune (melody) base to students and instructors alike. It is also intended to show creative arrangements of basic melodies with stylistic nuances designed to develop left and right hand skills (compare *Sally Ann 2*, *Martin's Waltz* and *Cotton Eyed Joe 2*). The tunes on the CD are intended to be instructional and enjoyable at the same time.

Preface

Arrangements

Cherokee Shuffle 1 (melody/harmony), *Cluck Old Hen, Cotton Eyed Joe 1, Cotton Eyed Joe 2, La Bastringue 1, President Garfield's Hornpipe 1, President Garfield's Hornpipe 2* and *Sally Ann 1* (melody/harmony) were arranged by Erik Neilson. All other parts in this book are arrangements by Mark Geslison. All 50 tunes are in the public domain or otherwise under licence.

Tune Order

Since this book is part of a series for various instruments, it is nearly impossible to arrange the tunes in a "beginning-to-advanced" order that fits every instrument. Therefore, the tunes have been placed in alphabetical order. In general, the tunes are organized so that "1" represents the simplest variation while "2" (and above) represents more difficult variations. In other words, *Mississippi Sawyer 1* is simpler than *Mississippi Sawyer 2*. You might want to start with *Old Joe Clark 1* or *Cripple Creek 1* and ultimately finish with *President Garfield's Hornpipe 2* or *Billy in the Lowground* (harmony). The end goal should be to use these tunes as stepping-stones toward a tremendous and enjoyable future in music.

Chords

Most chord sequences in this book are set according to tradition. However, the author has taken the liberty to set some chord sequences according to how they sound best to the ear of the author. Students and teachers are welcome to change chord sequences according to their preference. The chord diagrams found in the appendix are intended to be very extensive, but not all-inclusive. Pay close attention to how chords are constructed and you will gain the ability to create chords not found in the appendix.

Picking, Metronome Use and CD Tempo

It is vital to pick correctly in order to develop the speed necessary to play the enclosed tunes at CD speed (see appendix). Ultimately, you will want to gain the ability to play most of these tunes at 120-160 beats per minute (metronome speed). A very good way to gain speed in picking these tunes is to practice with the metronome at slower speeds always boosting your speed as you perfect the tune at each increase.

In order to keep the recorded tunes fast enough to be enjoyable for listening and yet slow enough for study, most of the tunes were recorded at 100 beats per minute. The following tunes were recorded at the listed tempo:

Tune	Tempo
Aura Lee	80
Battle Cry of Freedom	76
Carthage Waltz	108
Cluck Old Hen	120
Cotton-eyed Joe	120
Down Yonder	120
Gardenia Waltz	112
Indian's Farewell Waltz	112
Irish Washerwoman	100-120
La Bastringue	120
Martin's Waltz	112
Red Wing	120
Swallowtail Jig	100-120
Turkey in the Straw	120

Special Thanks

I am grateful to Erik Neilson for adding his professionalism to this project. Erik helped in the arranging (see above) and proofreading of many of these tunes. Erik's sincere and thoughtful suggestions have improved this series tremendously.

-Mark Geslison

Angus Campbell

Mandolin

Scottish

Disc 1
Track 1

Disc 1
Track 2

Arkansas Traveler

Mandolin 1*

North American

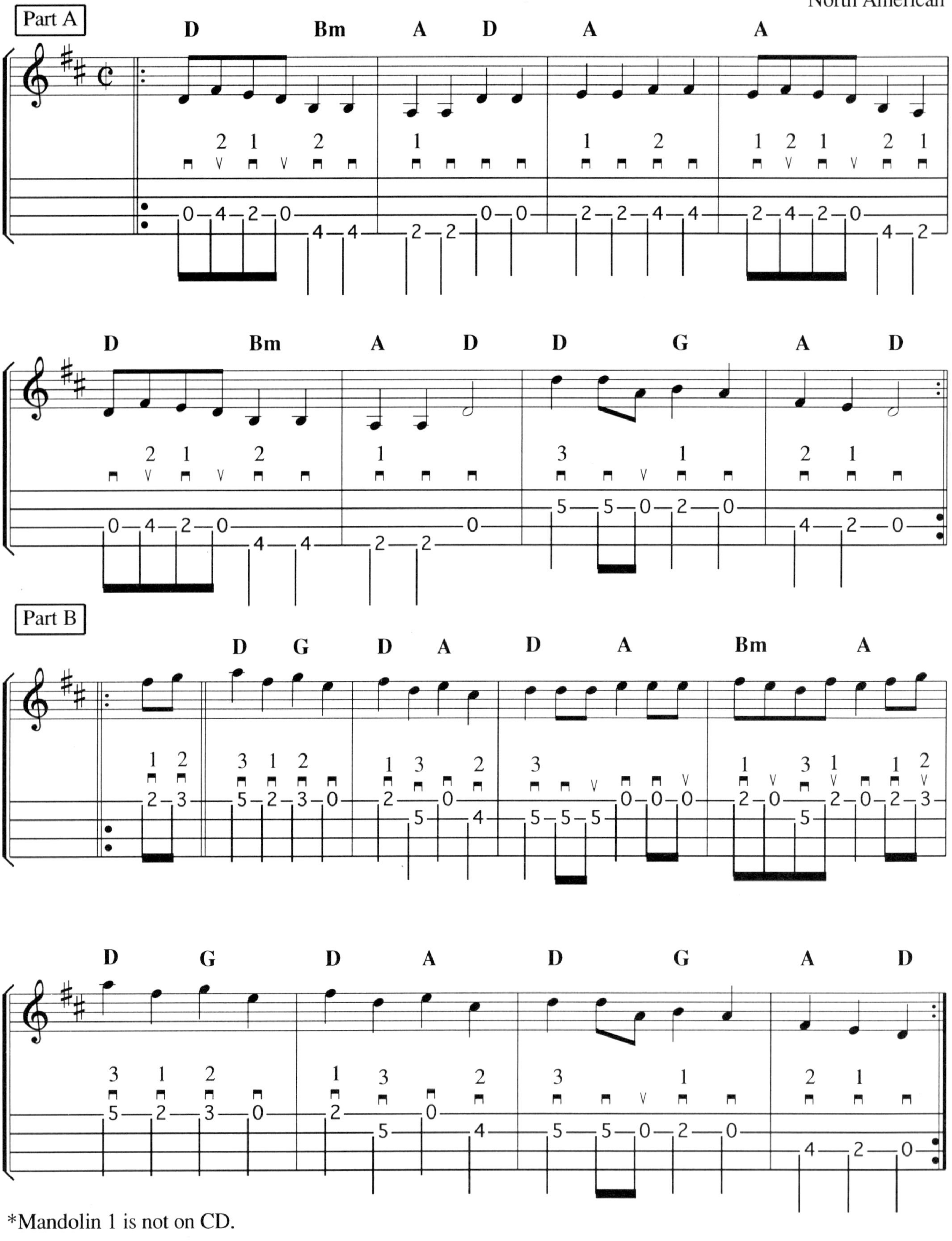

*Mandolin 1 is not on CD.

Arkansas Traveler

Mandolin 2 (melody)

Arkansas Traveler

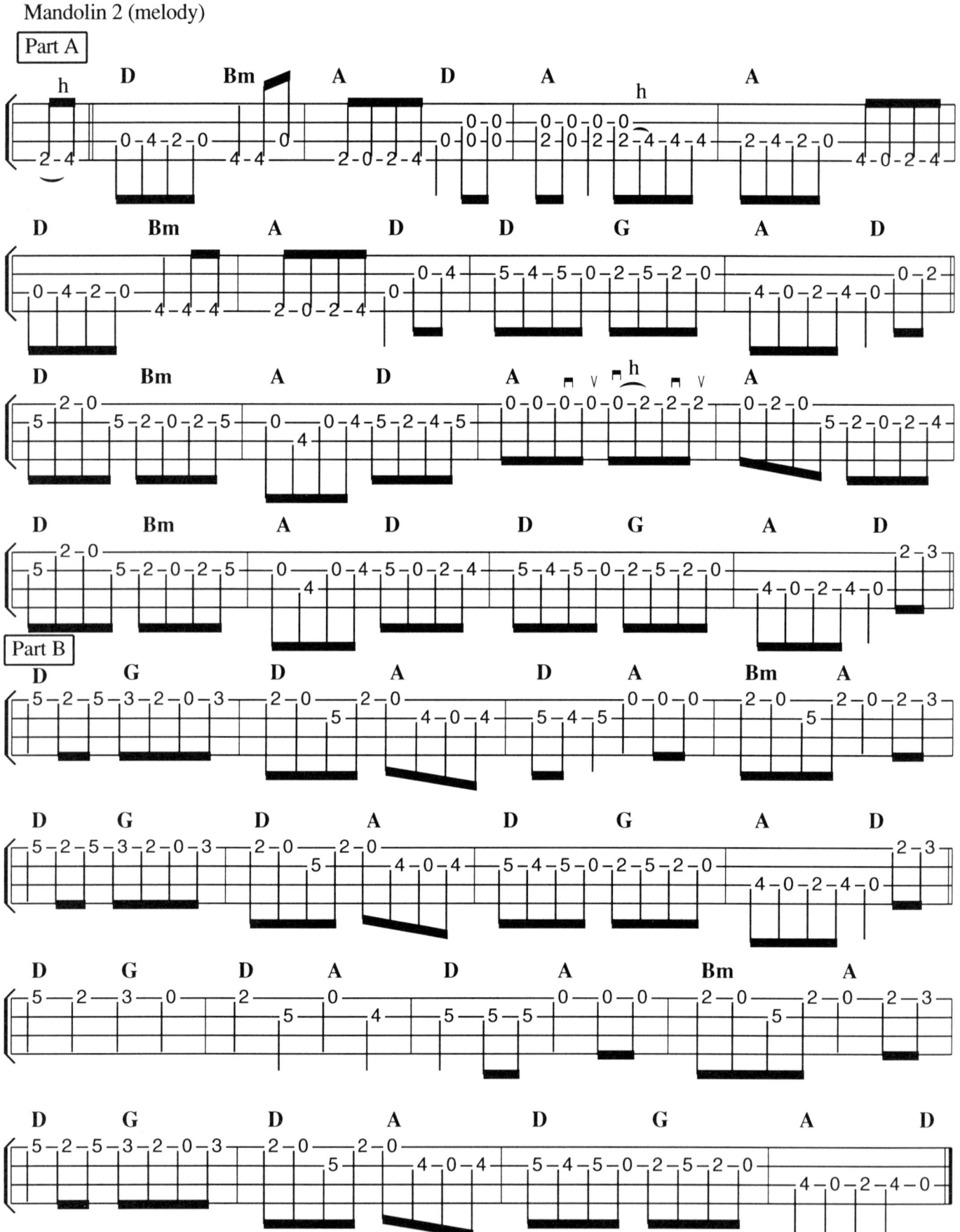

Arkansas Traveler

Disc 1
Track 3

Aura Lee

Mandolin

Irish

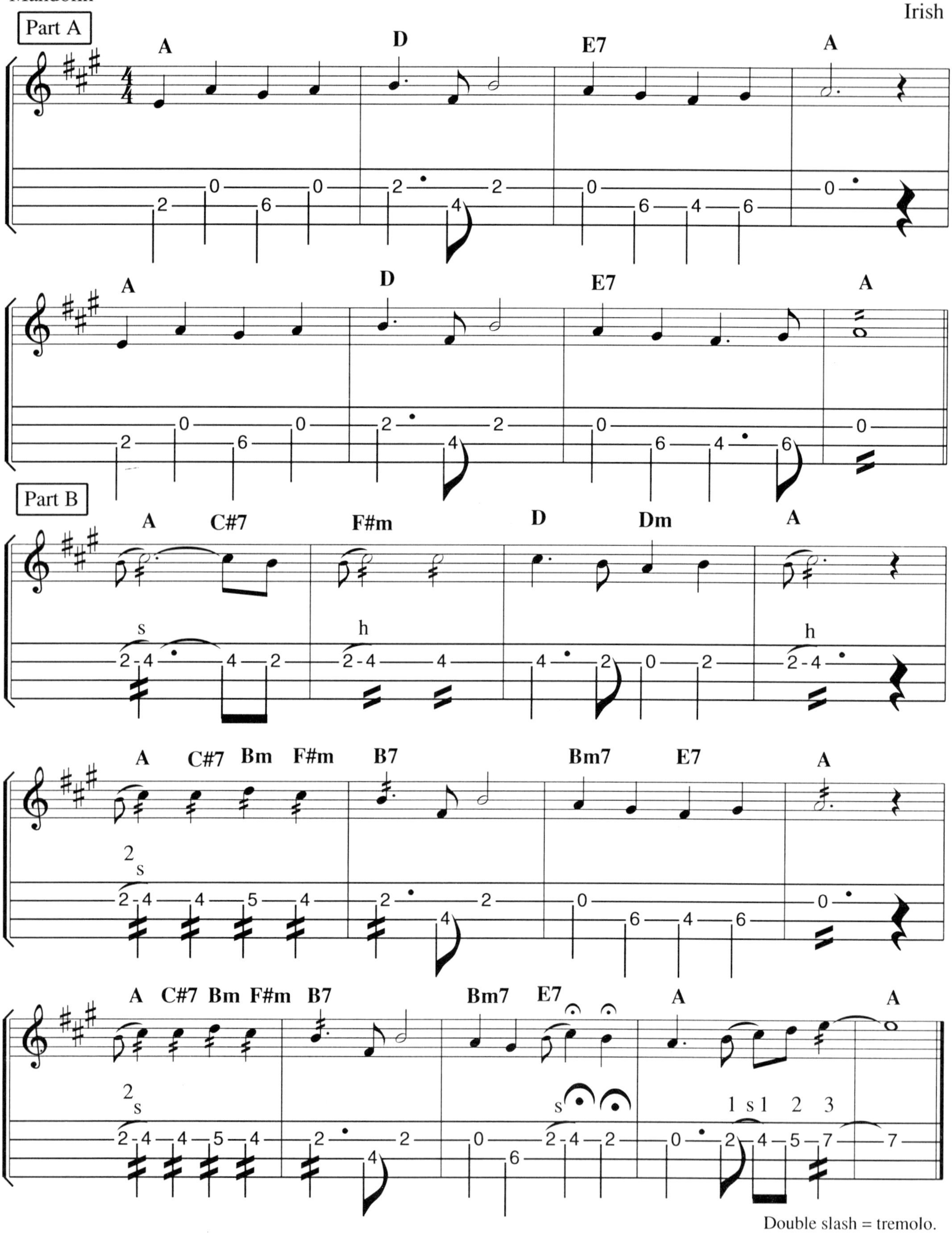

Double slash = tremolo.

Disc 1
Track 4

The Battle Cry of Freedom

Mandolin (melody)

North American

Part A

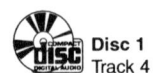

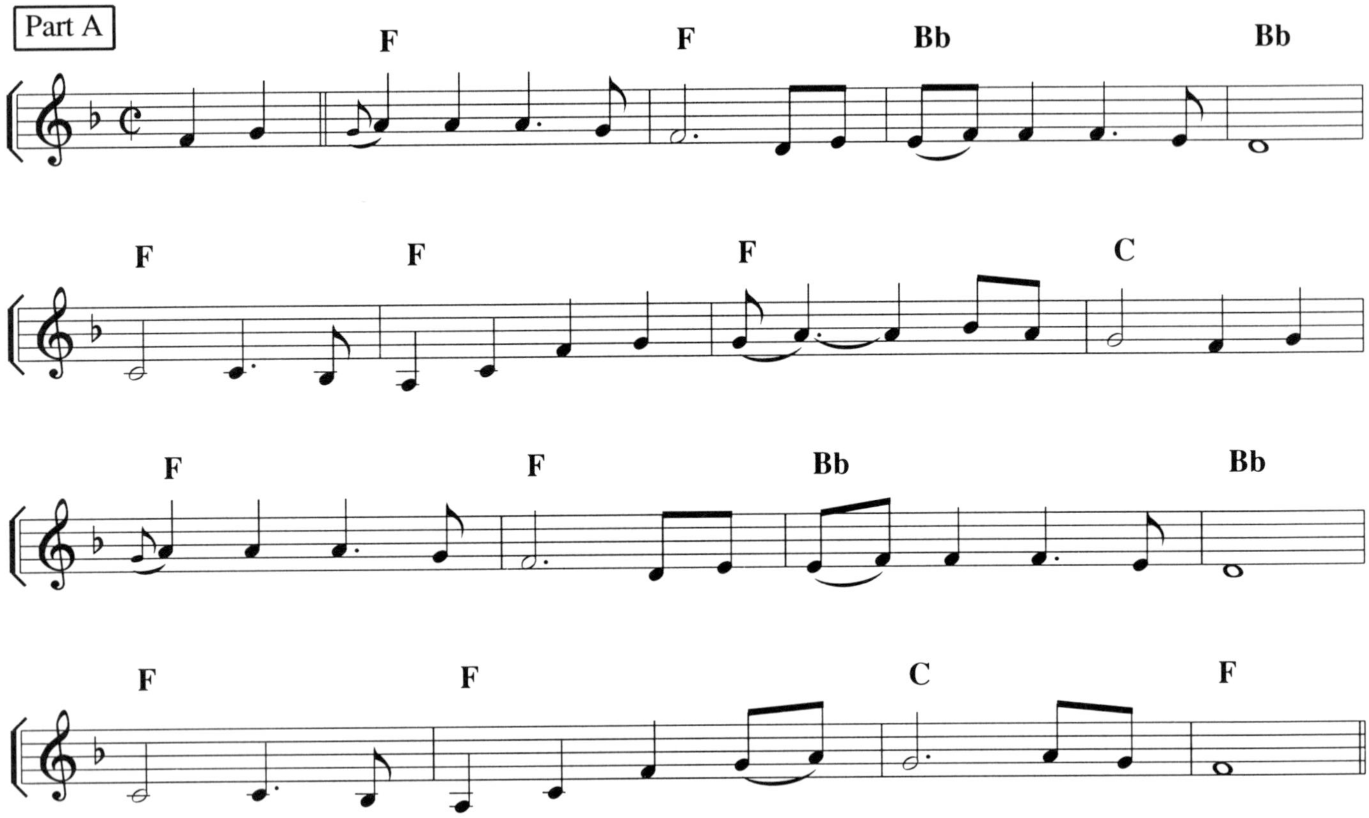

Part B

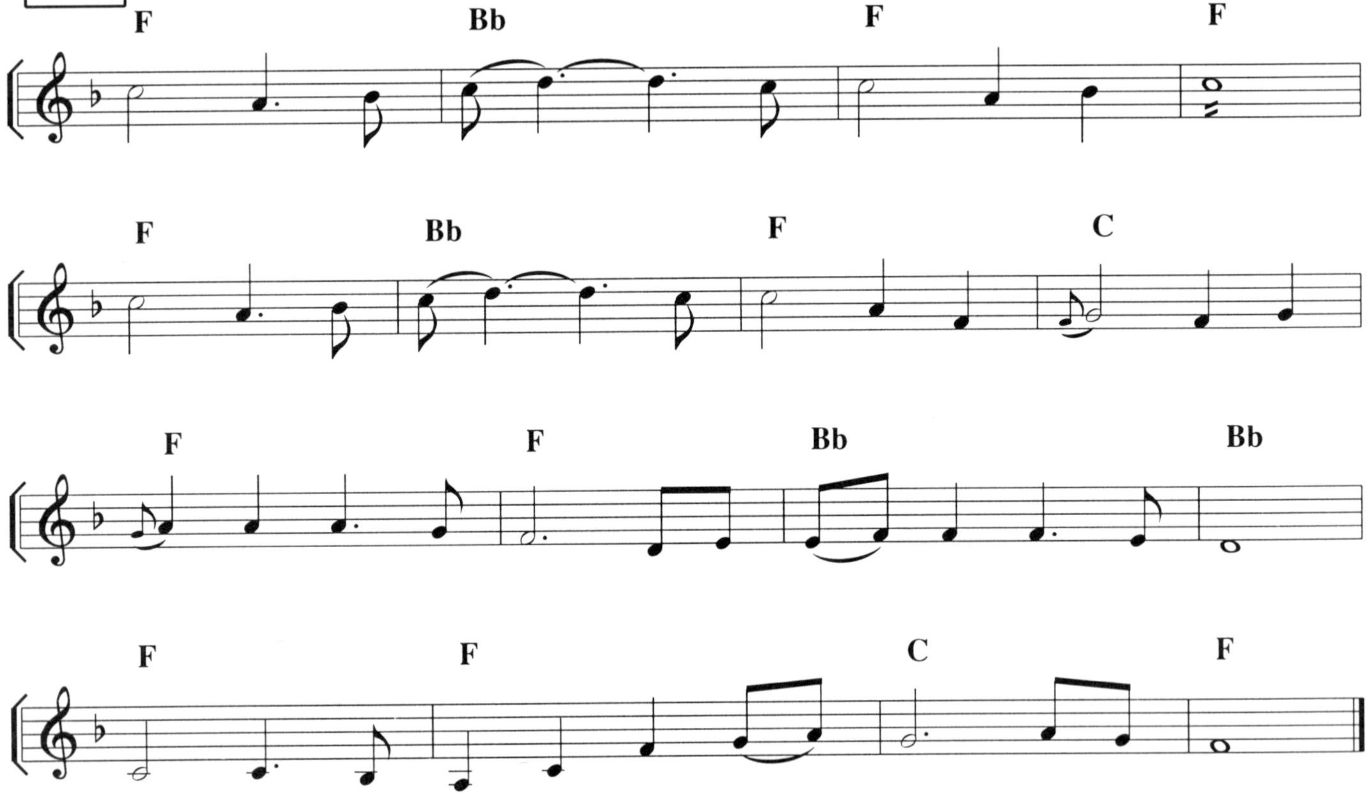

The Battle Cry of Freedom

Mandolin (harmony)*

*Mandolin harmony is not on CD.

The Battle Cry of Freedom

The Battle Cry of Freedom

Mandolin (harmony)*

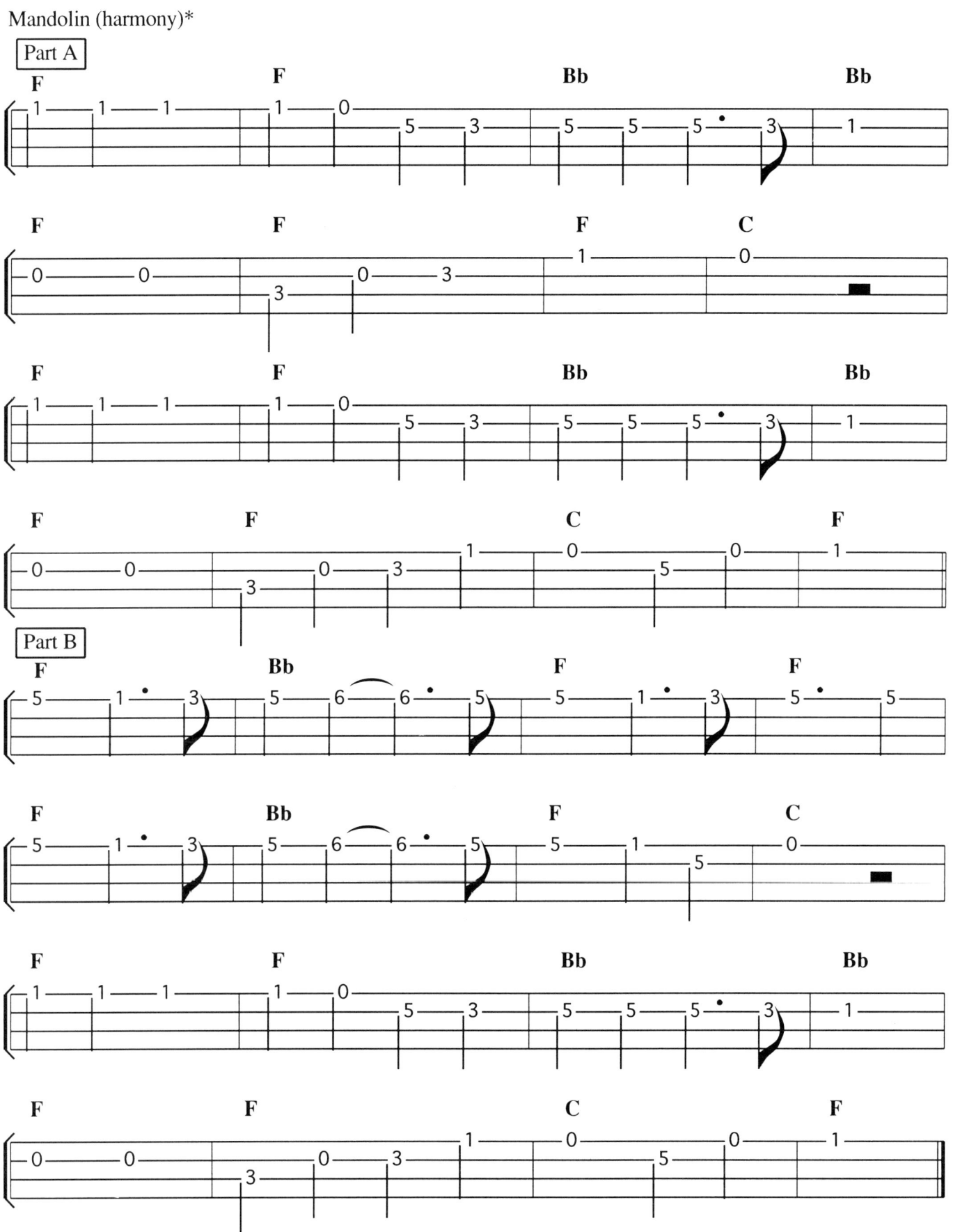

*Mandolin harmony is not on CD.

Beaumont Rag

Mandolin

North American

Beaumont Rag

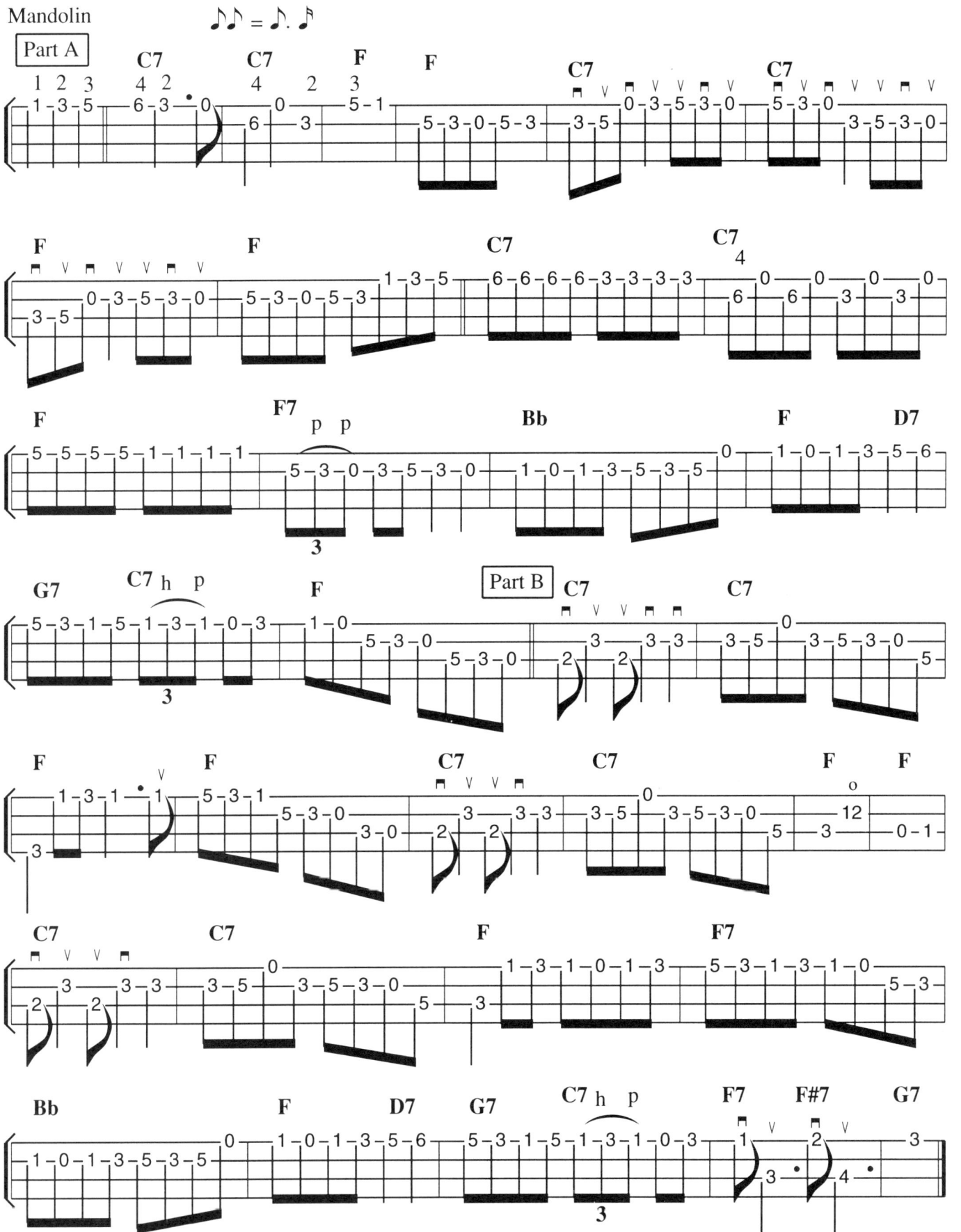

Billy in the Lowground

Mandolin (melody)

North American

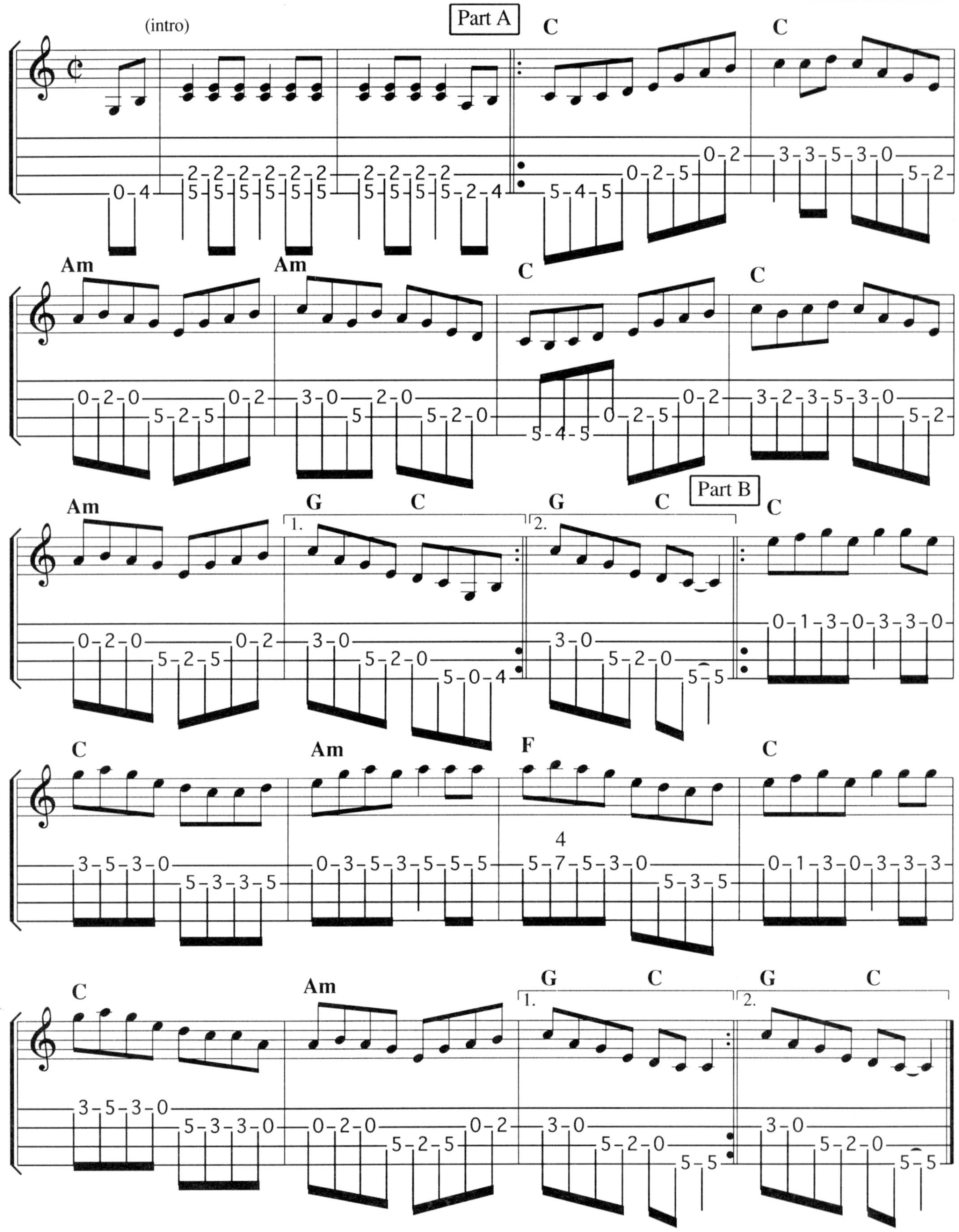

Billy in the Lowground

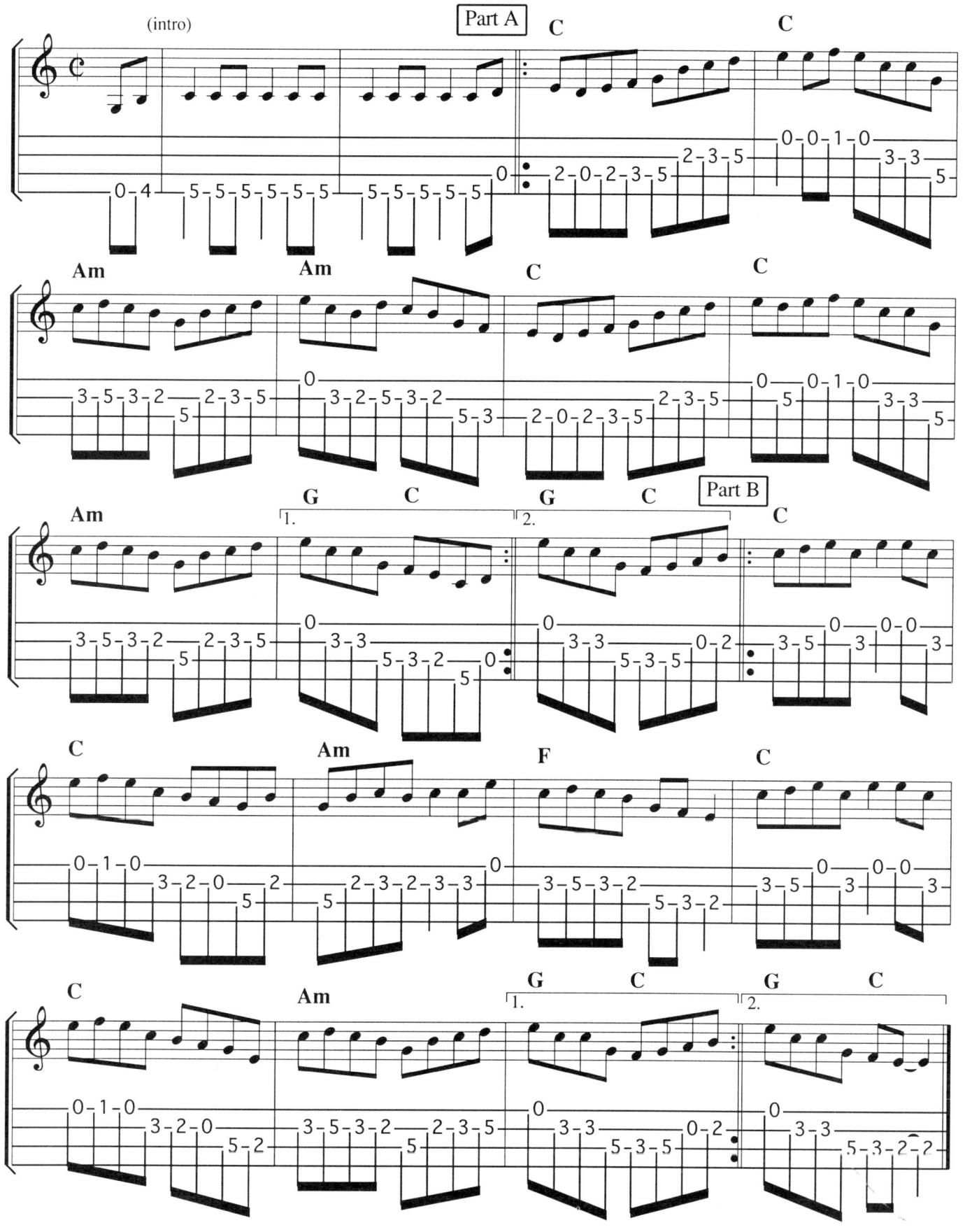

Blackberry Blossom

Mandolin 1

Australian

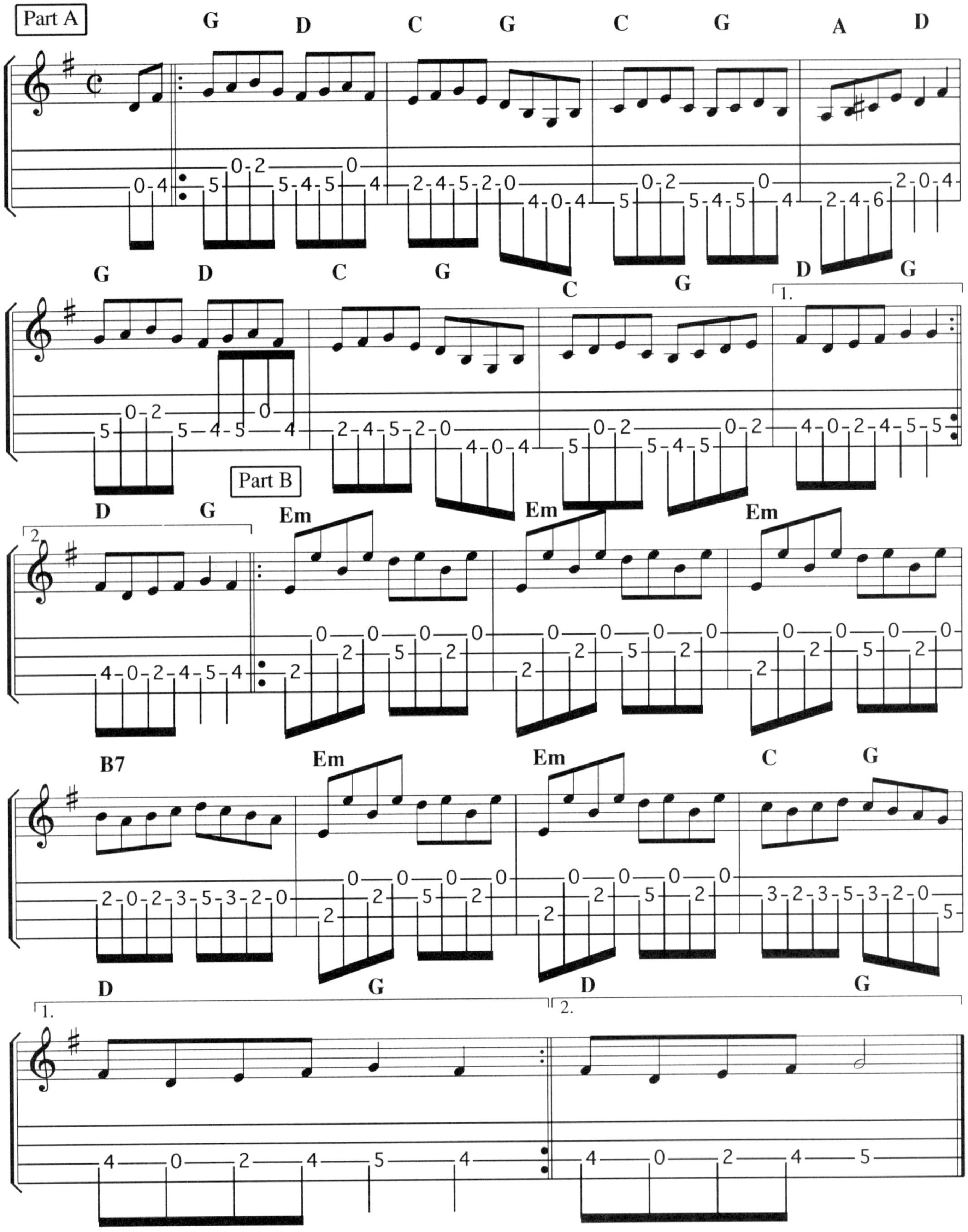

Blackberry Blossom

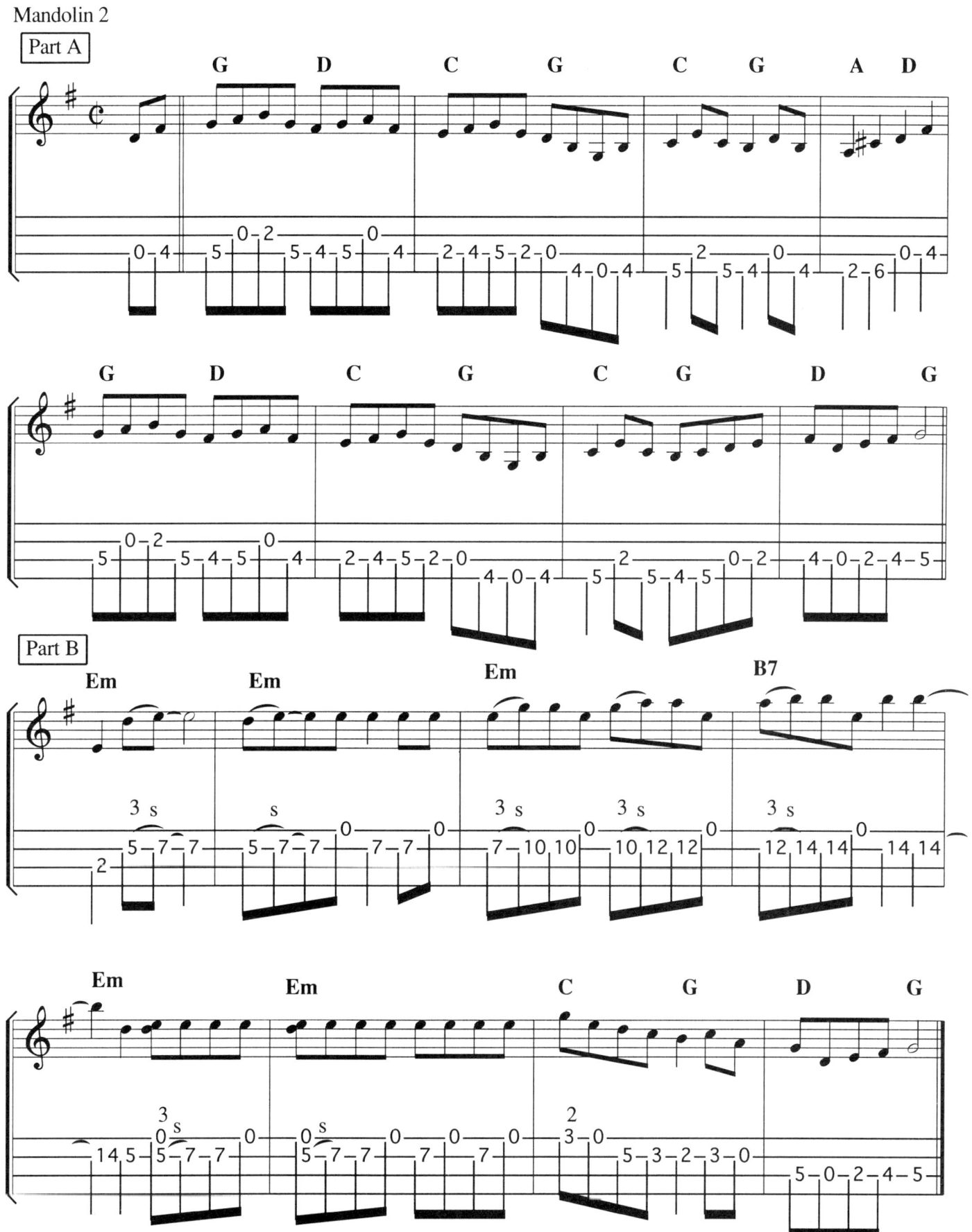

Bonaparte's Retreat

Disc 1
Track 8

Mandolin 1 (melody)

North American

Part A

Part B

24

Bonaparte's Retreat

Mandolin 1 (harmony)

Bonaparte's Retreat

Mandolin 1 (melody w/B1)*

*Part B1 represents the first B part played by the fiddle. This is not played by the mandolin on the audio CD.

Bonaparte's Retreat

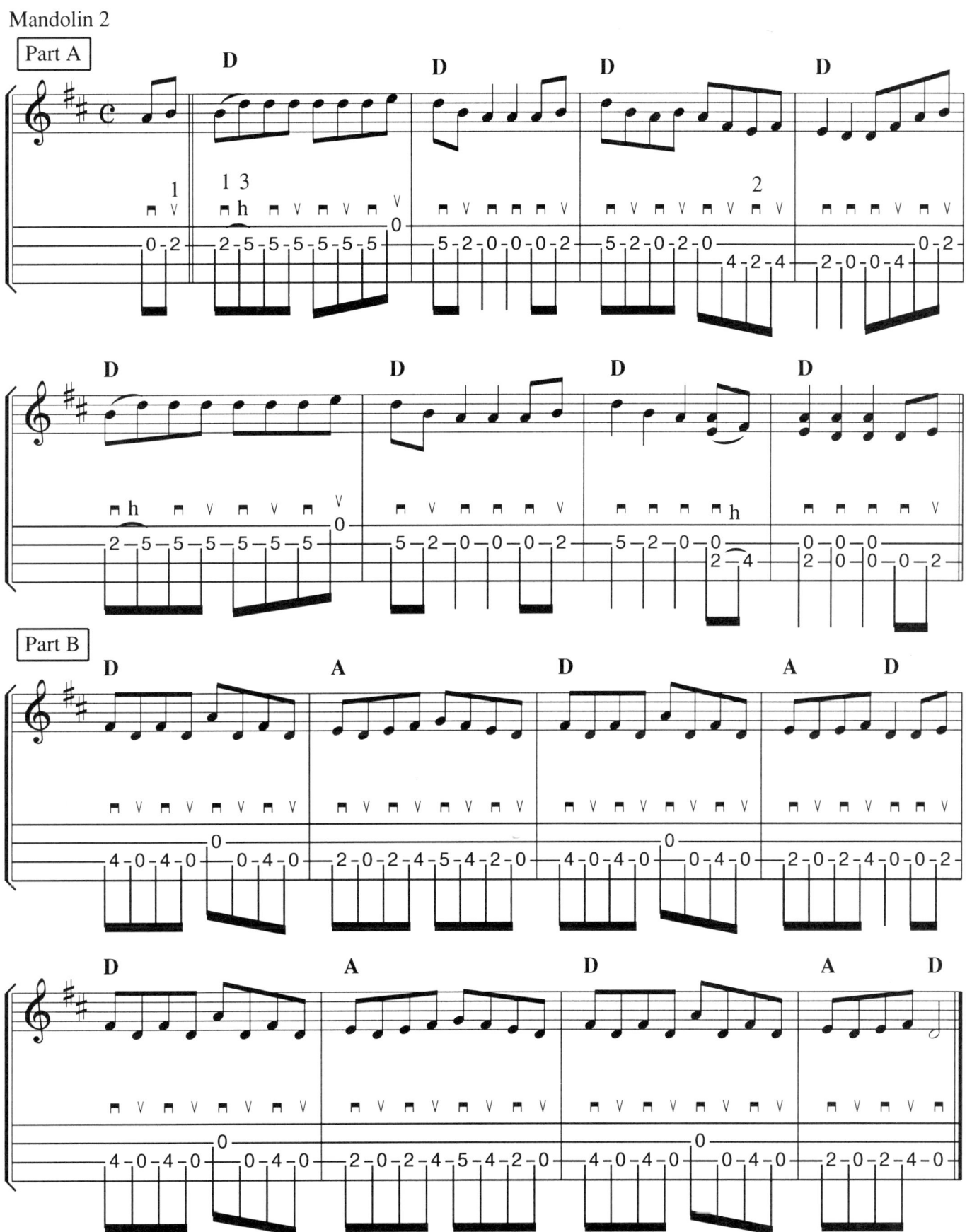

Carthage Waltz

Mandolin 1

North American

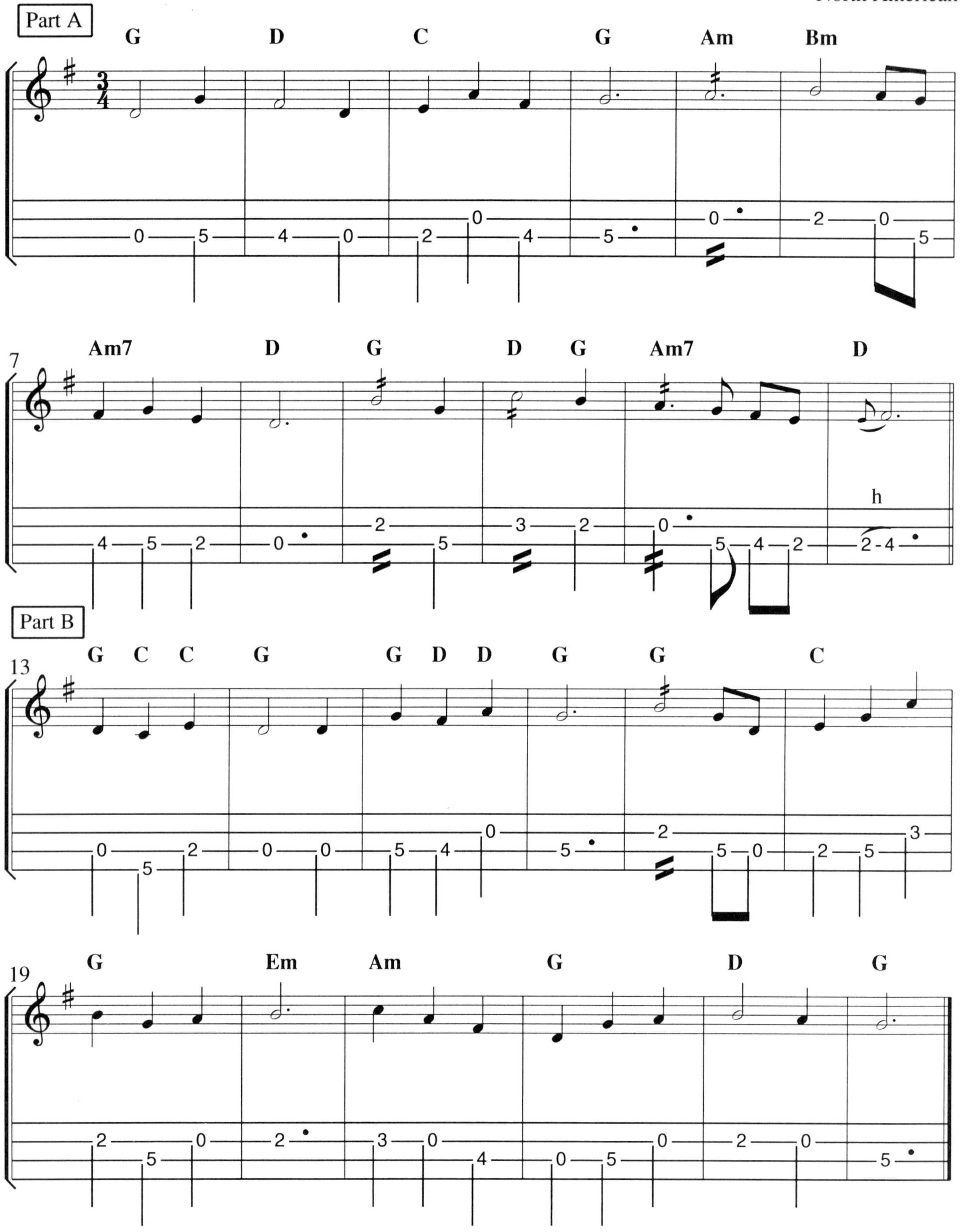

Carthage Waltz

Carthage Waltz

Mandolin 1 and 2 (harmony for measures 13-16)

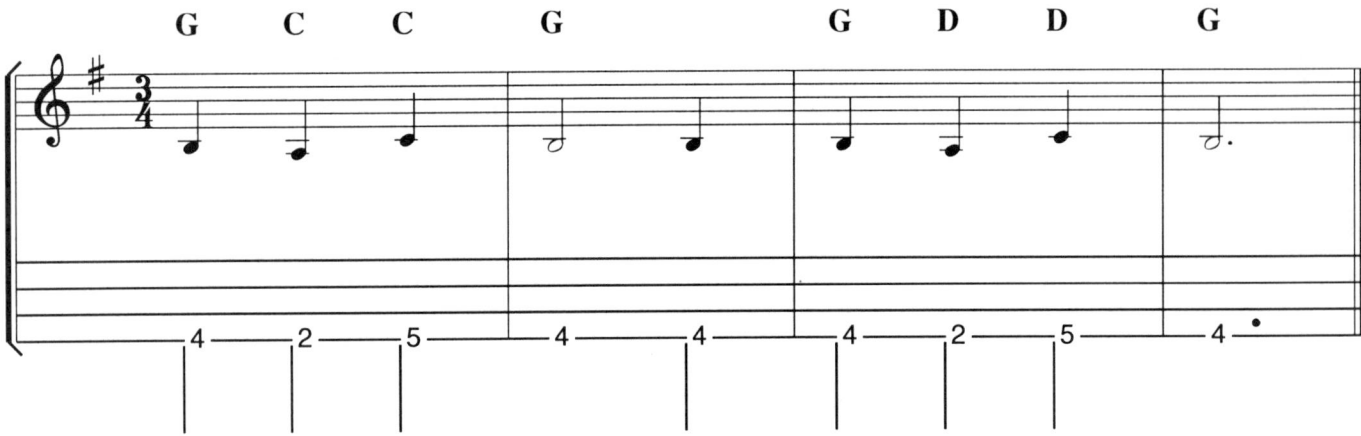

30

Disc 1
Track 10

Cherokee Shuffle

Mandolin 1 (melody)*

North American

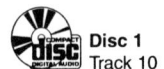

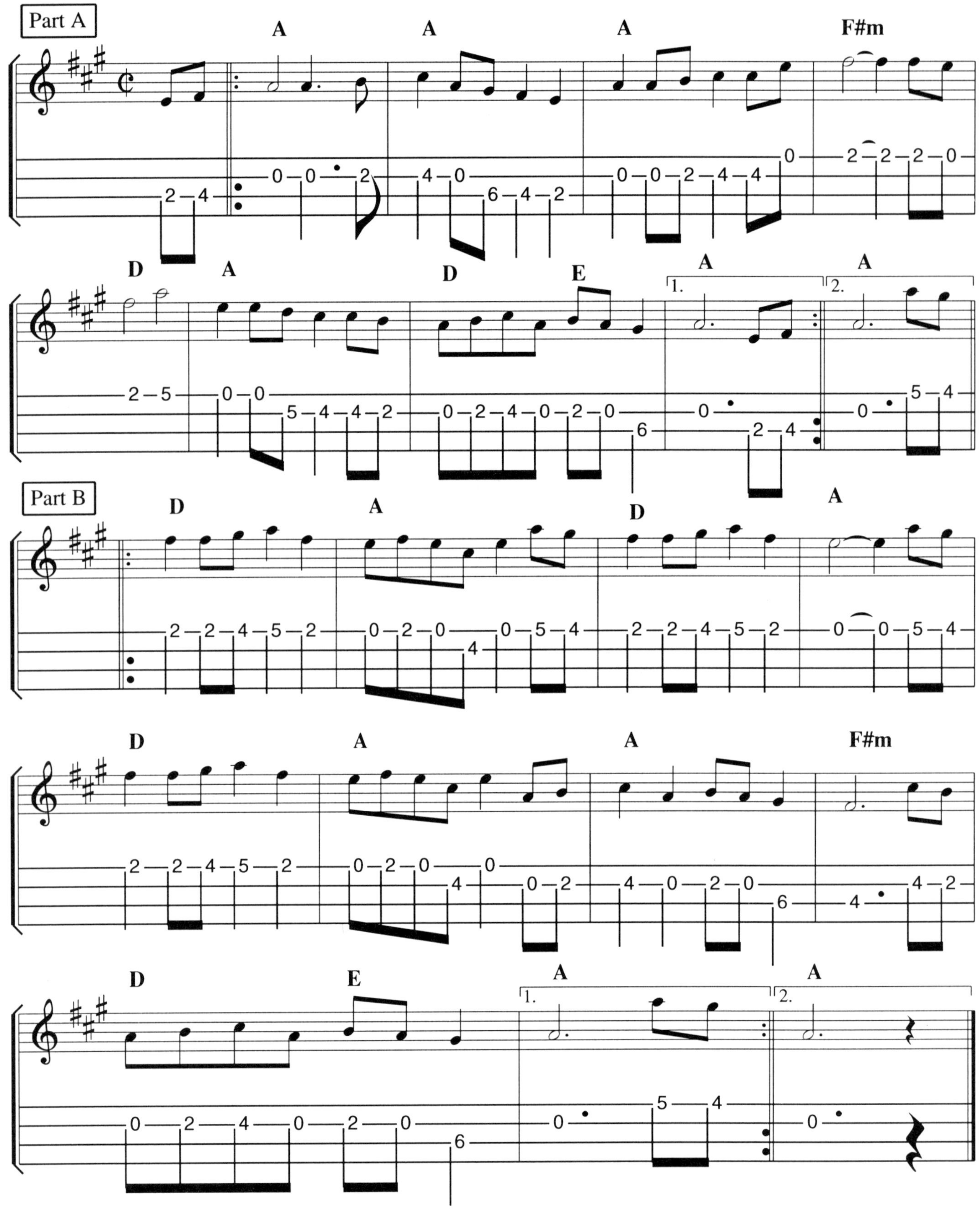

*Mandolin 1 melody is not on CD.

Cherokee Shuffle

*Mandolin 1 harmony is not on CD.

Cherokee Shuffle

*Mandolin 2 is not on CD.

Cherokee Shuffle

Cluck Old Hen

Disc 1
Track 11

Mandolin

North American

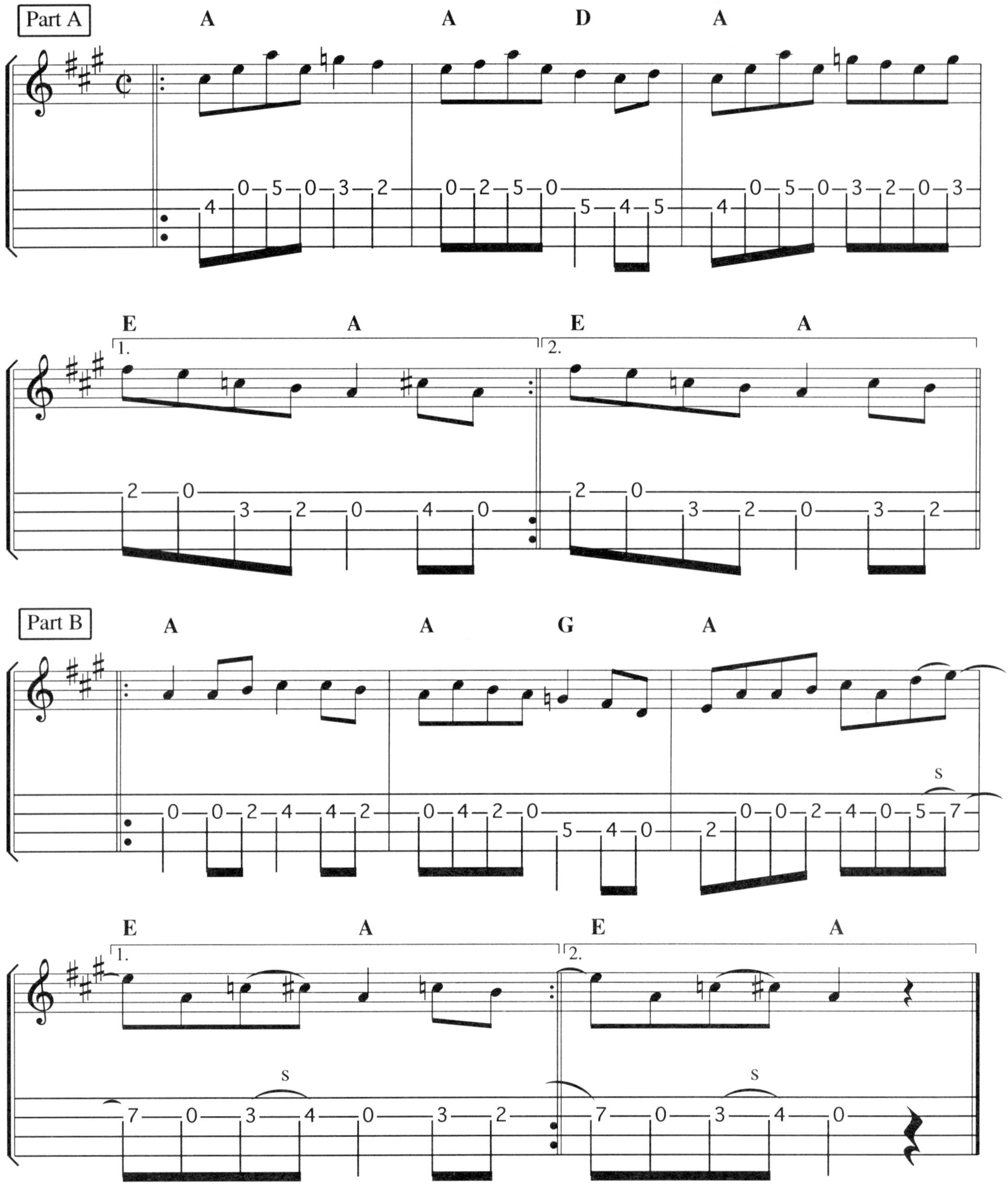

Part A

Cotton-eyed Joe

Mandolin 1* (key of A)

North American

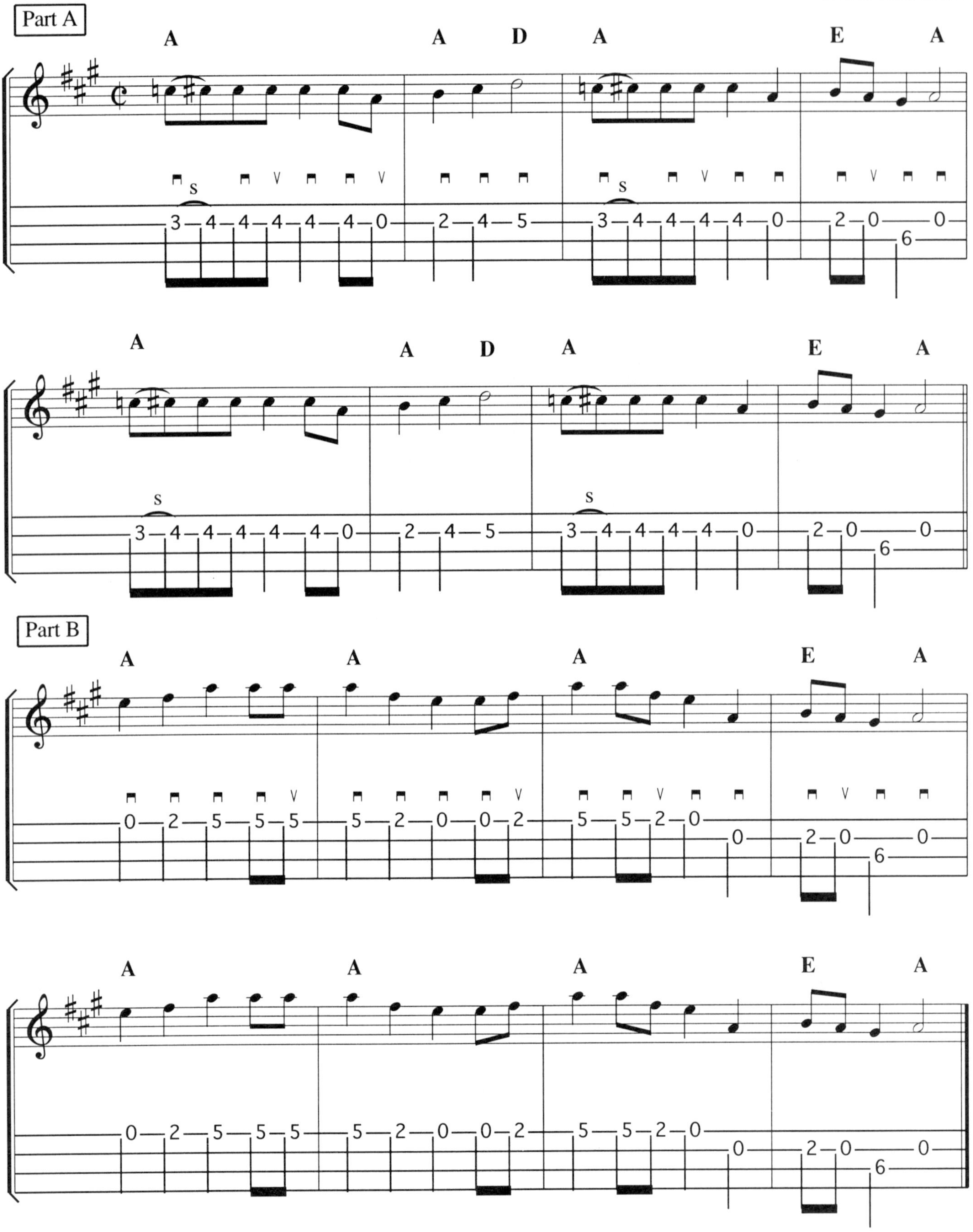

Part A

Part B

*Mandolin 1 in A is not on CD.

Cotton-eyed Joe

Mandolin 1* (key of D)

*Mandolin 1 in D is not on CD.

Cotton-eyed Joe

Mandolin 2 (key of A)

Cotton-eyed Joe

Mandolin 2 (key of D)

Disc 1
Track 13

Cotton Patch Rag

Mandolin

North American

Part A

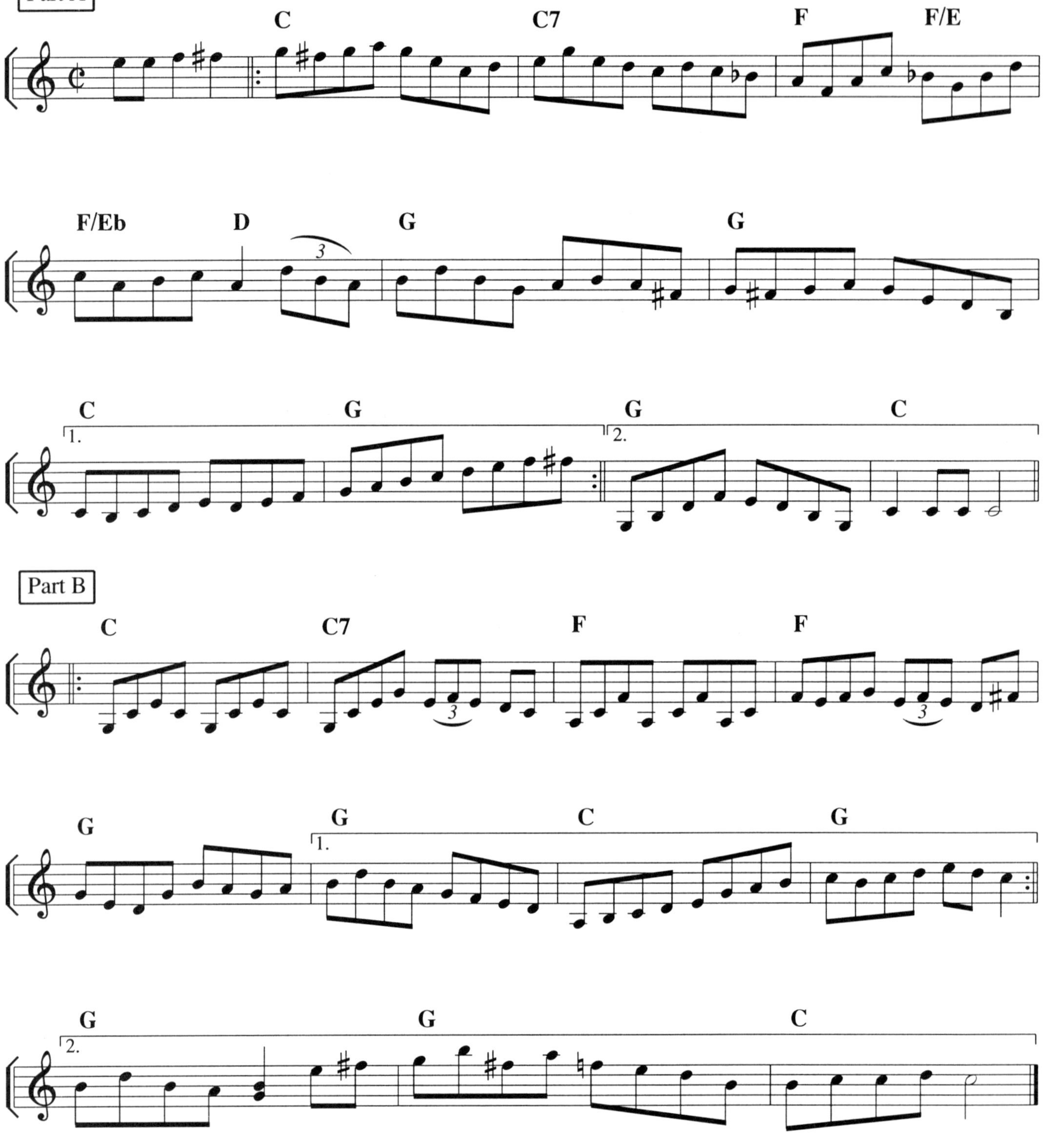

Cotton Patch Rag

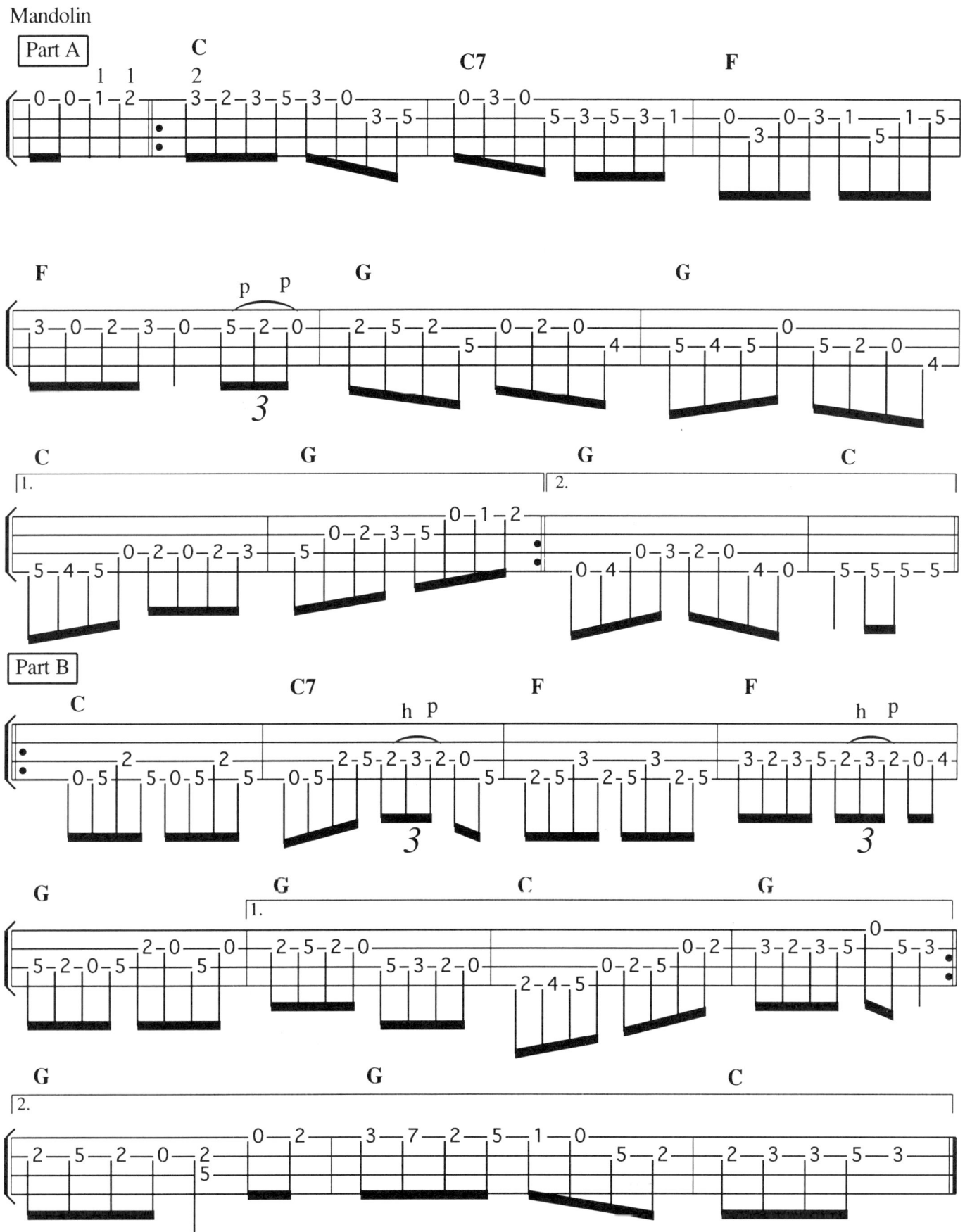

Cripple Creek

Disc 1
Track 14

Mandolin 1*

North American

Part A

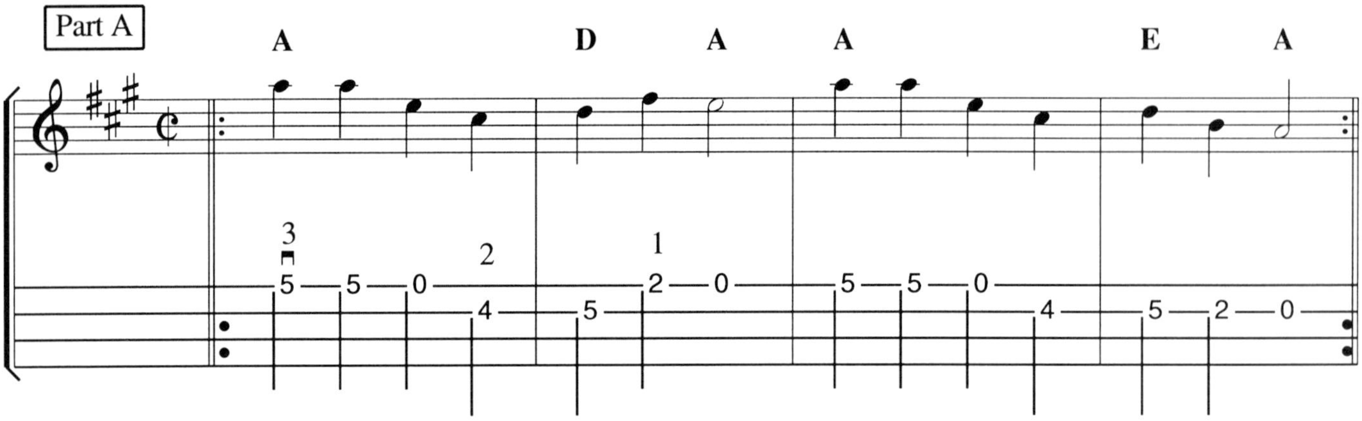

Part B

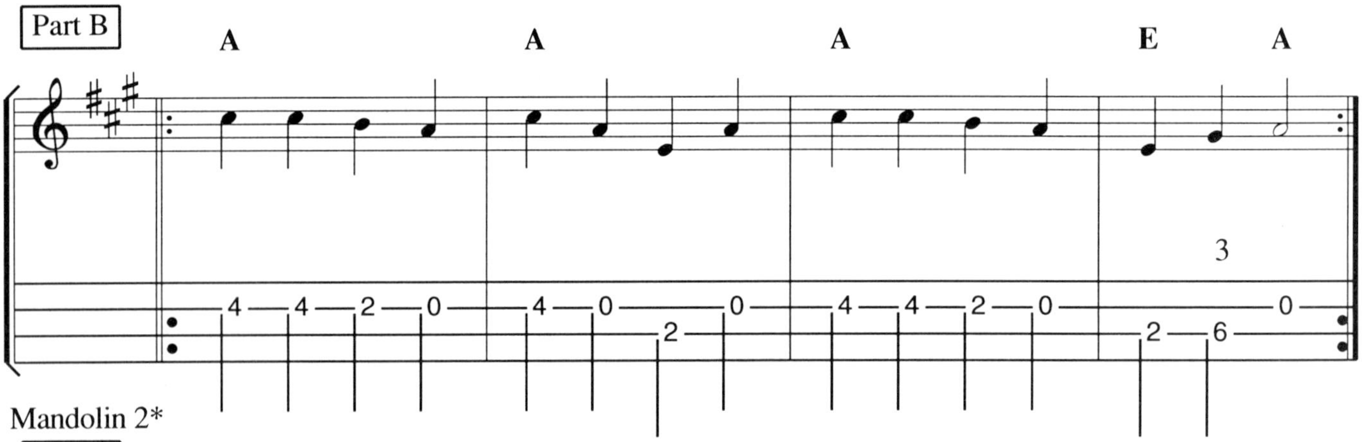

Mandolin 2*

Part A

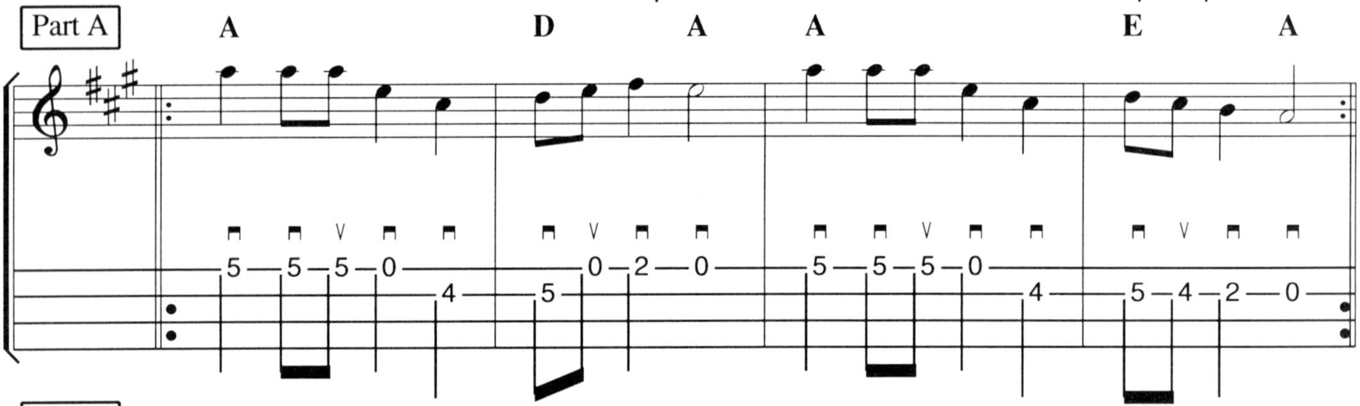

Part B

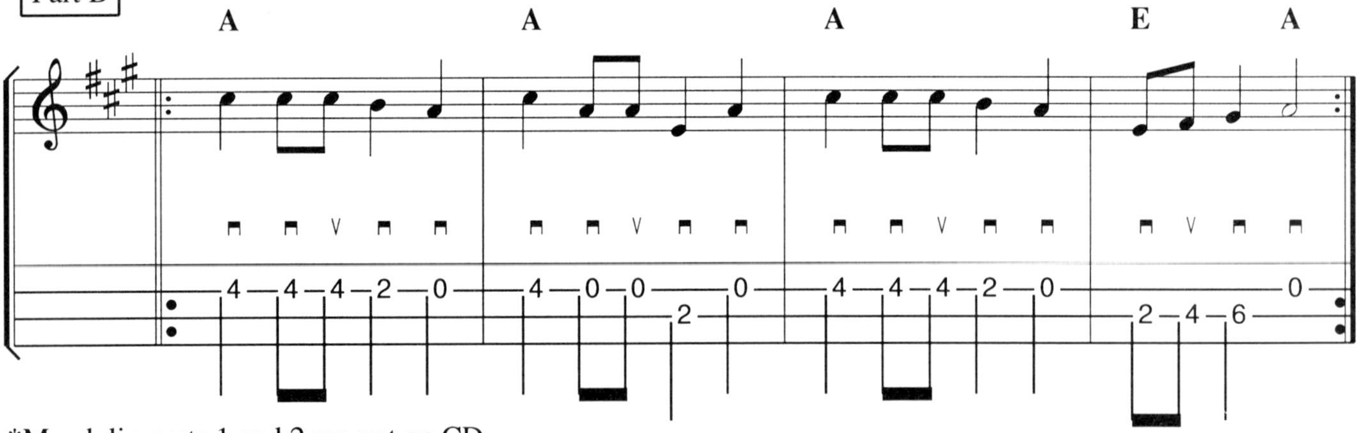

*Mandolin parts 1 and 2 are not on CD.

Cripple Creek

Mandolin 3

Cripple Creek

Mandolin 4*

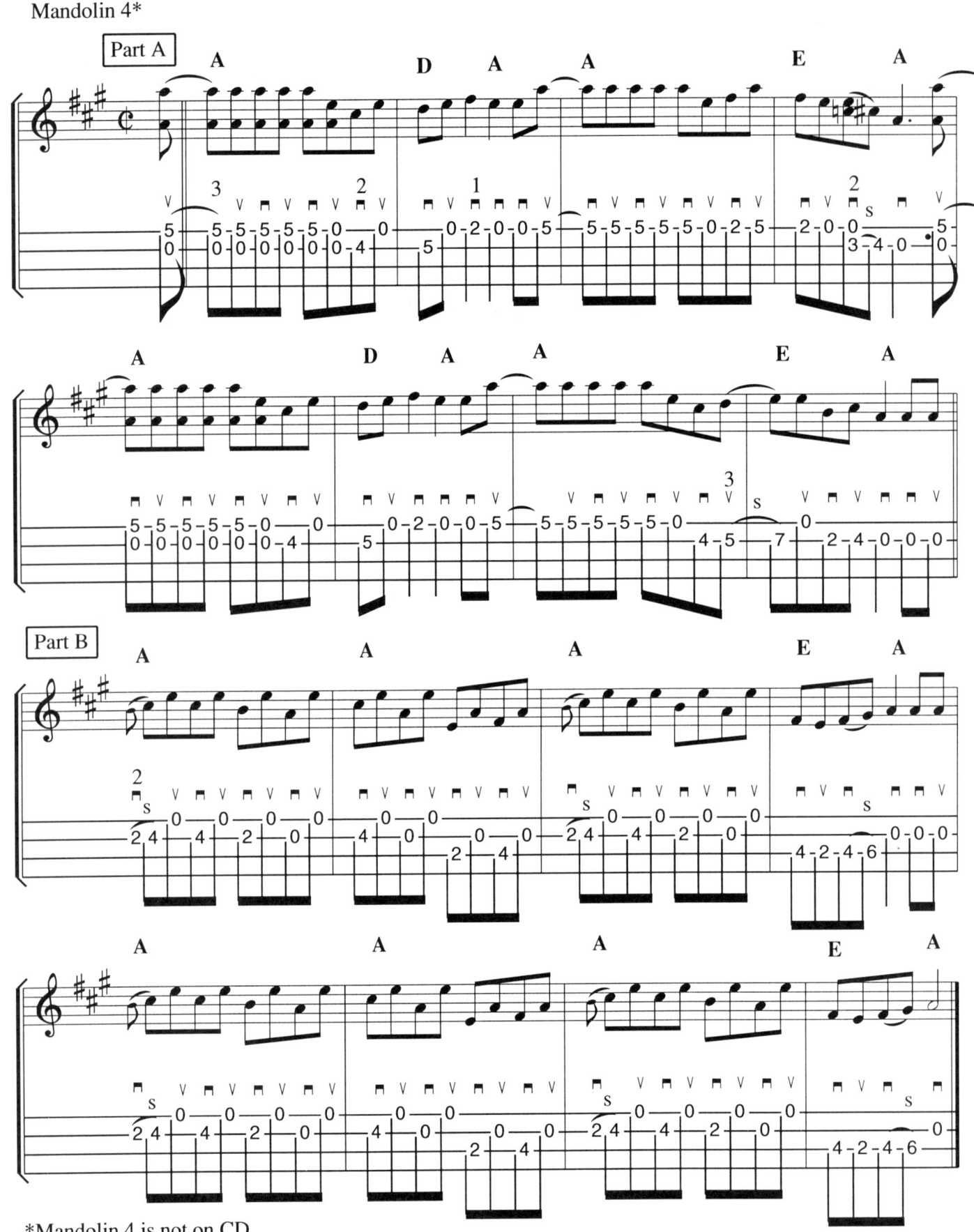

*Mandolin 4 is not on CD.

This page has been left blank to avoid awkward page turns.

Devil's Dream

Mandolin 1 (melody in G)
North American

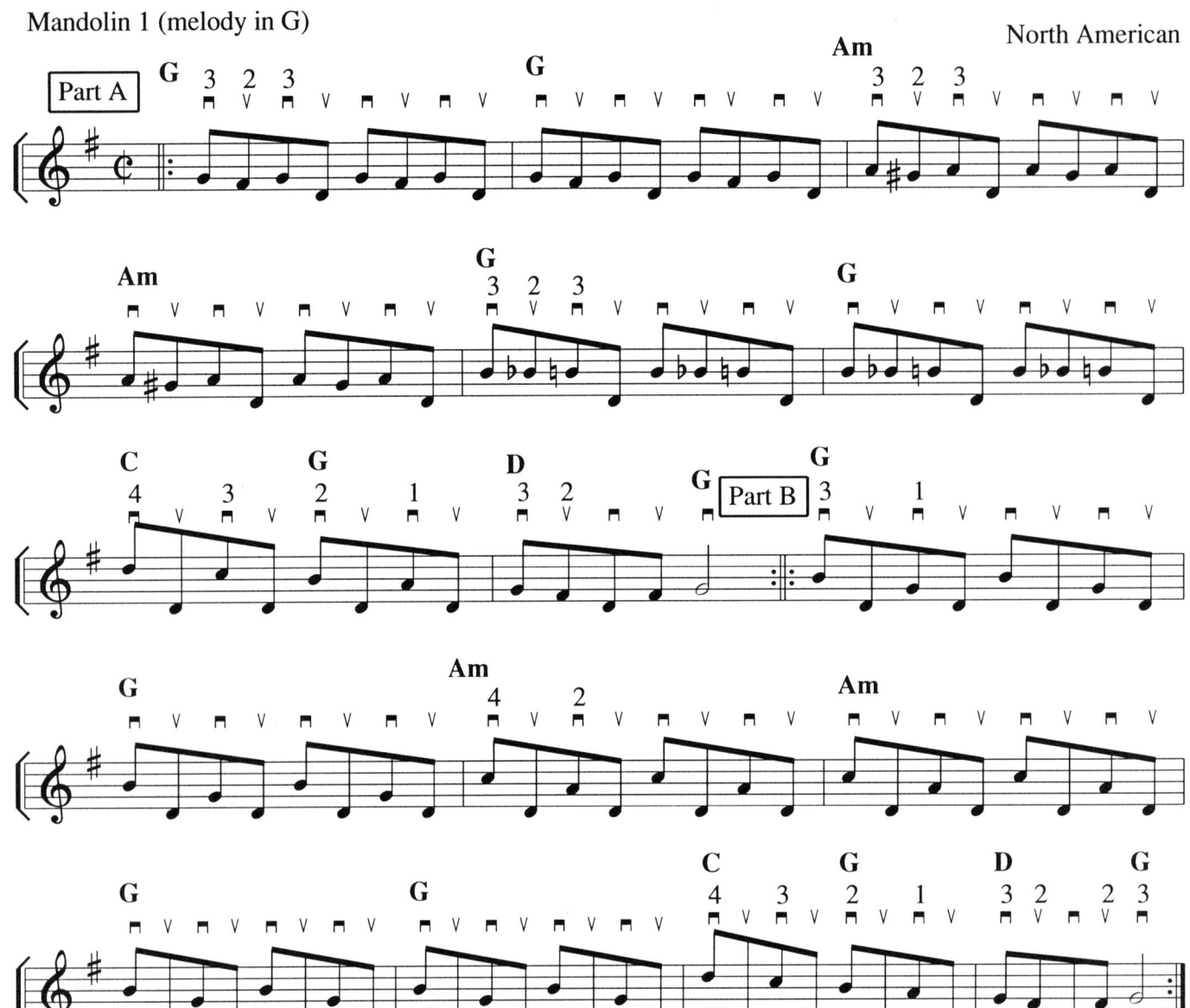

Devil's Dream

Mandolin 1 (melody in G)

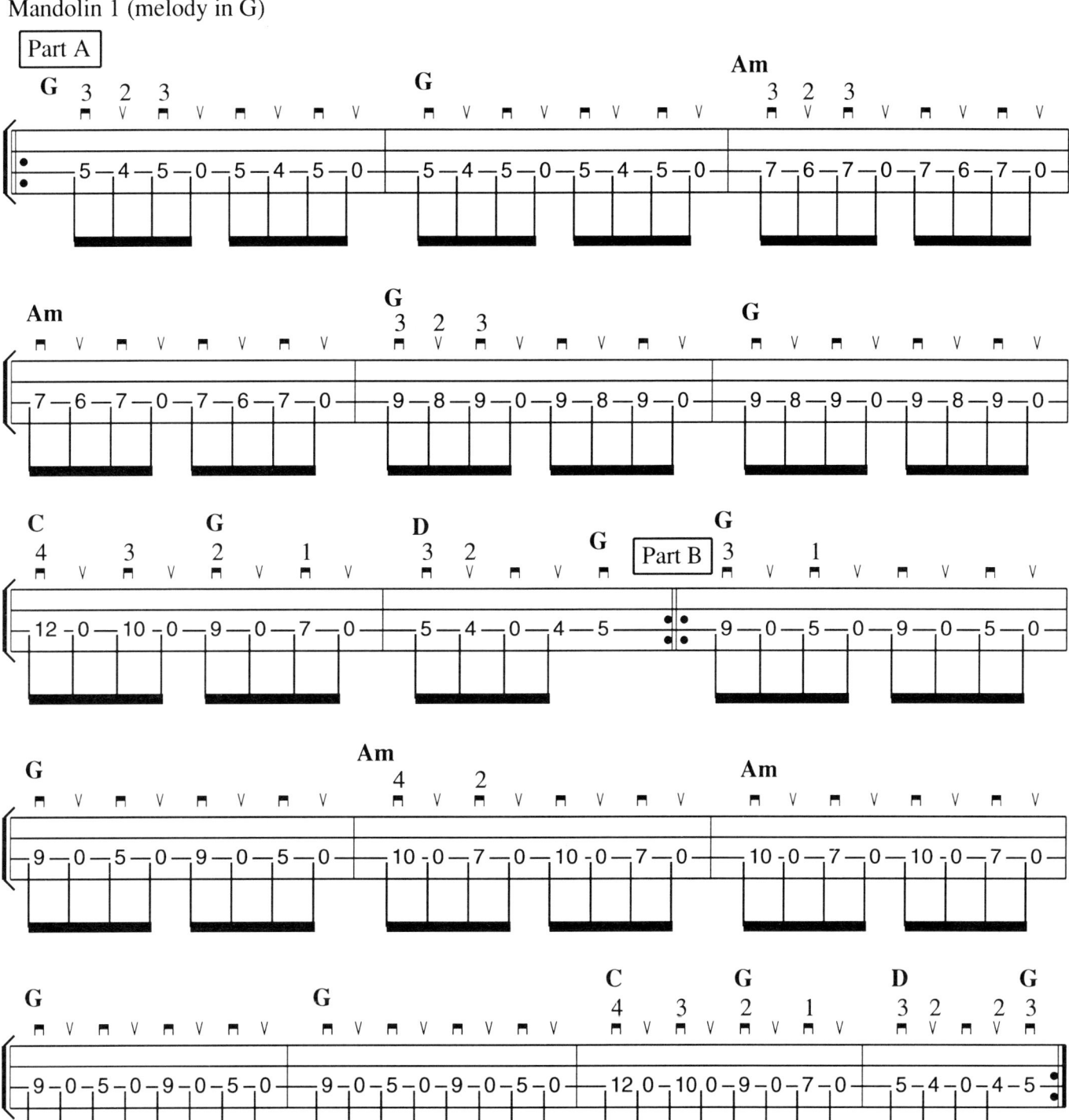

Devil's Dream

Mandolin 1 (melody in A)*

*Mandolin 1 (key of A) is not on CD.

Devil's Dream

Mandolin 1 (melody in A)*

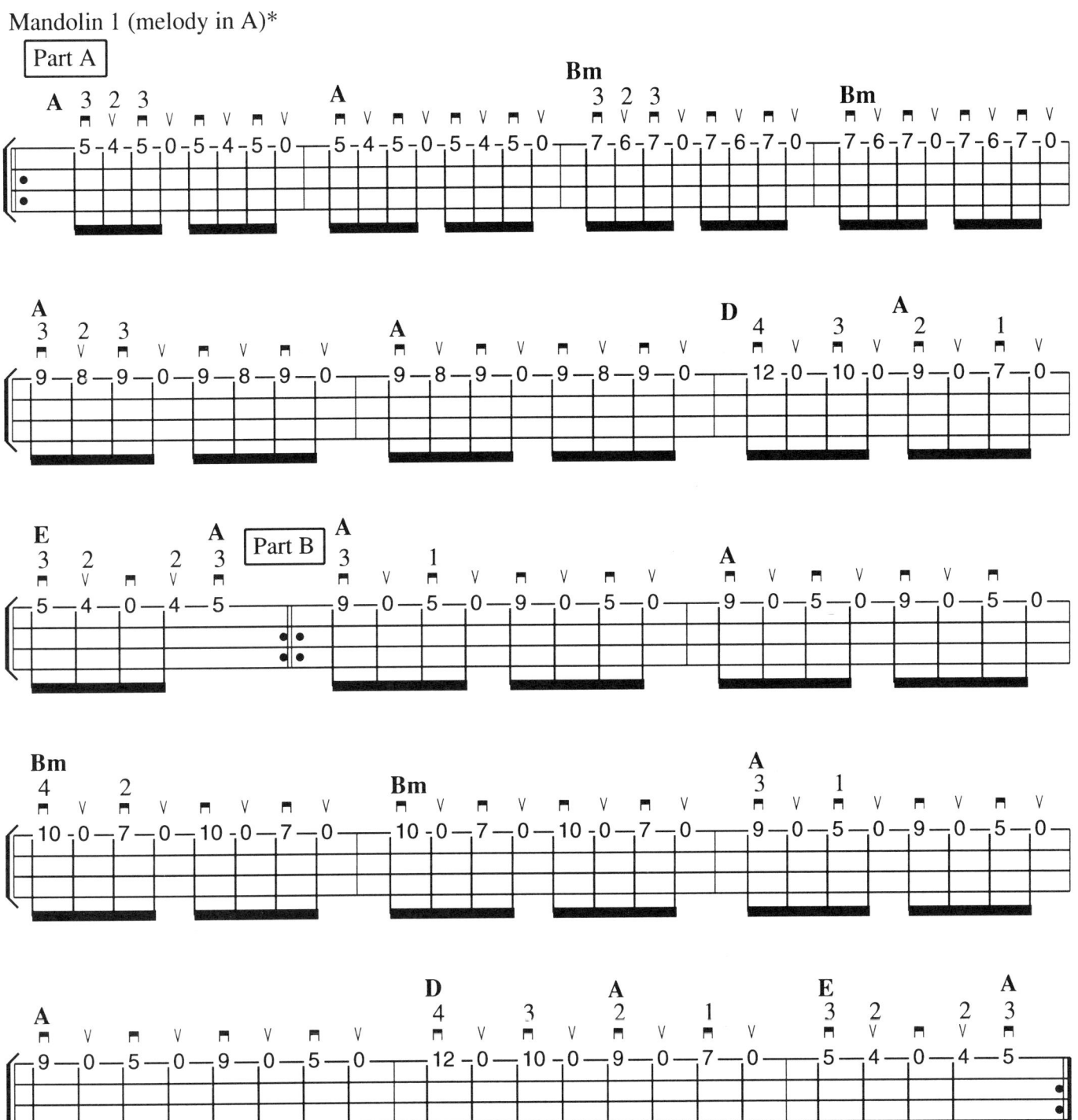

*Mandolin 1 (key of A) is not on CD.

Devil's Dream

Mandolin 1 (harmony in G)*

*Mandolin 1 harmony in G is not on CD.

Devil's Dream

Mandolin 1 (harmony in G)*

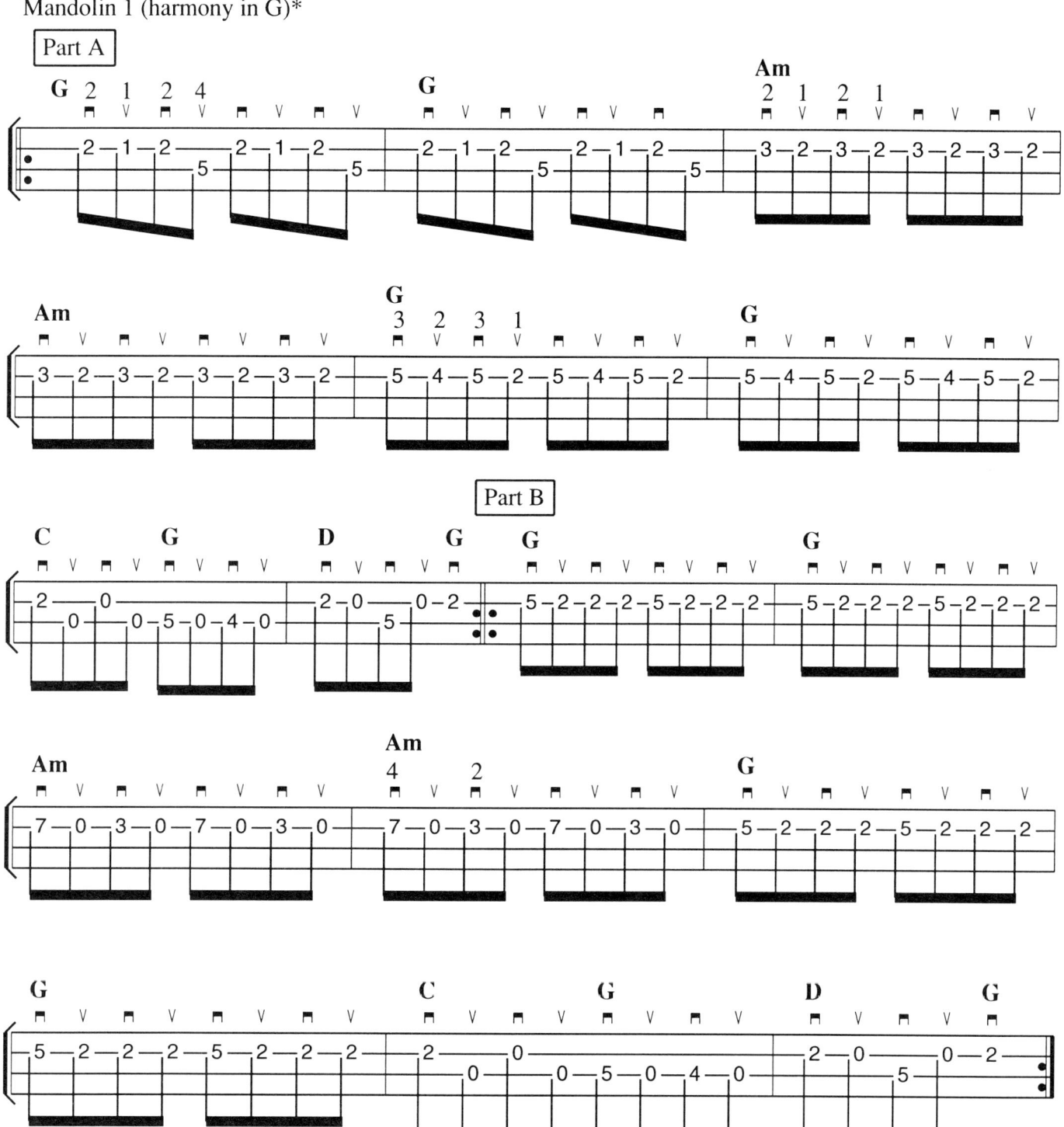

*Mandolin 1 harmony in G is not on CD.

Devil's Dream

Mandolin 2 (key of A)

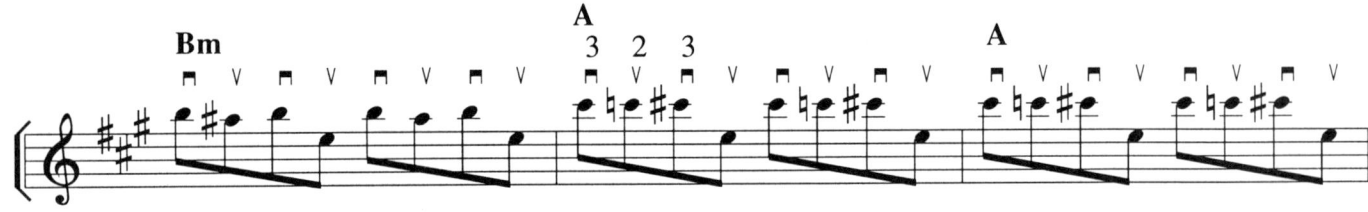
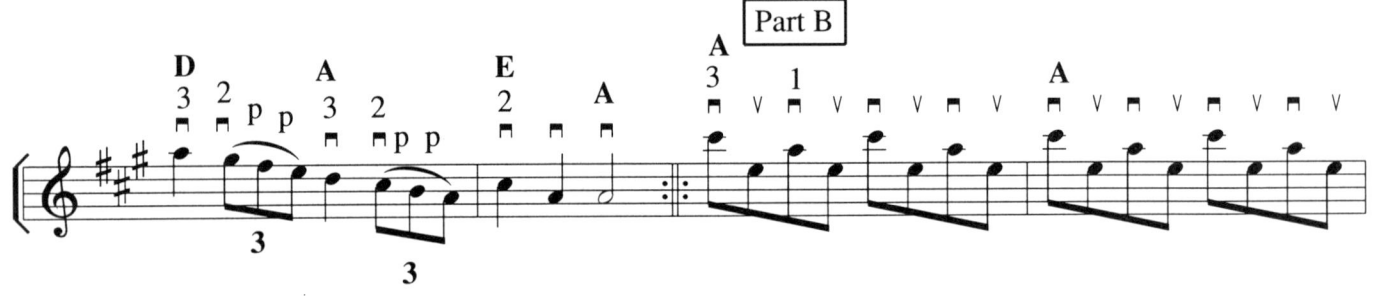
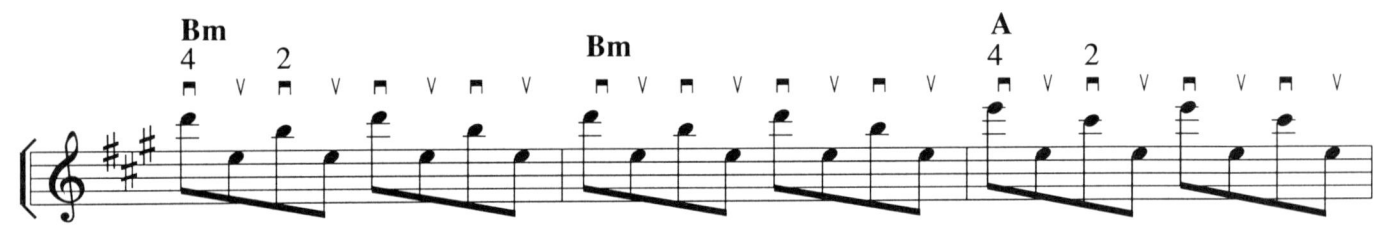
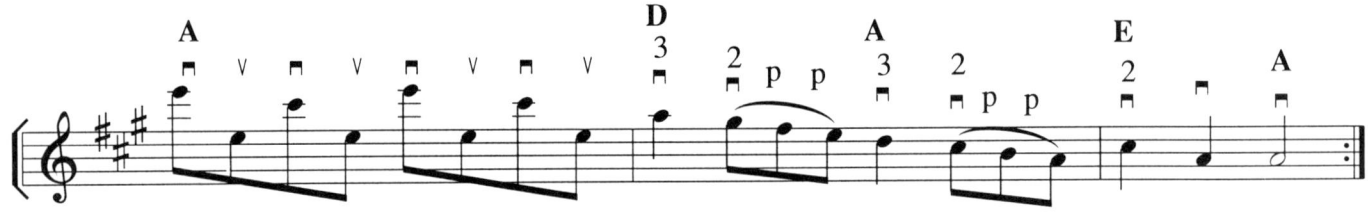

Devil's Dream

Mandolin 2 (key of A)

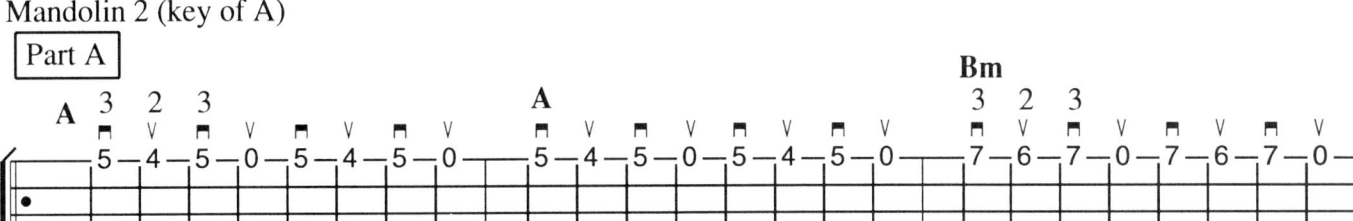
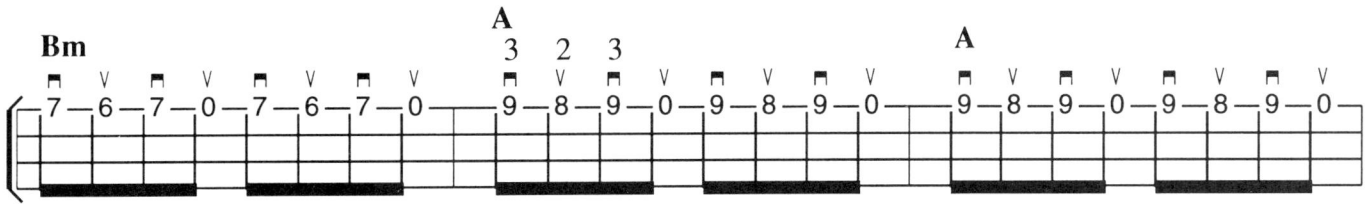
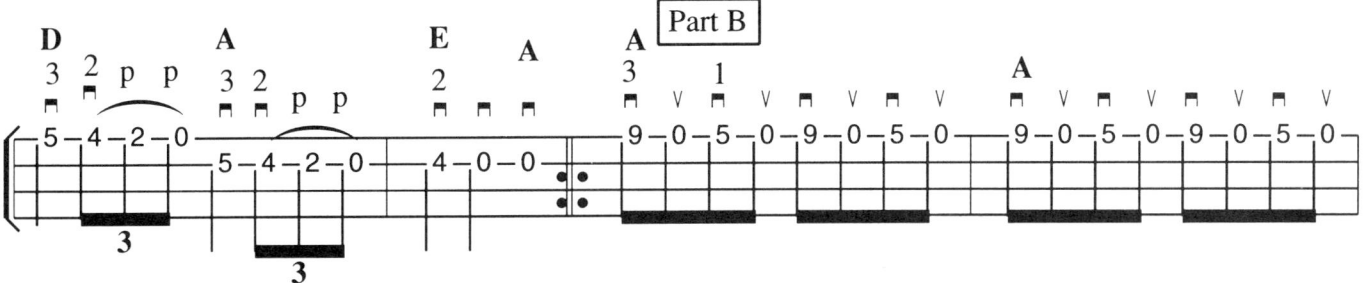
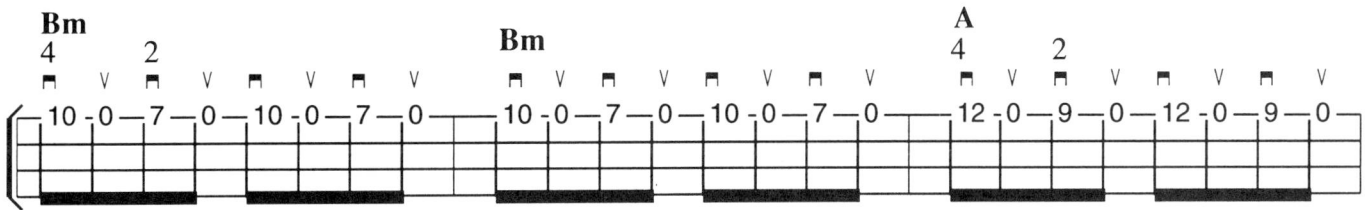
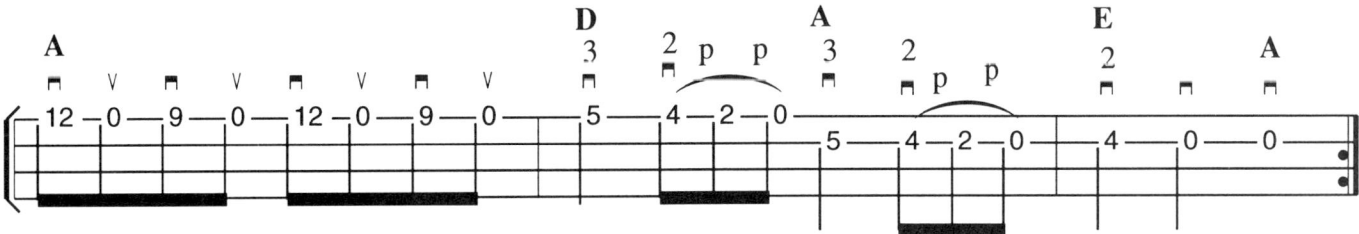

Down Yonder

Mandolin

North American

Disc 1
Track 16

Down Yonder

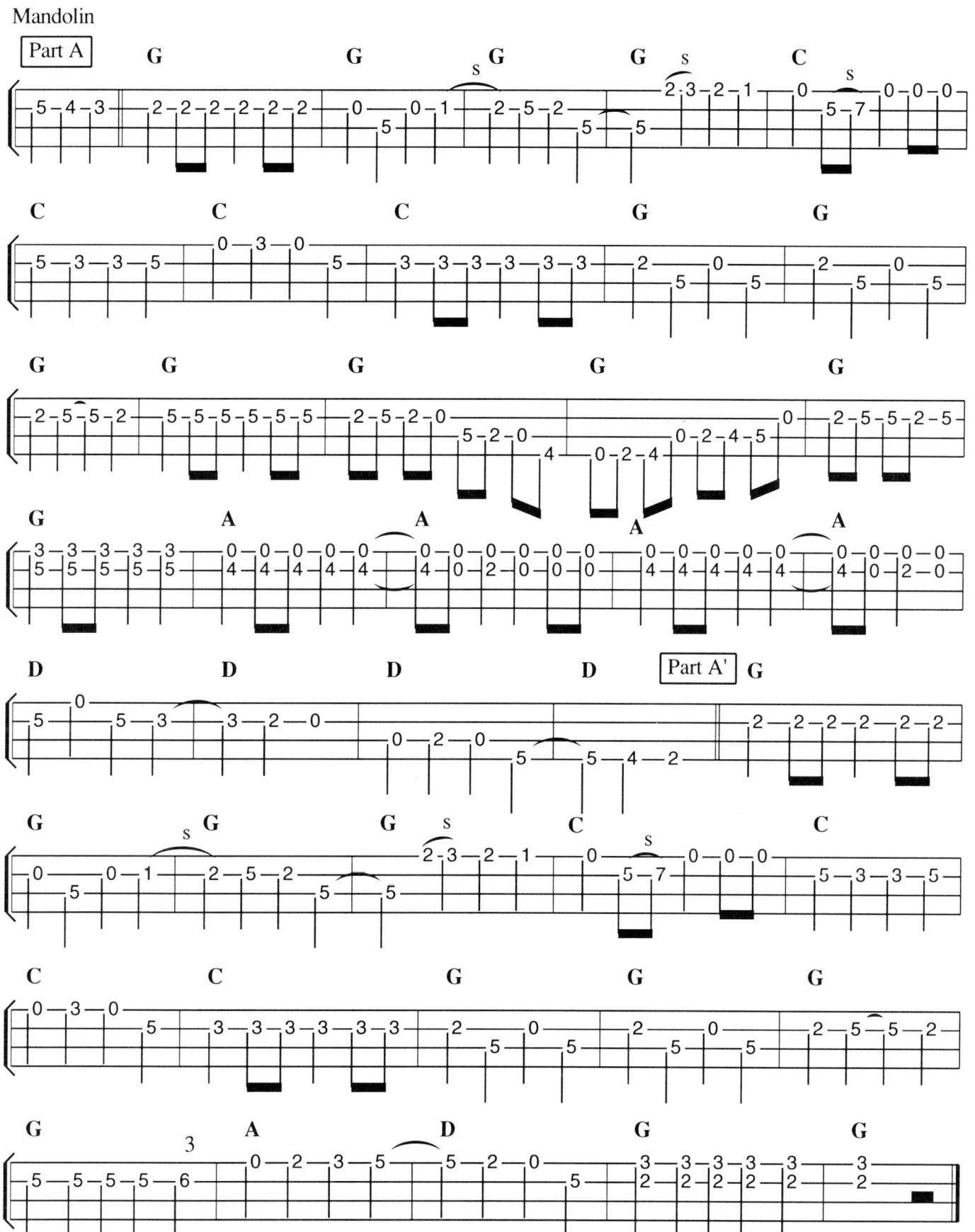

Eighth of January

North American

Mandolin 1

Part A

Part B

Mandolin 2

Part A

Part B

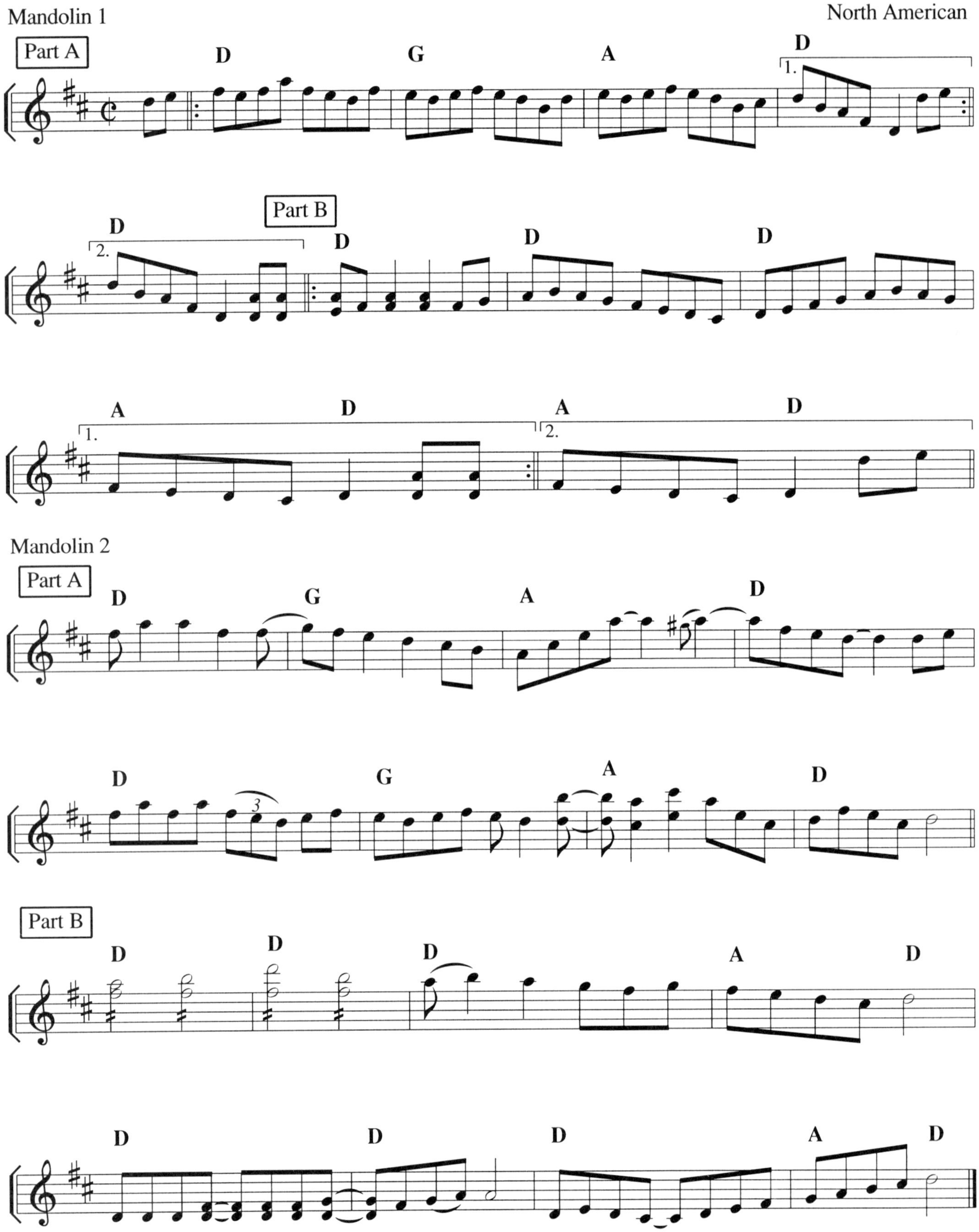

Eighth of January

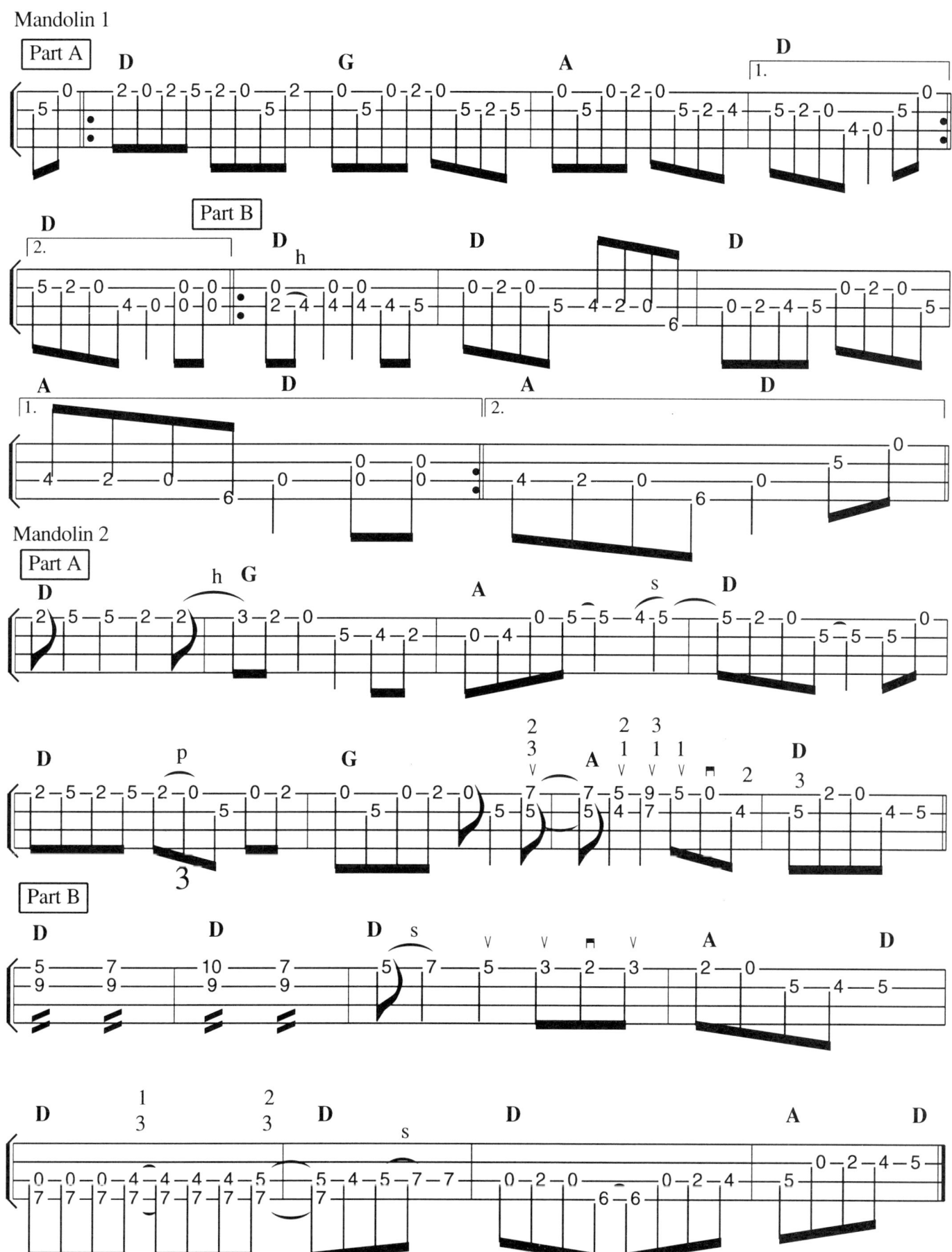

Eighth of January

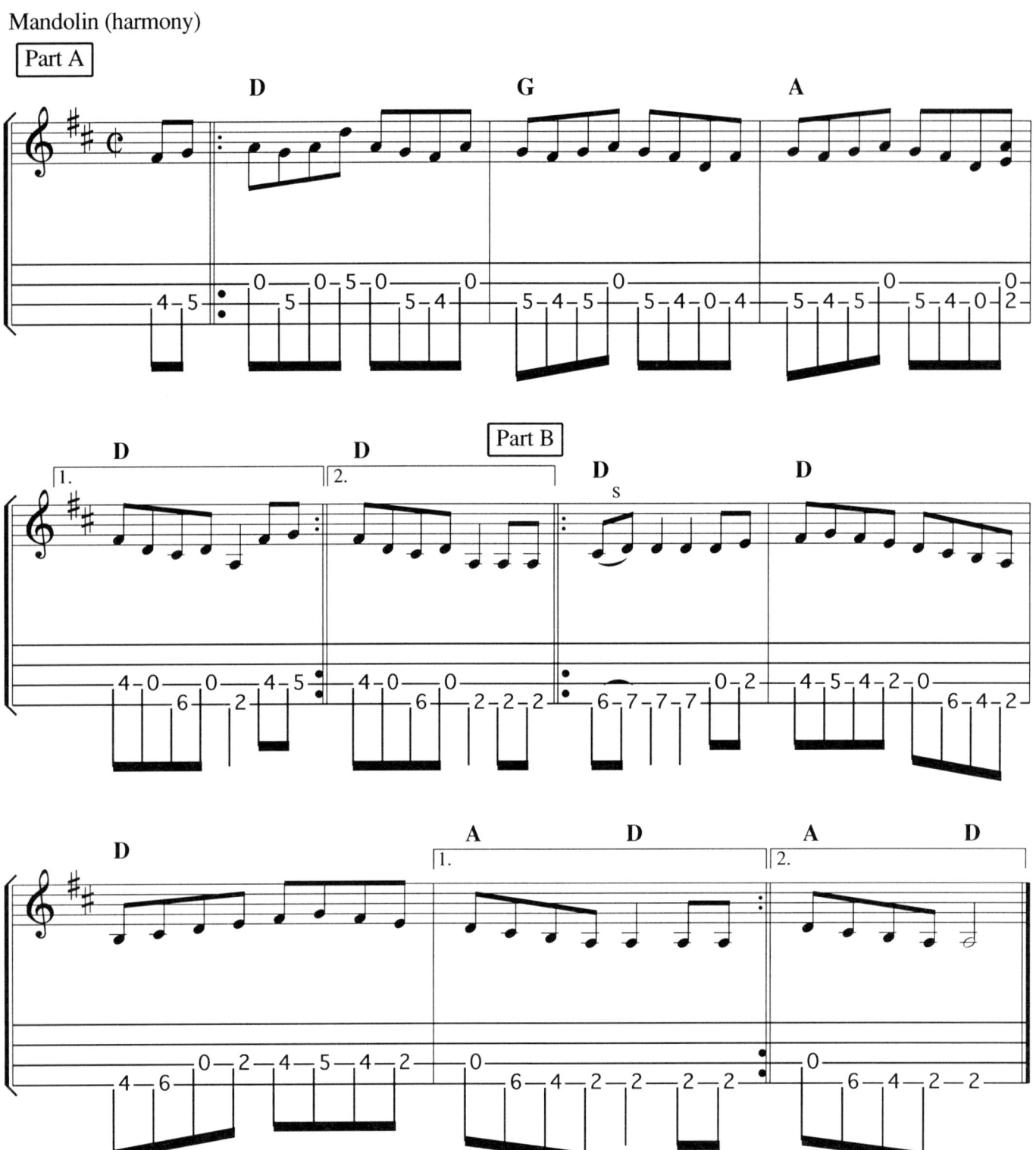

Forked Deer

Mandolin

North American

Disc 2
Track 1

Part A

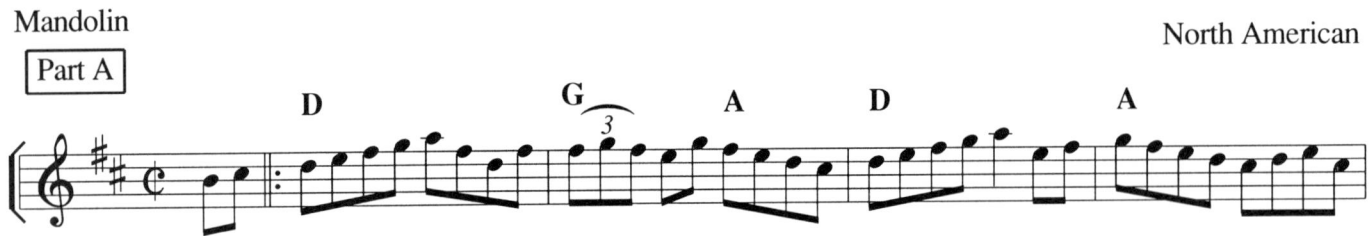

*Part B is played first on CD (part A comes later).

Forked Deer

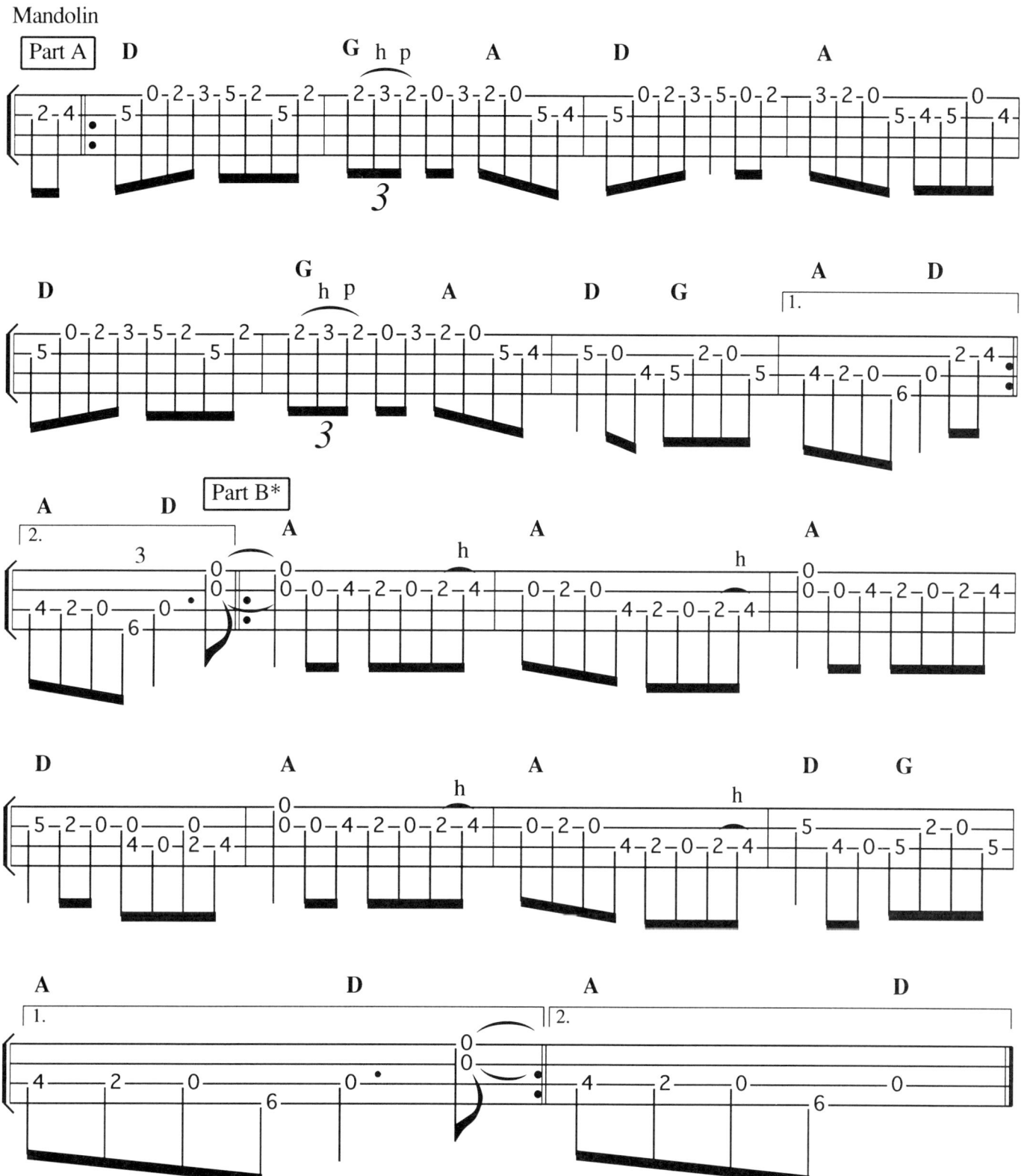

*Part B is played first on CD (part A comes later).

Gardenia Waltz

Mandolin*

North American

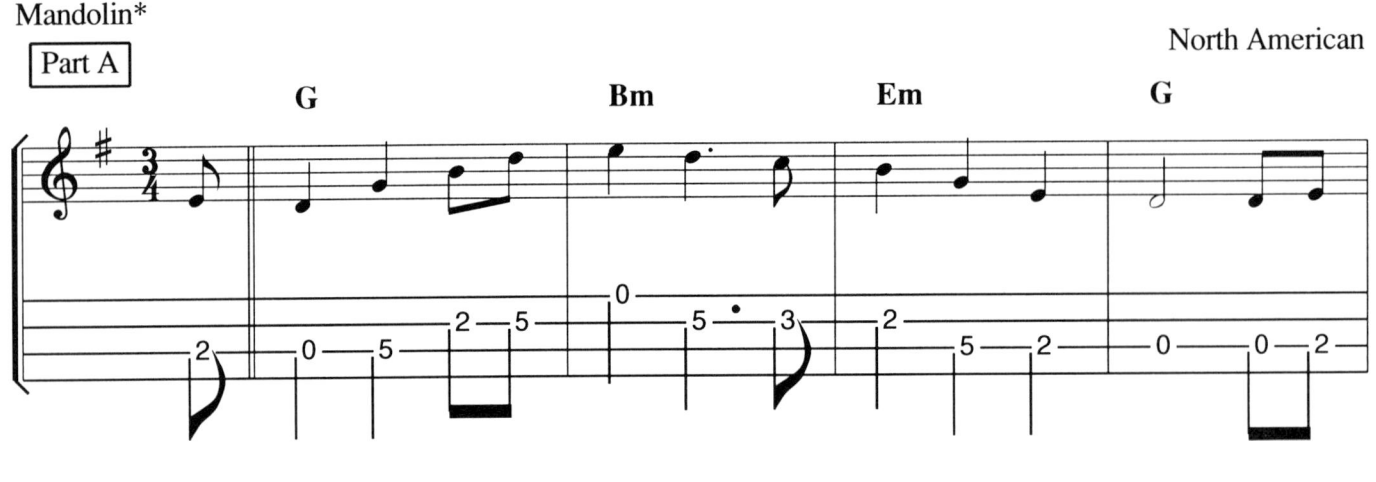
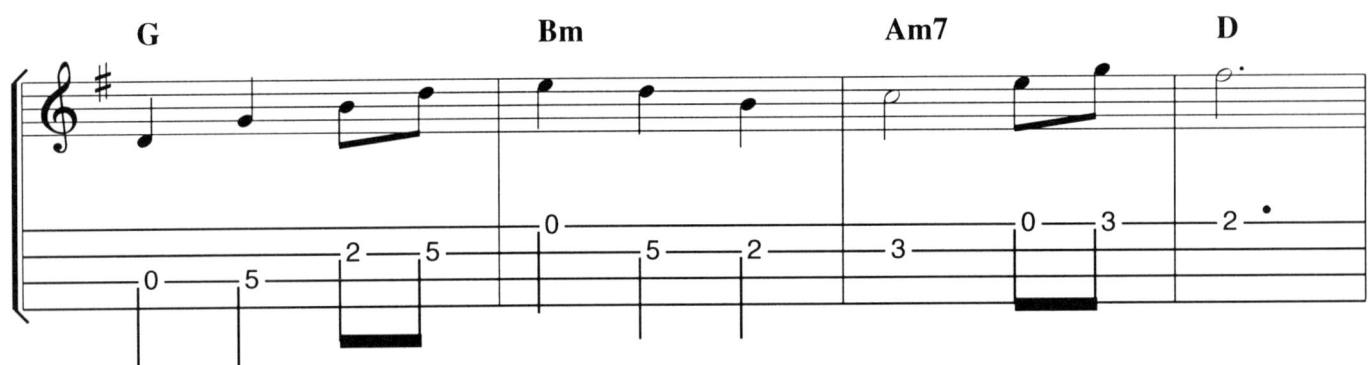
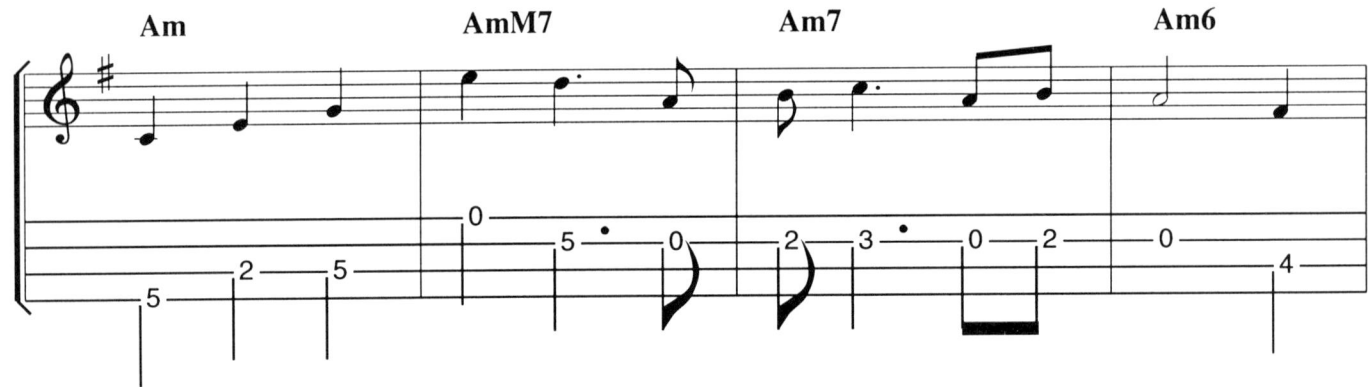
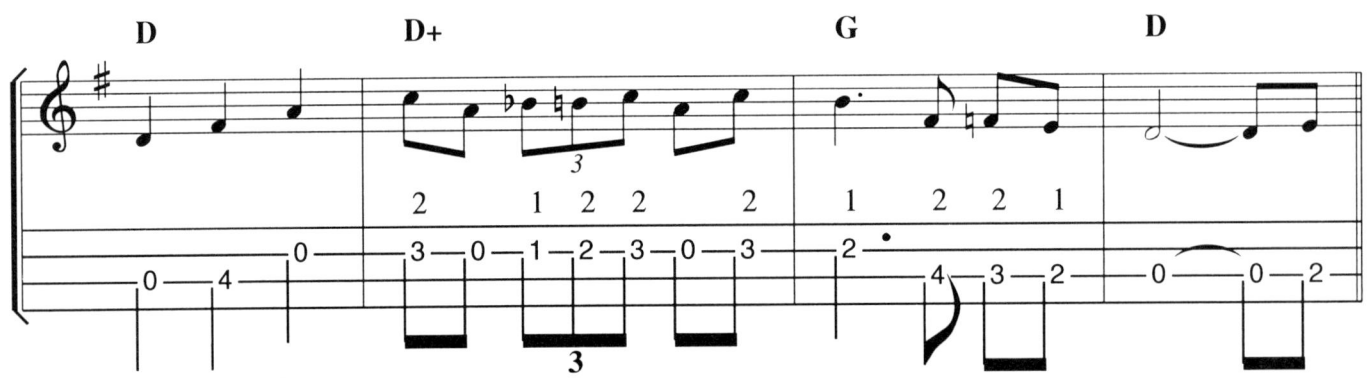

*Mandolin is not on CD.

Gardenia Waltz by Johnny Gimble
© 1974 by Gardenia Music. All Rights Reserved. Used by Permission.

Gardenia Waltz

Mandolin (cont.)

Part A'

Grandfather's Clock

Mandolin

North American

Grandfather's Clock

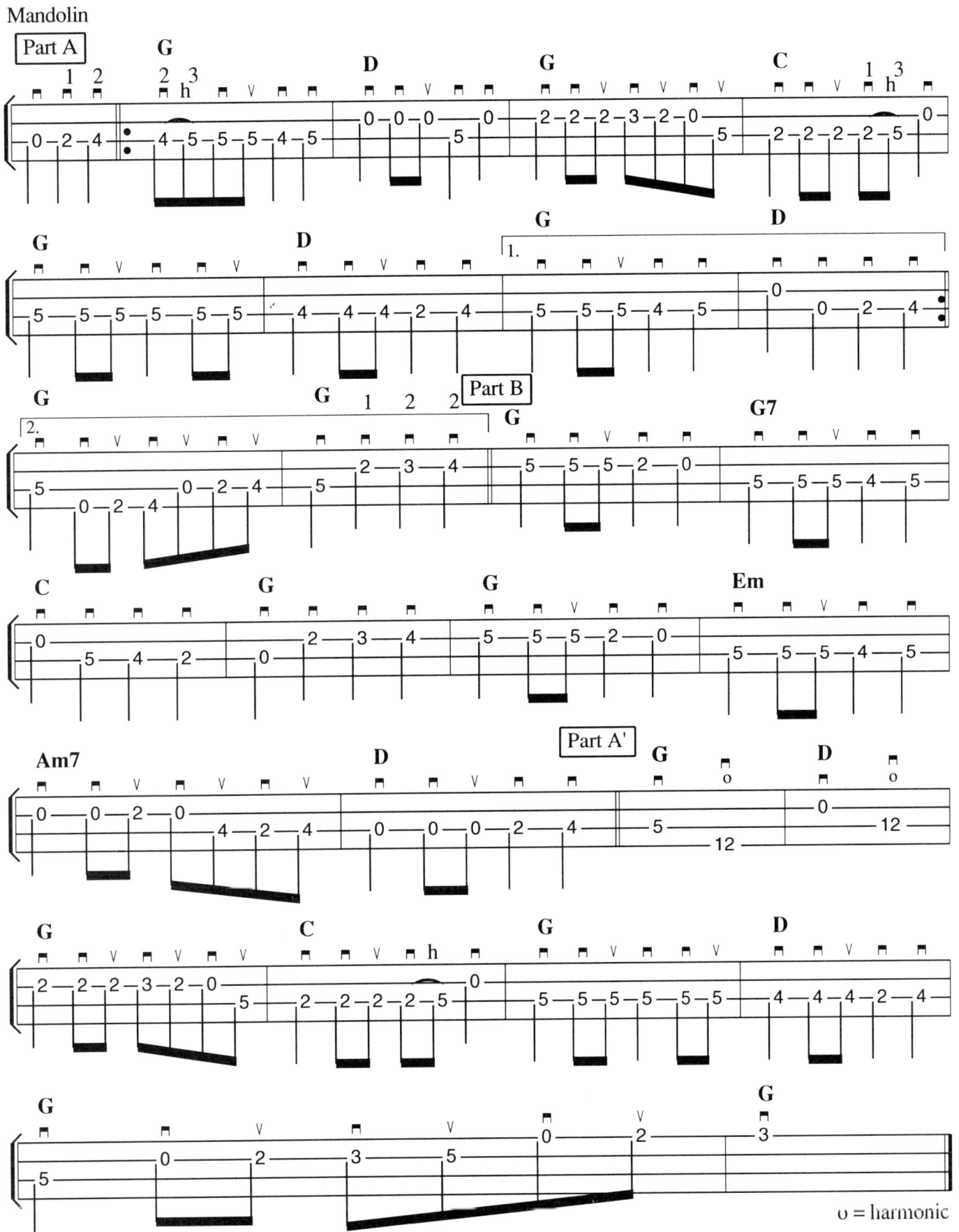

Disc 2
Track 4

Green Willis

Mandolin

Irish/American

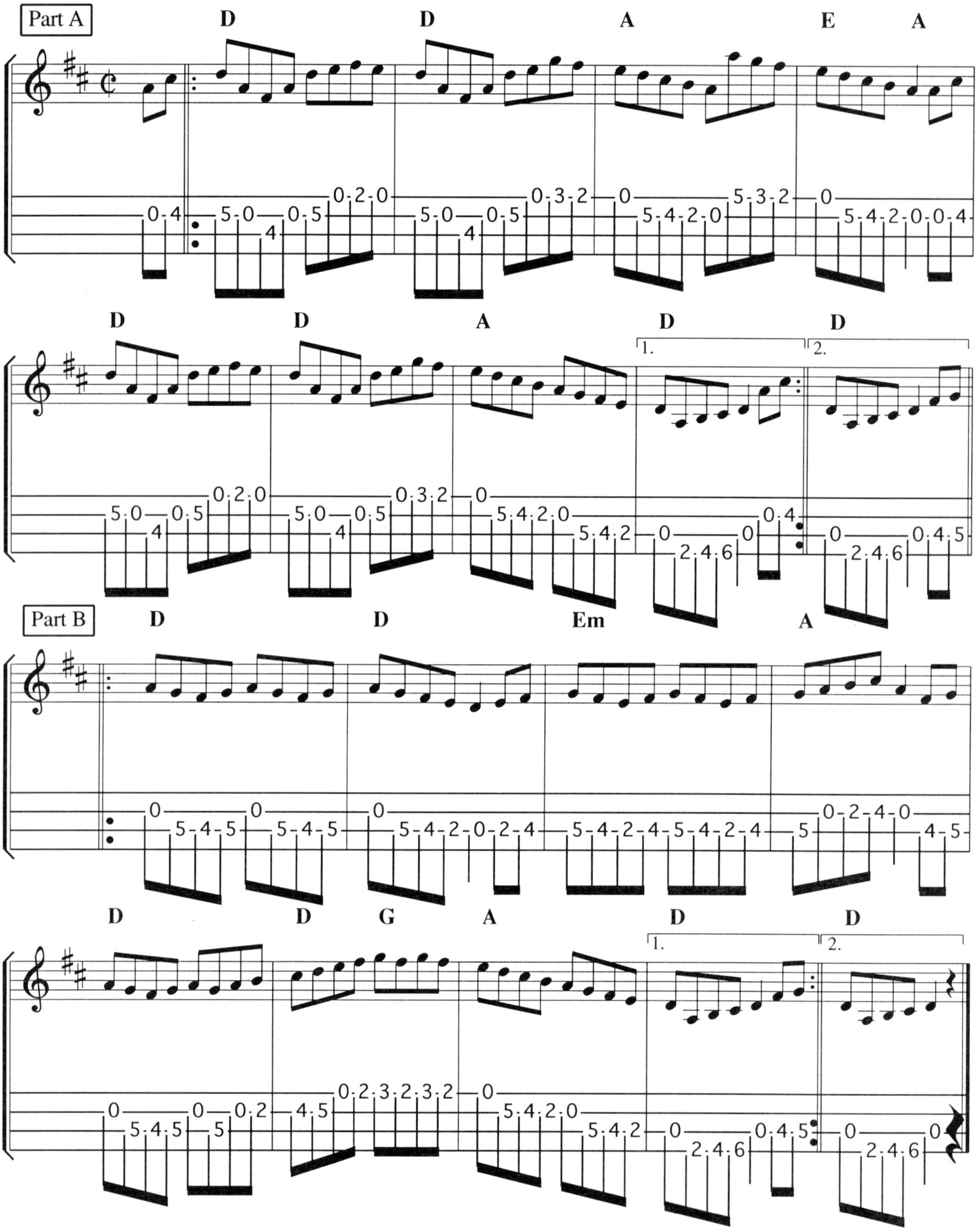

Disc 2
Track 5

Indian's Farewell Waltz

Mandolin

North American

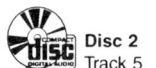

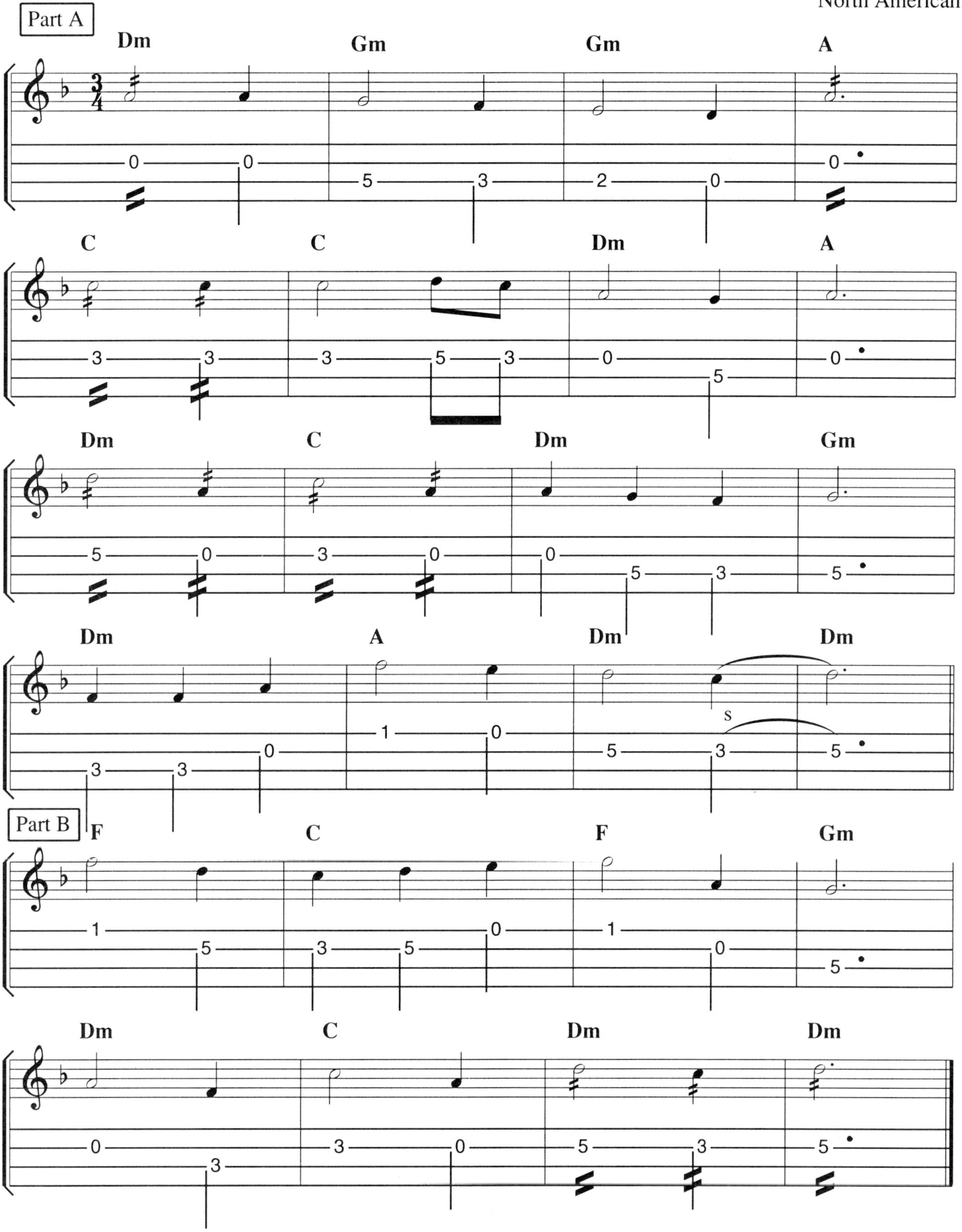

Irish Washerwoman

Irish Washerwoman

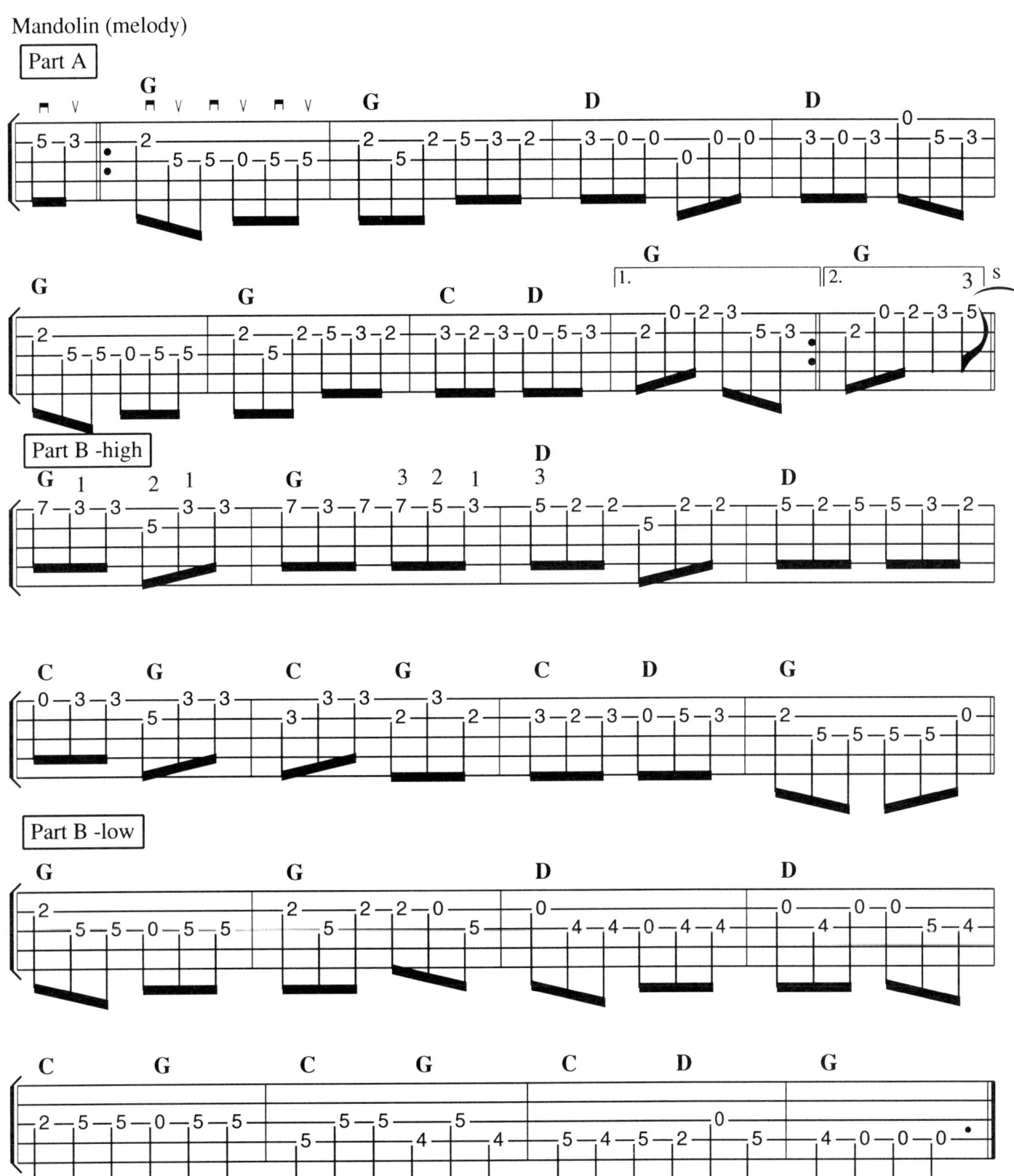

Irish Washerwoman

Mandolin (harmony 1)*

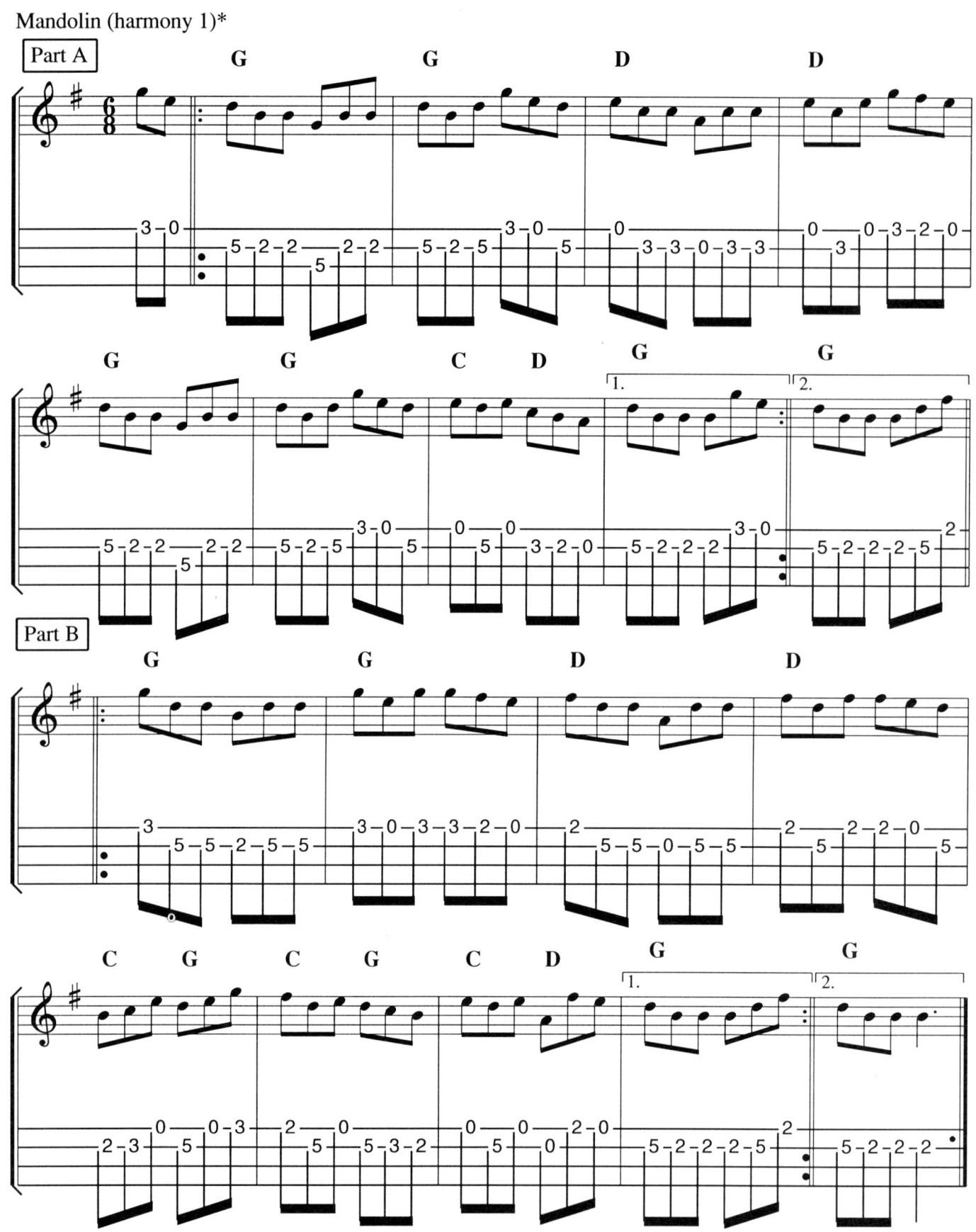

*Mandolin harmony 1 is not on CD.

Irish Washerwoman

Mandolin (harmony 2)*

*Mandolin harmony 2 is not on CD.

Disc 2
Track 7

La Bastringue

Mandolin 1*

French Canadian

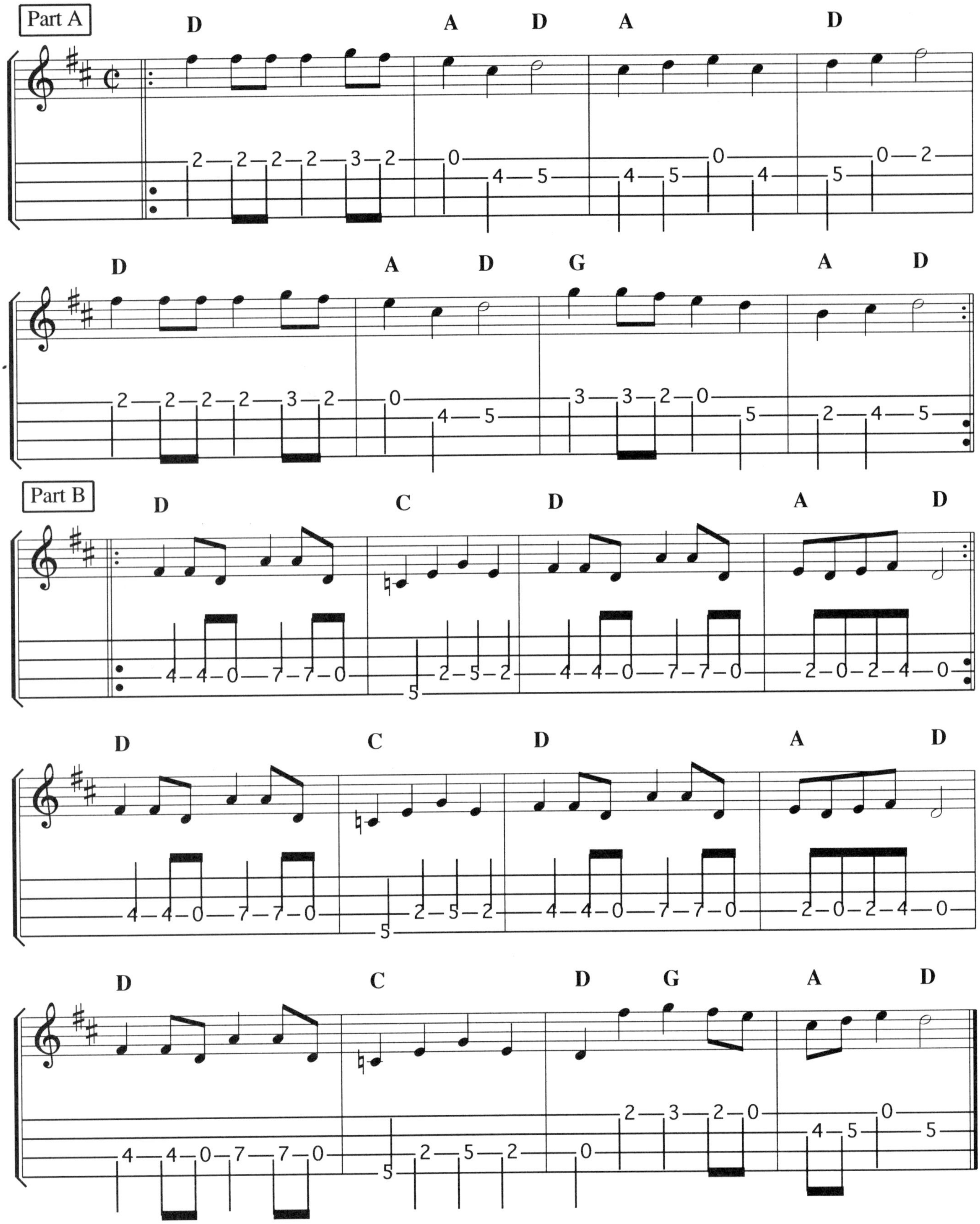

*Mandolin 1 is not on CD.

La Bastringue

La Bastringue

*All notes for this part are harmonics.
o = harmonics.

Leather Britches

Disc 2
Track 8

Mandolin (intro)*

North American

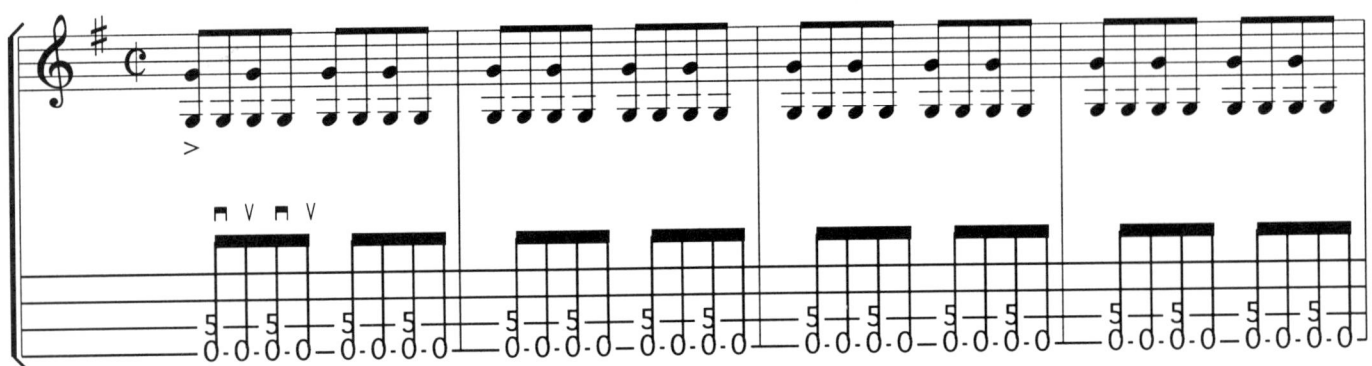

> Accent every beat. (The beat is on the first of every 4 notes).

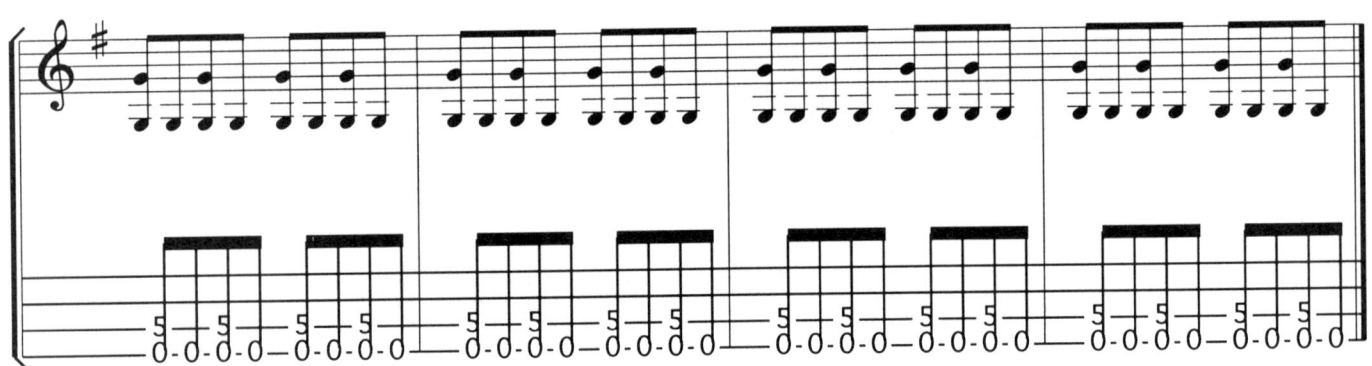

*This part occurs during the guitar intro.

Leather Britches

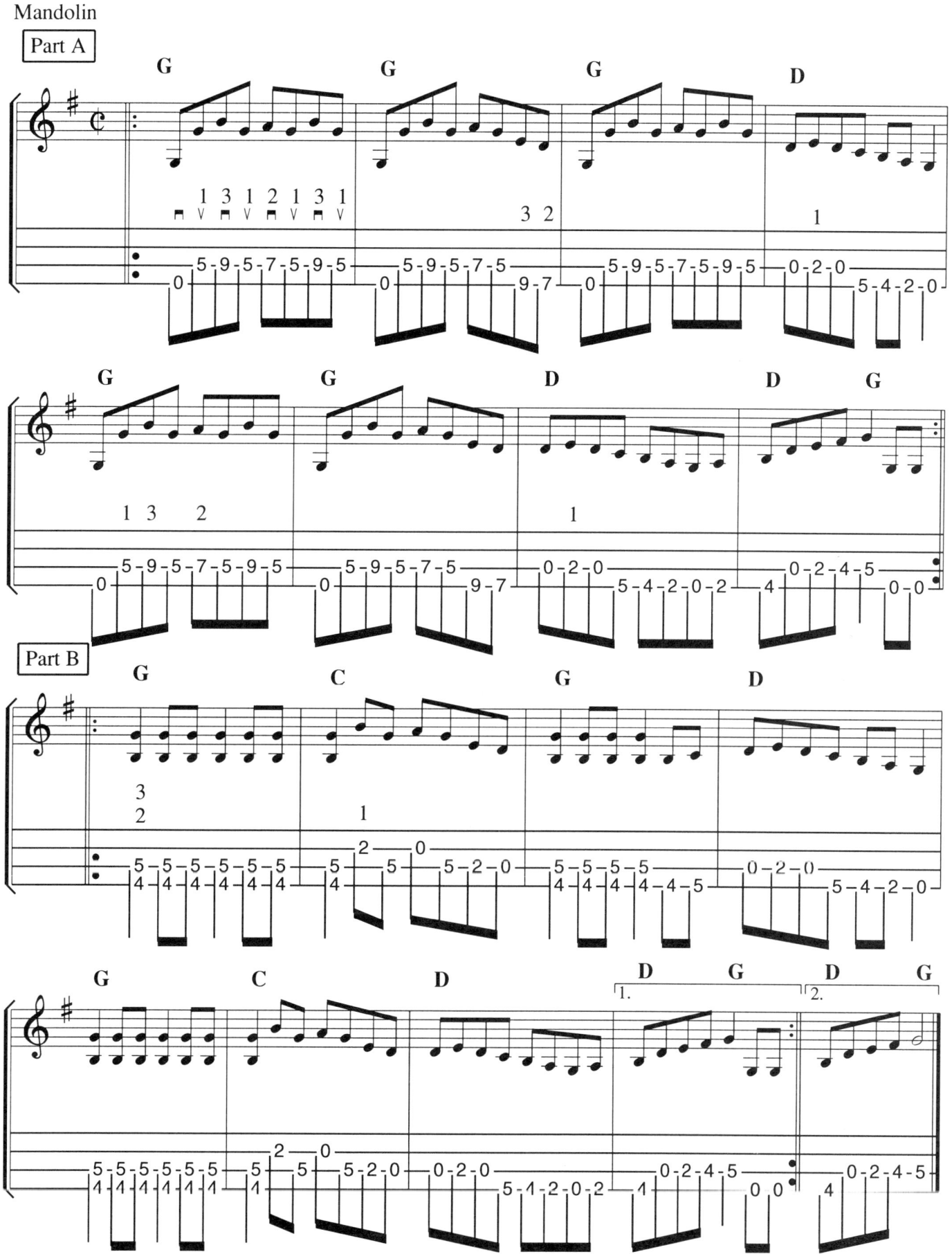

Liberty

Mandolin (melody)

North American

Part A

Part B

Ending

o = harmonic

Liberty

Mandolin (harmony)*

o = harmonic

*Mandolin harmony is not on CD.

Liberty

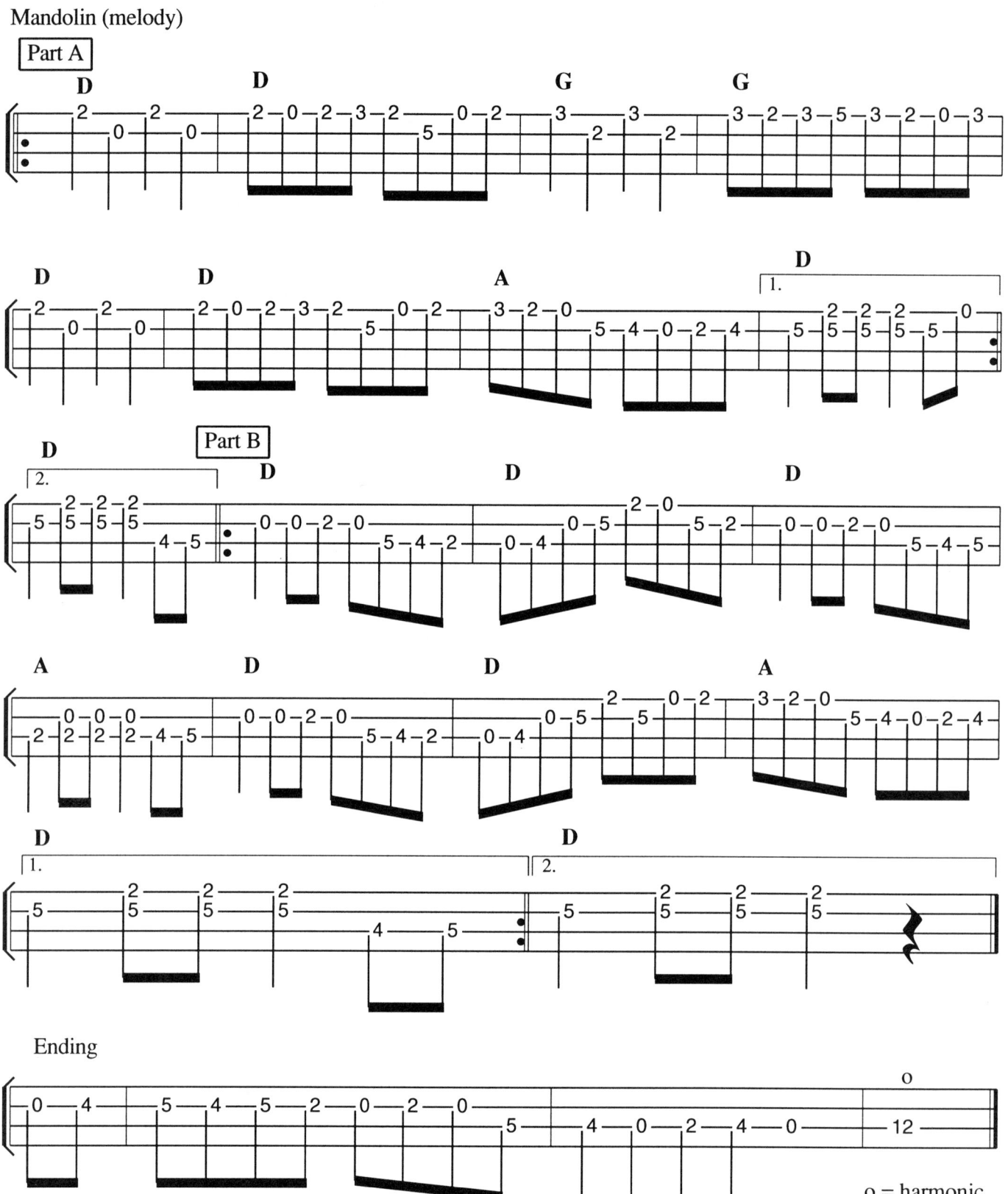

Liberty

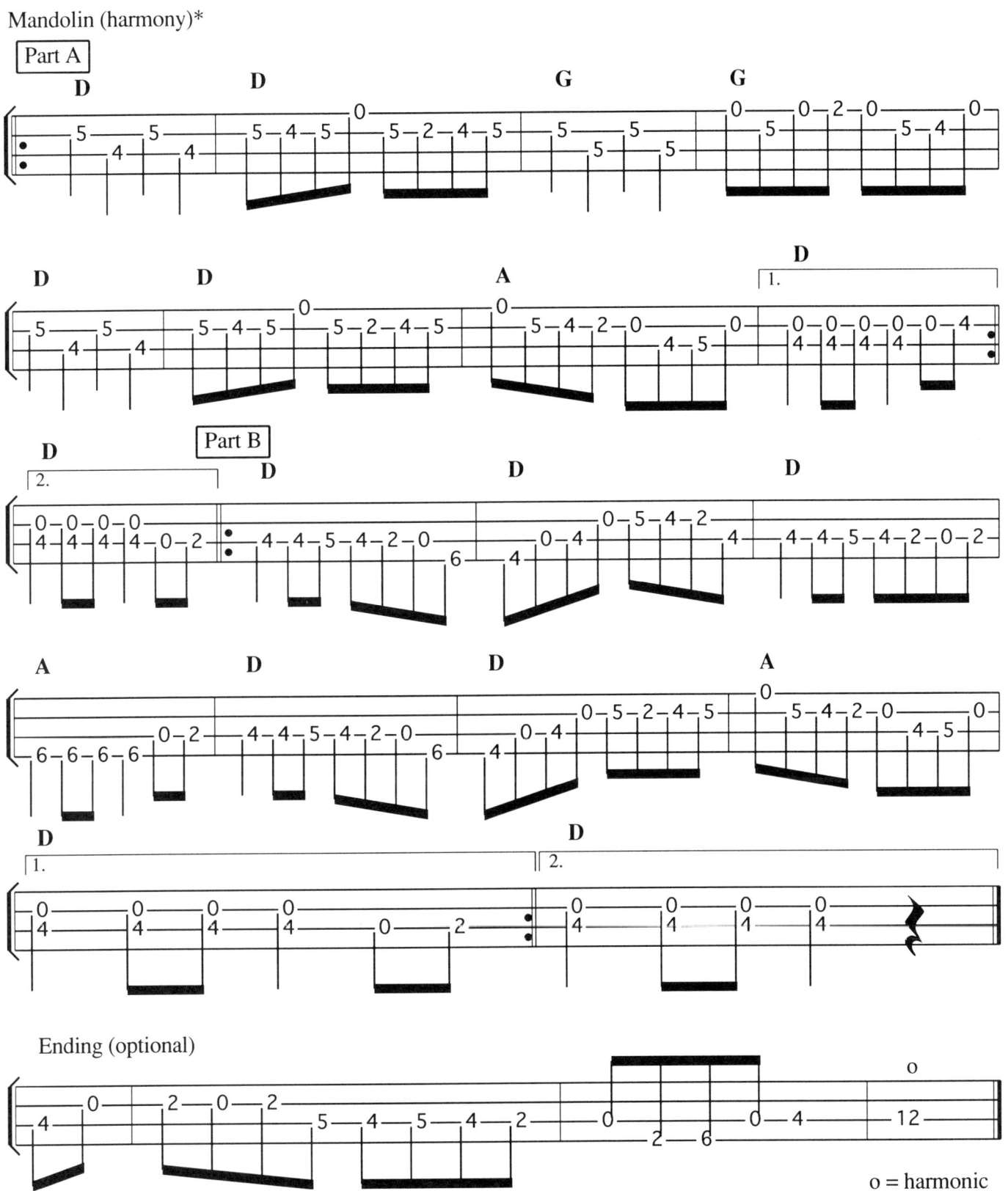

*Mandolin harmony is not on CD.

Martin's Waltz

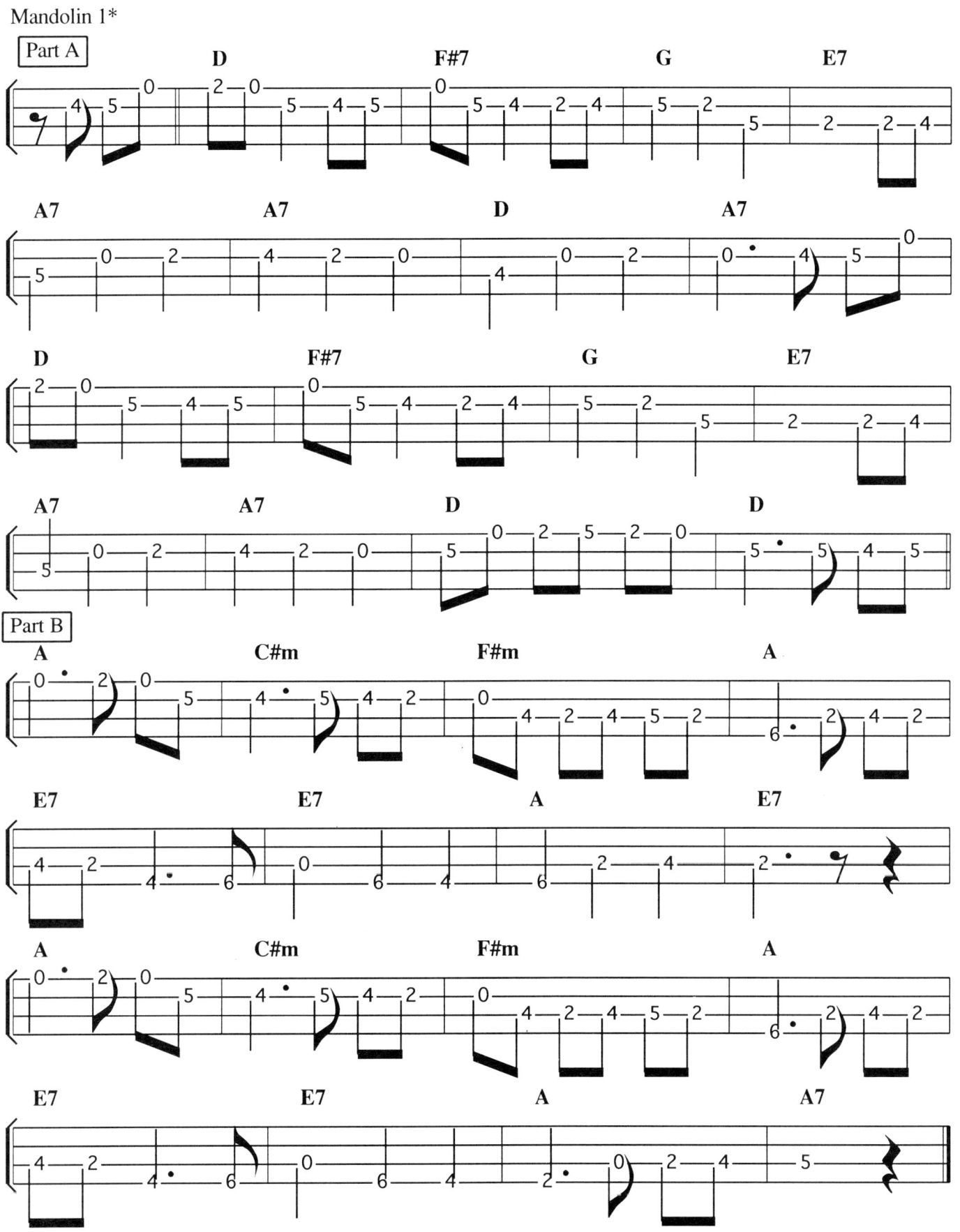

*Mandolin 1 is not on CD.

Martin's Waltz

Martin's Waltz

Mason's Apron

Mandolin — Irish

Part A

Disc 2
Track 12

Mississippi Hornpipe

Mandolin*

North American

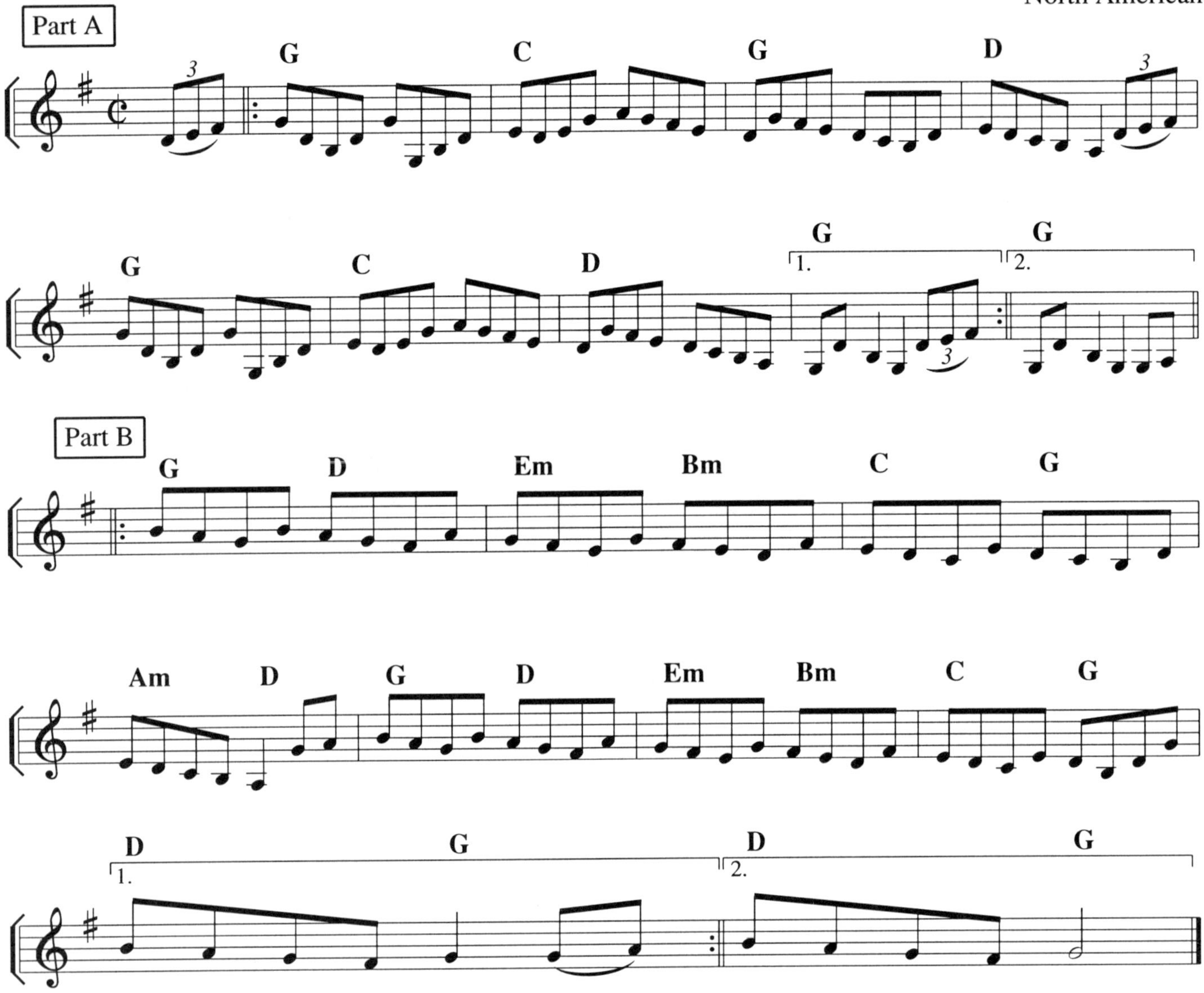

*Mandolin is not on CD.

Mississippi Hornpipe

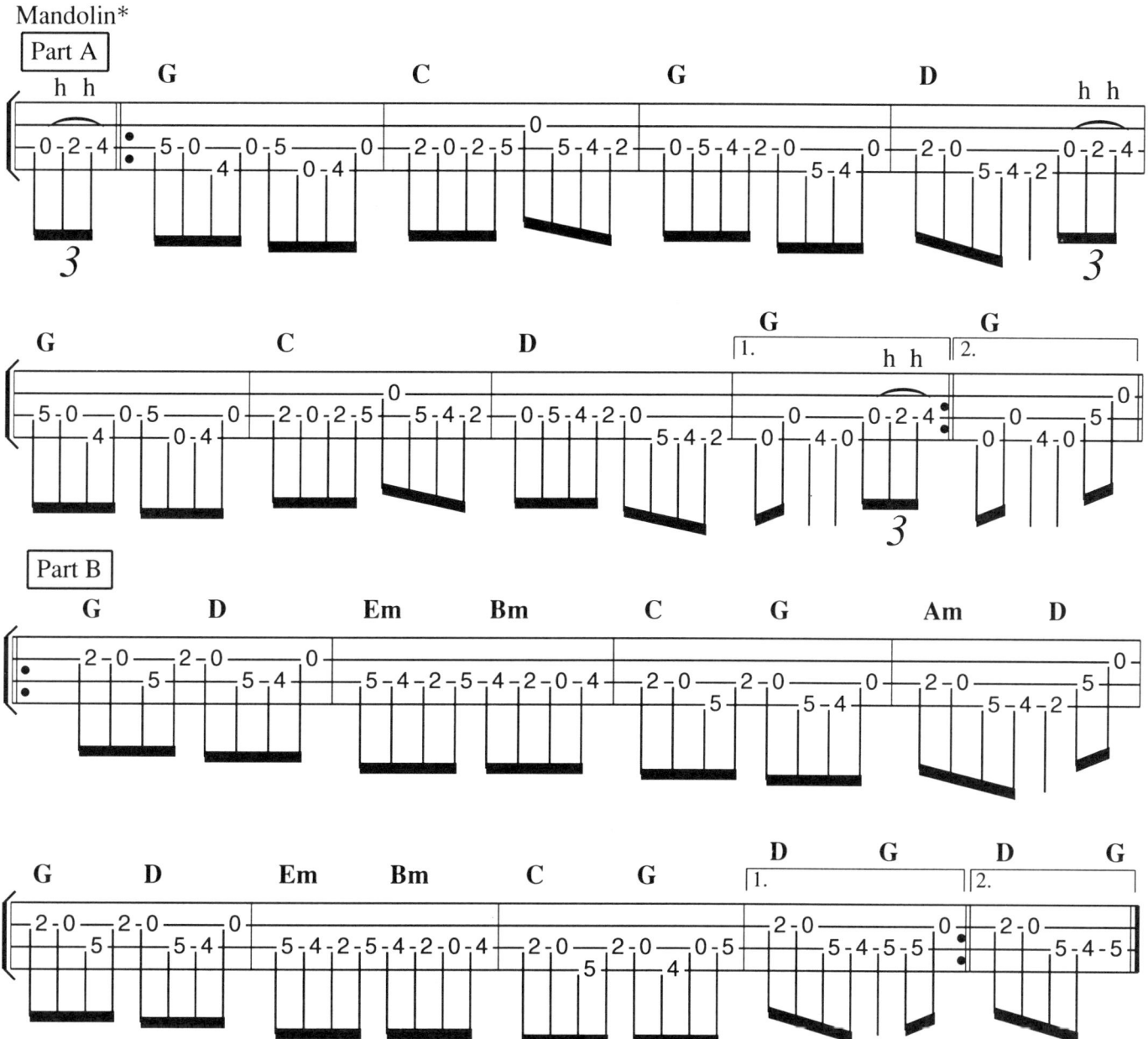

*Mandolin is not on CD.

Mississippi Sawyer

Mandolin (melody)

North American

Disc 2 Track 13

Mississippi Sawyer

*Mandolin harmony is not on CD.

Old Dan Tucker

Mandolin

North American

Old Dan Tucker

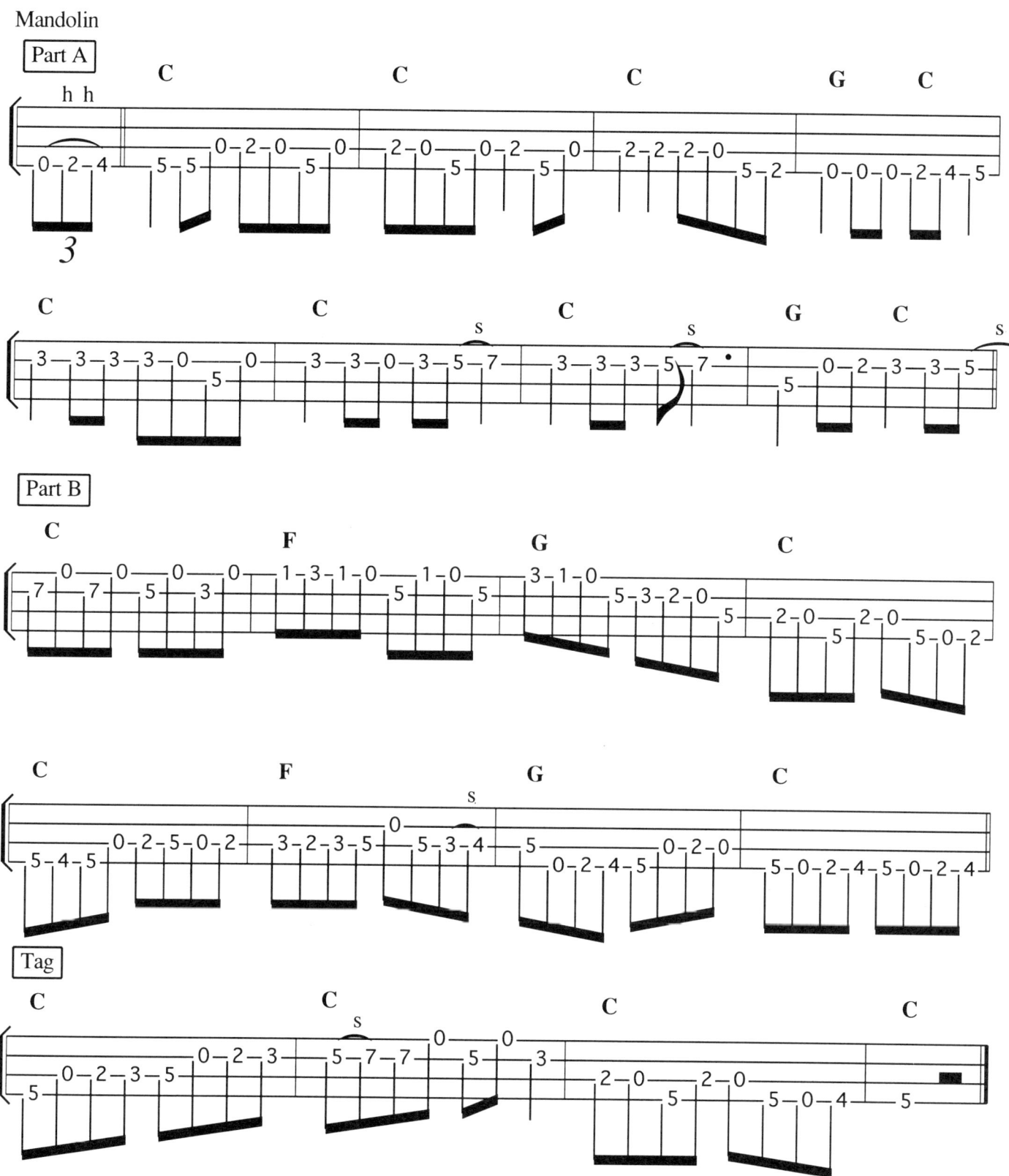

Old Joe Clark

Mandolin 1

North American

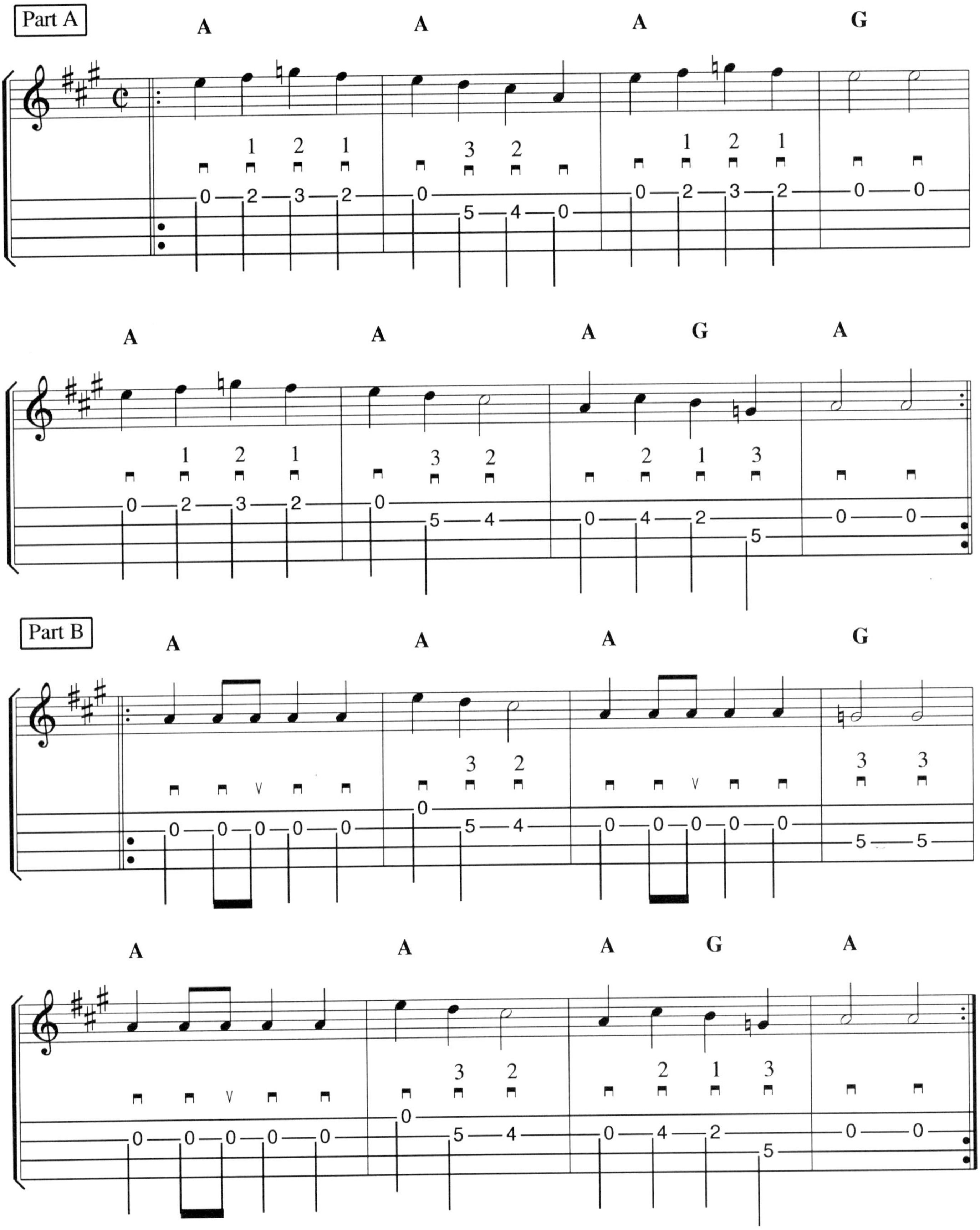

Part A

Part B

Old Joe Clark

Mandolin 2

President Garfield's Hornpipe

Mandolin 1*
North American

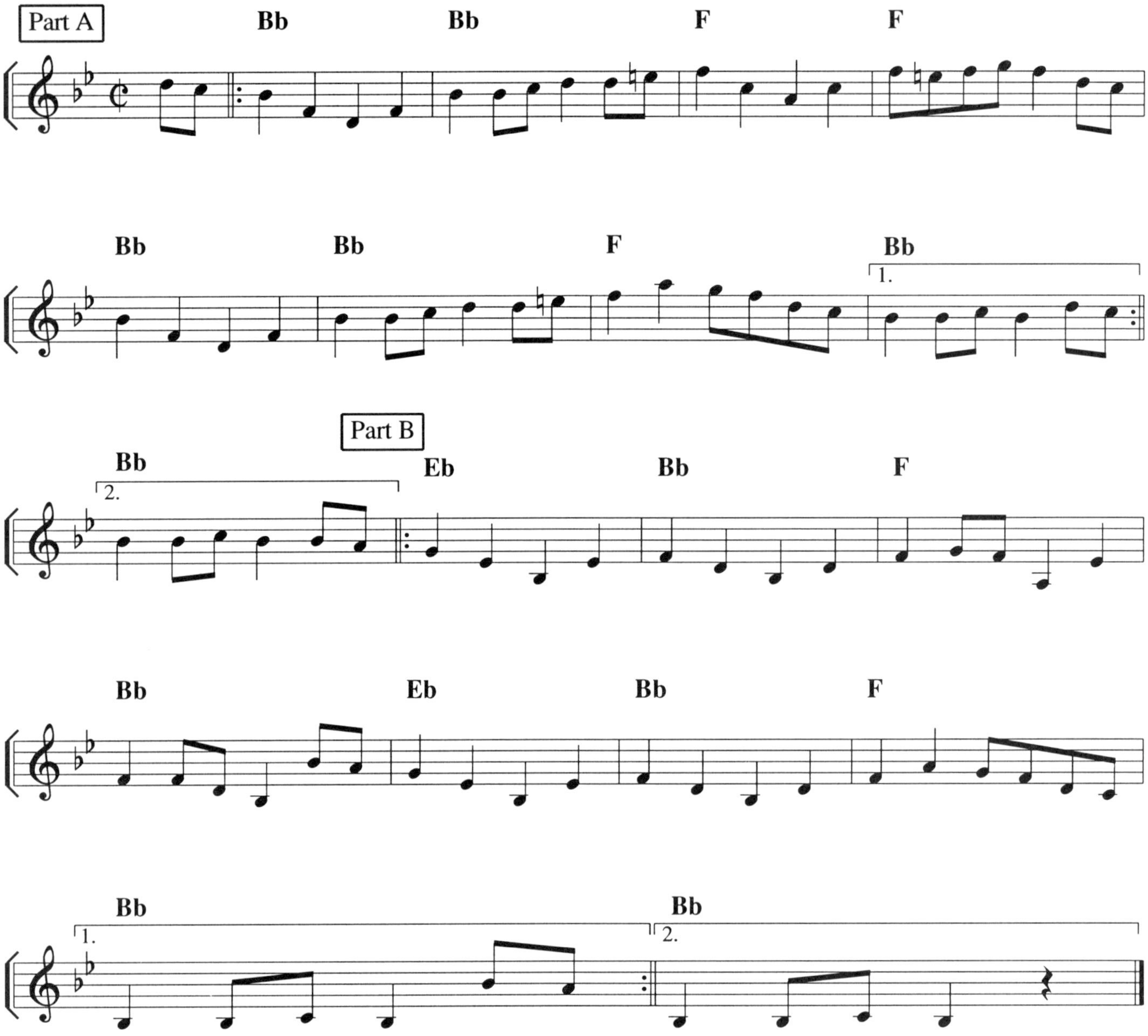

Part A

*Mandolin 1 is not on CD.

President Garfield's Hornpipe

Mandolin 1*

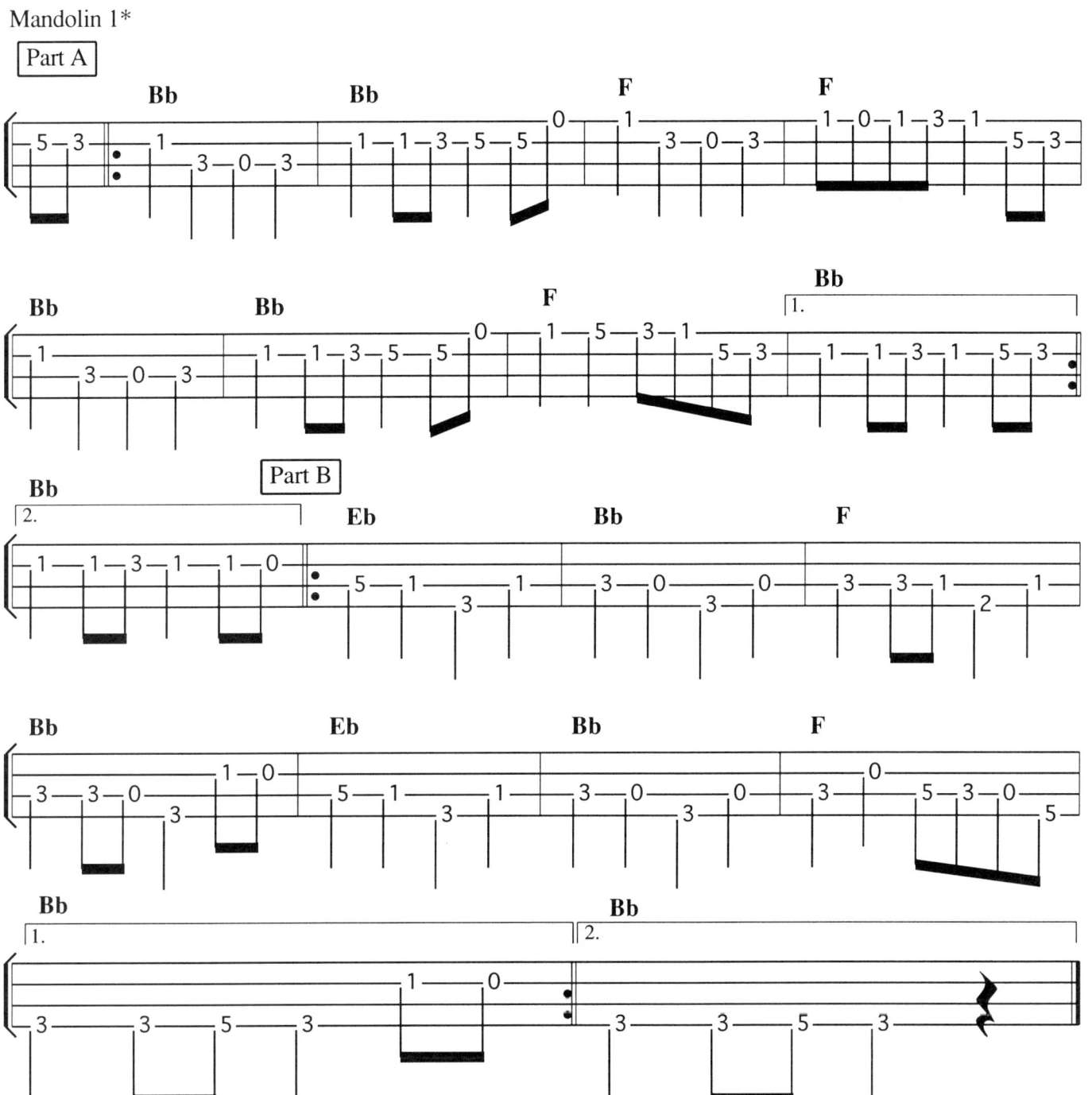

*Mandolin 1 is not on CD.

President Garfield's Hornpipe

Mandolin 2*

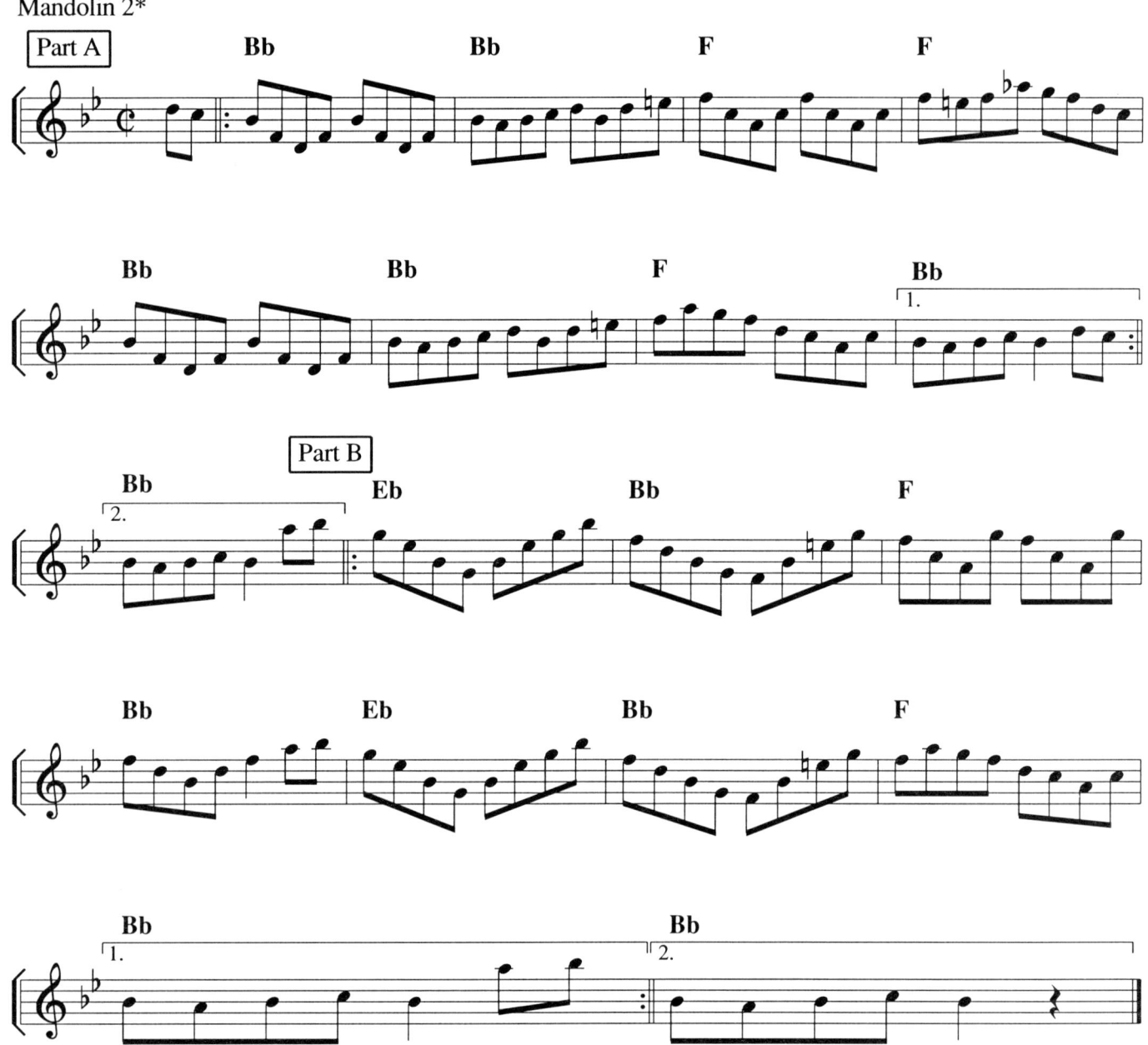

*Mandolin 2 is not on CD.

President Garfield's Hornpipe

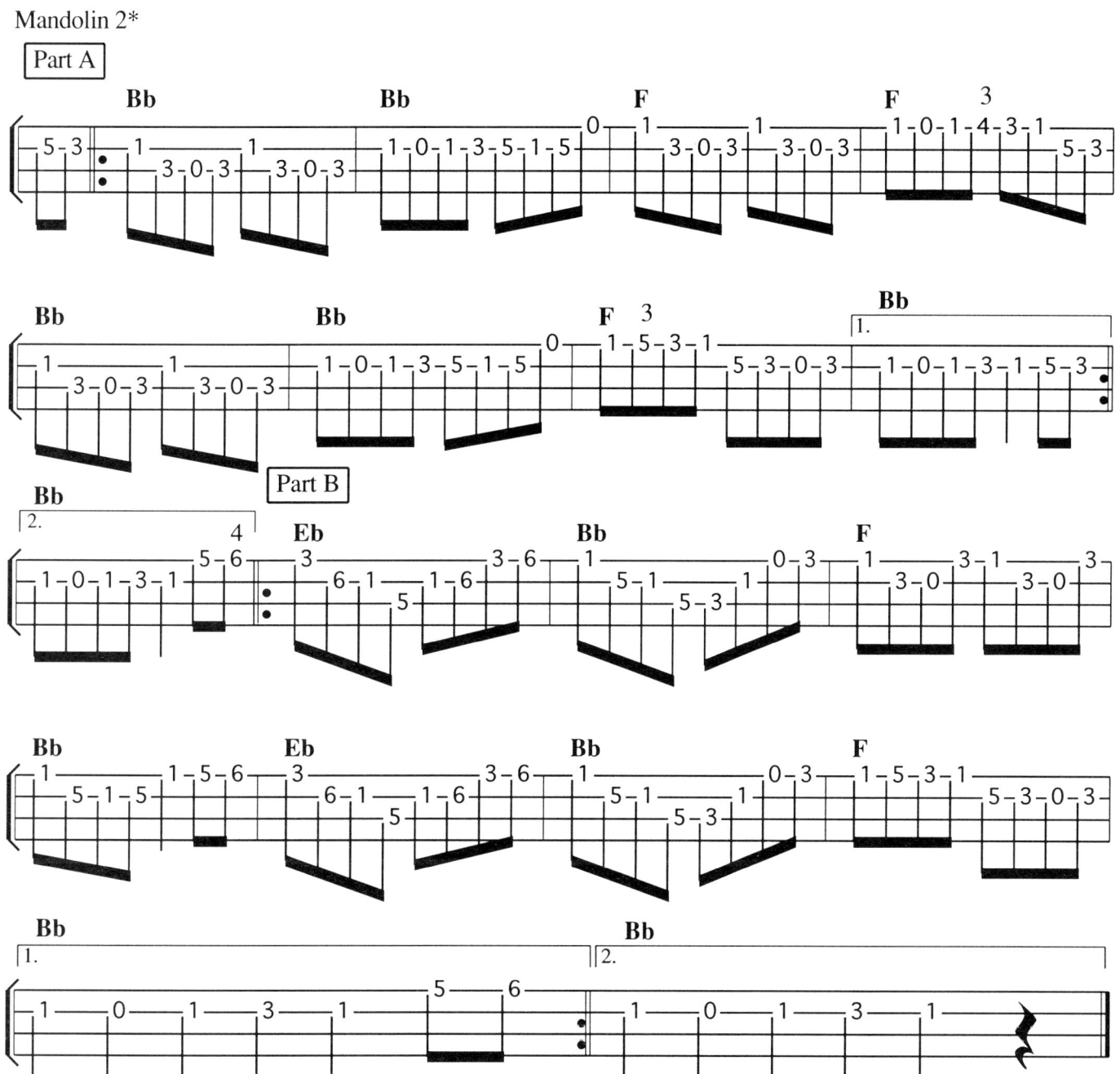

*Mandolin 2 is not on CD.

Pretty Peg

Scottish

Mandolin

Part A

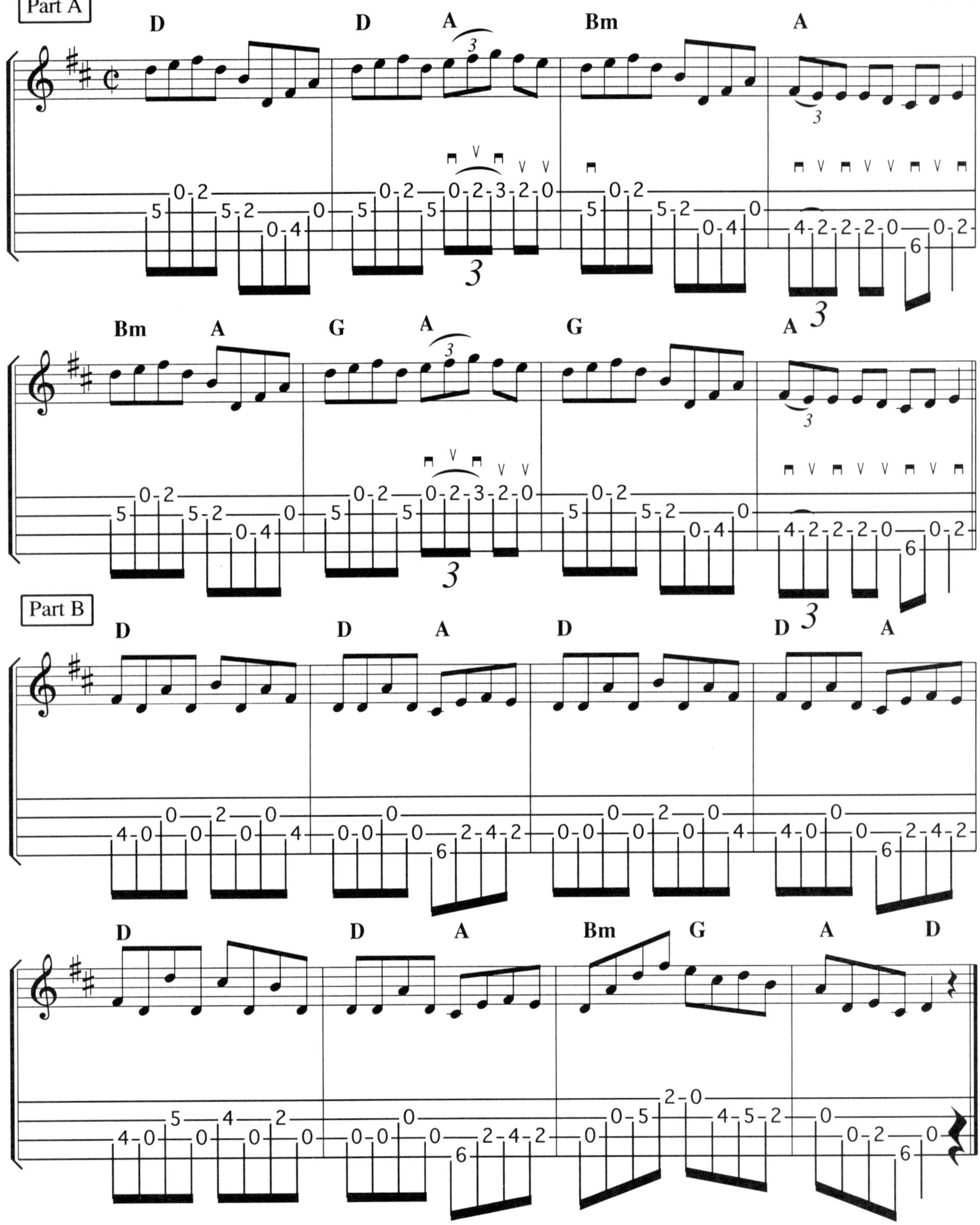

Red-haired Boy

Mandolin (melody)

Irish

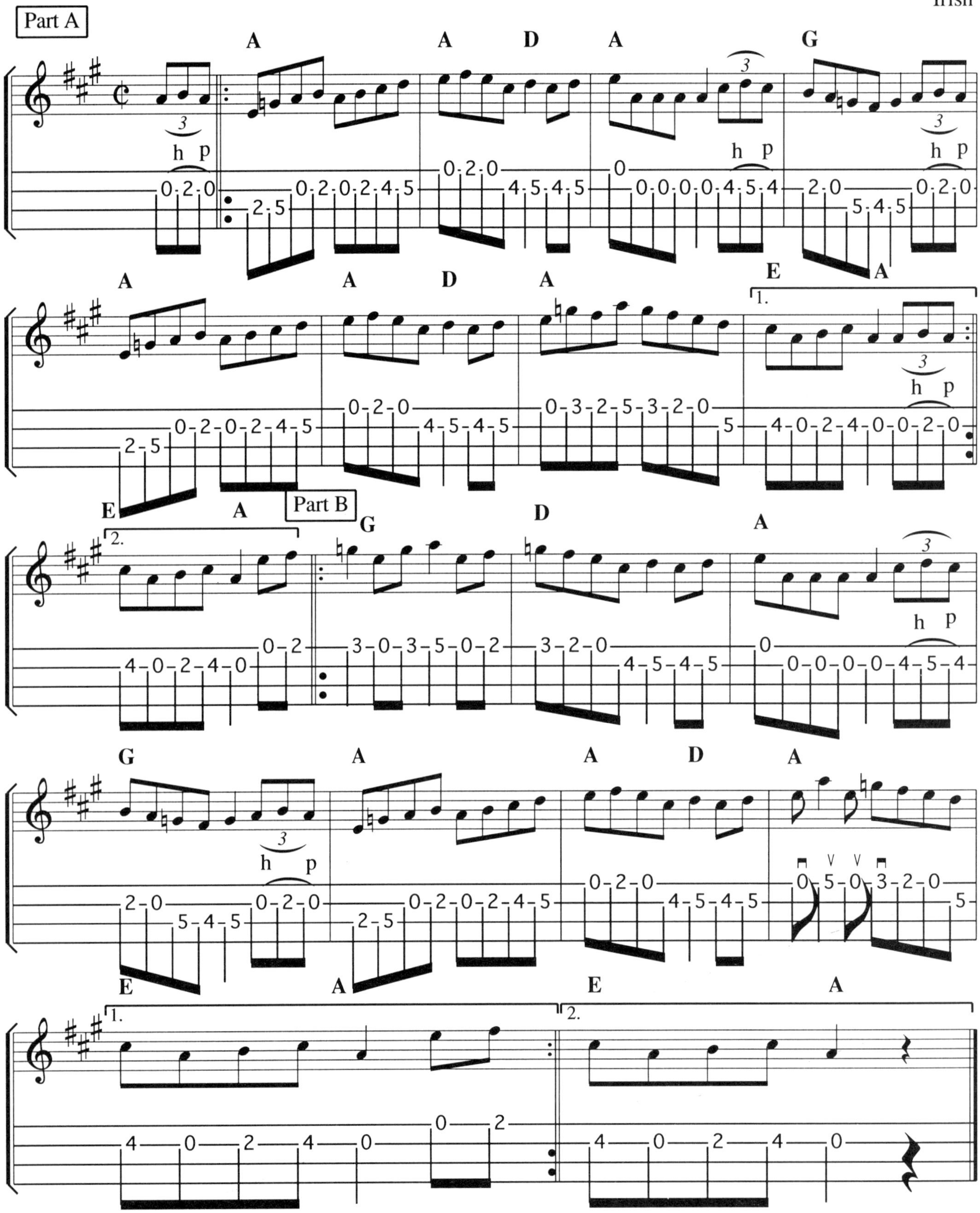

Part A

Red-haired Boy

Mandolin (harmony)

Red Wing

Mandolin

North American

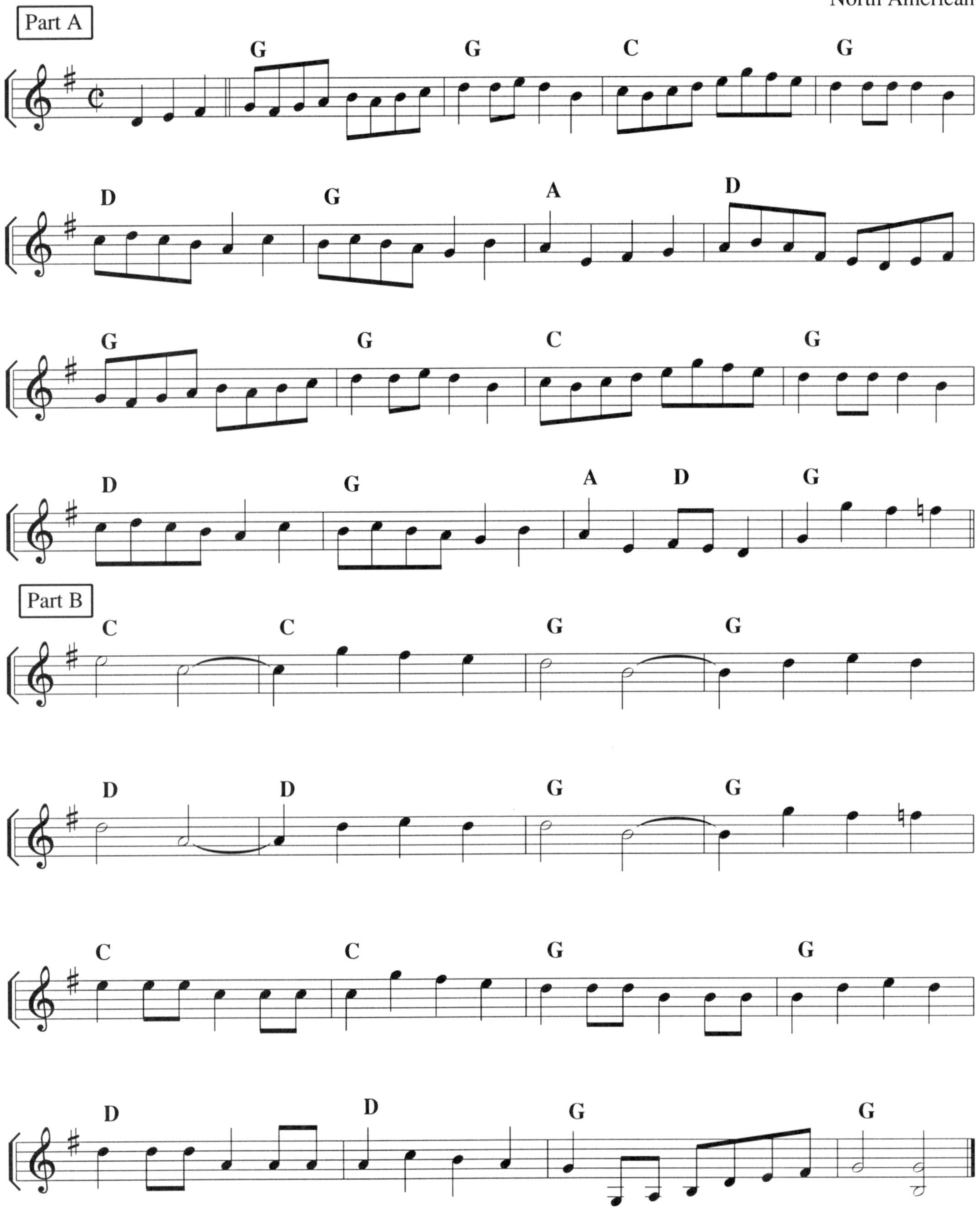

Part A

Part B

Red Wing

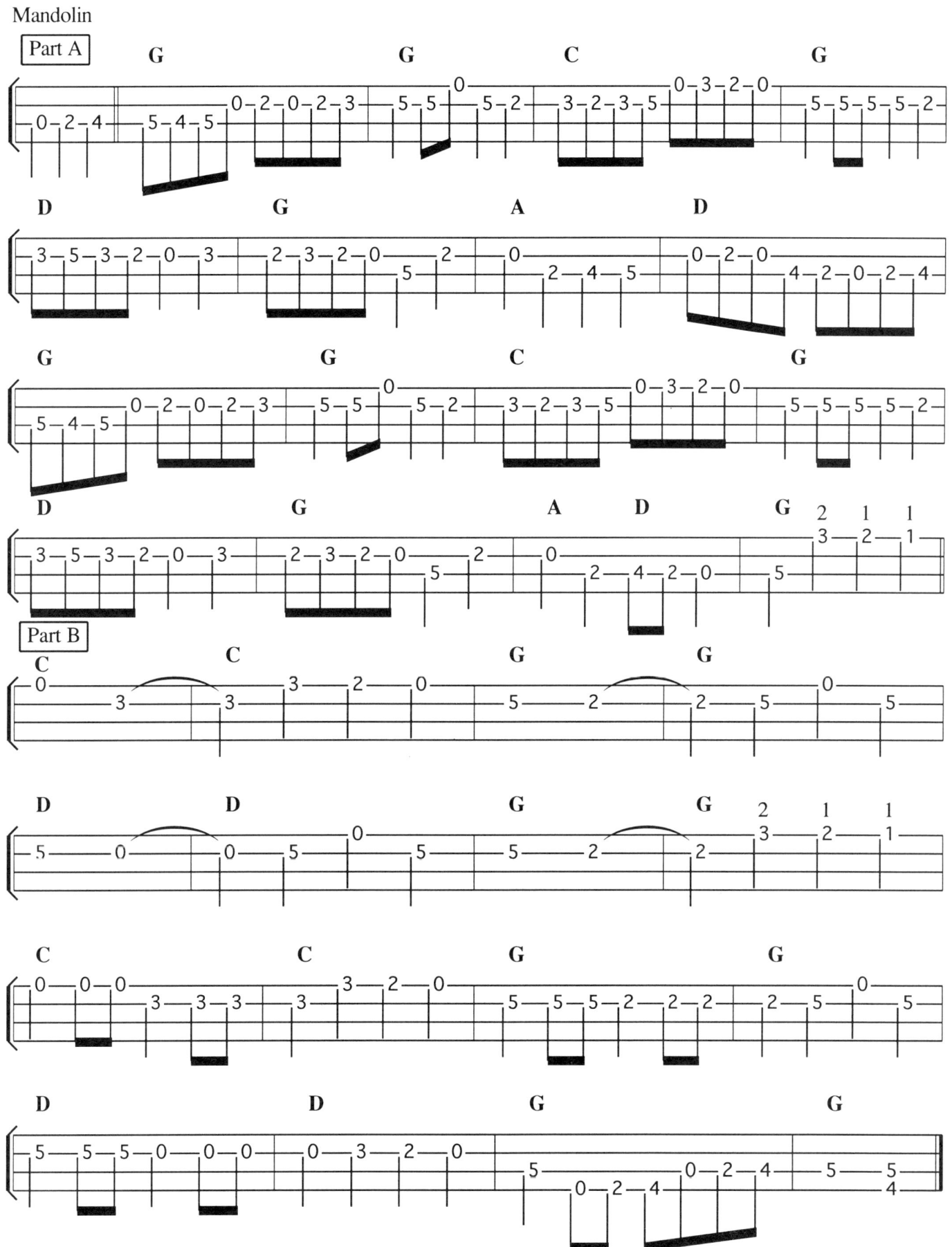

Sailor's Hornpipe

Mandolin

English

Part A

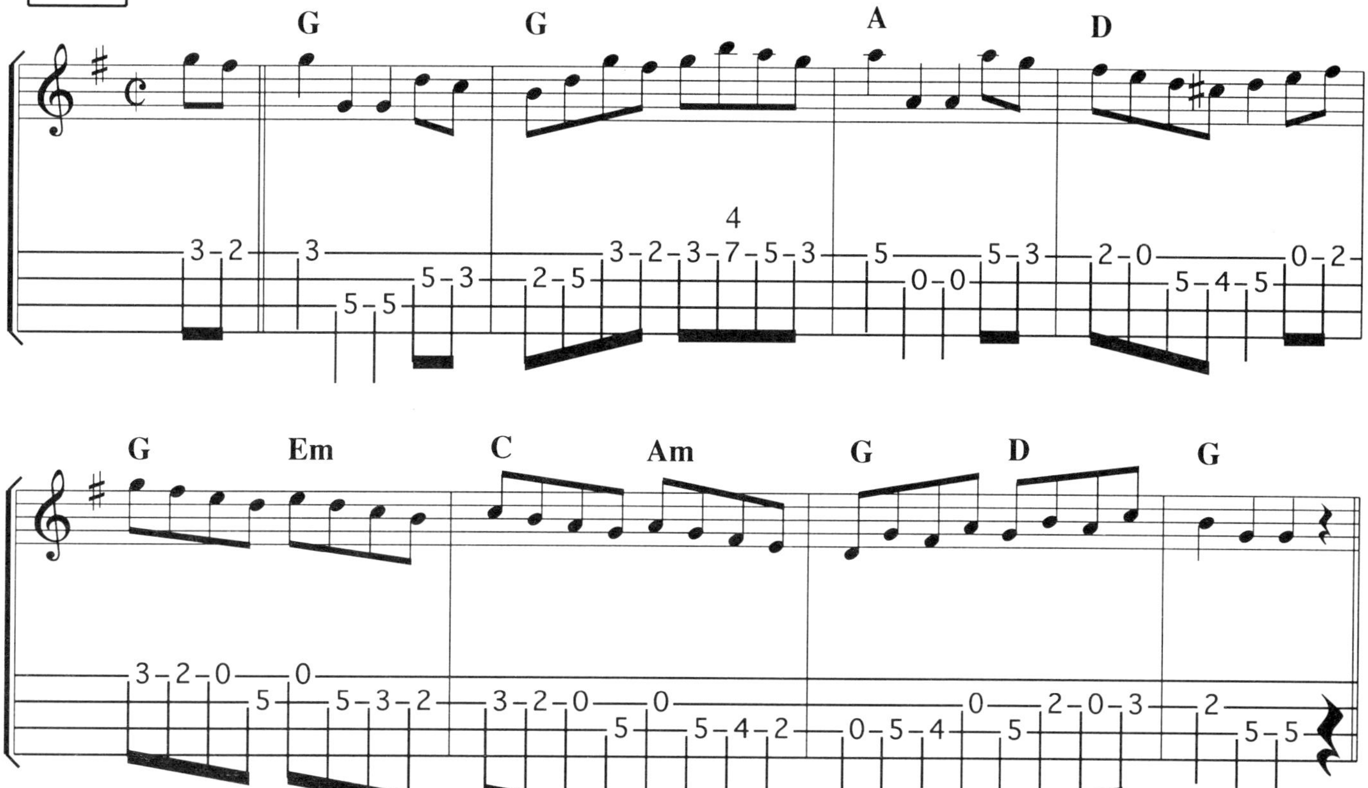

Part B*

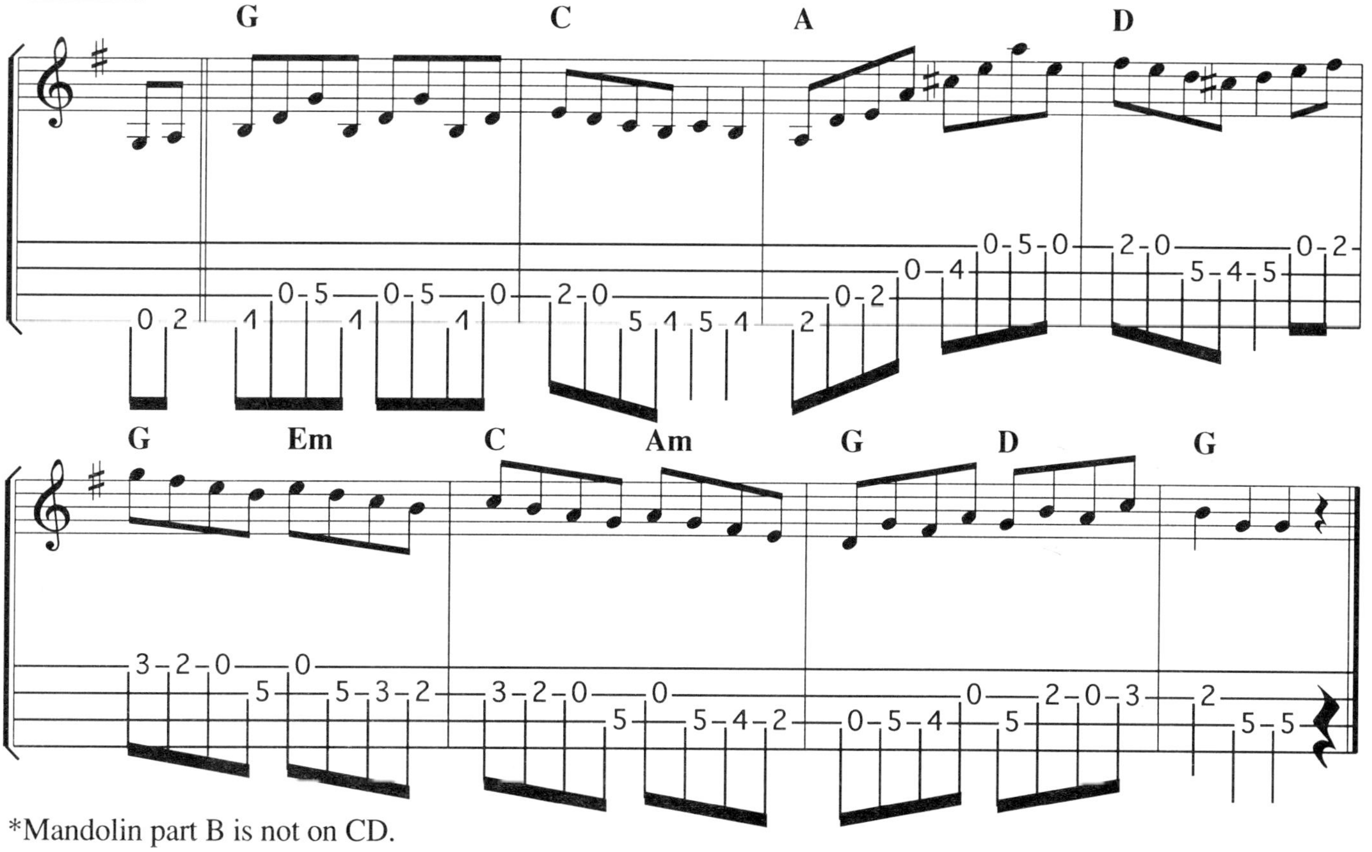

*Mandolin part B is not on CD.

College Hornpipe

Mandolin* North American

North American

College Hornpipe

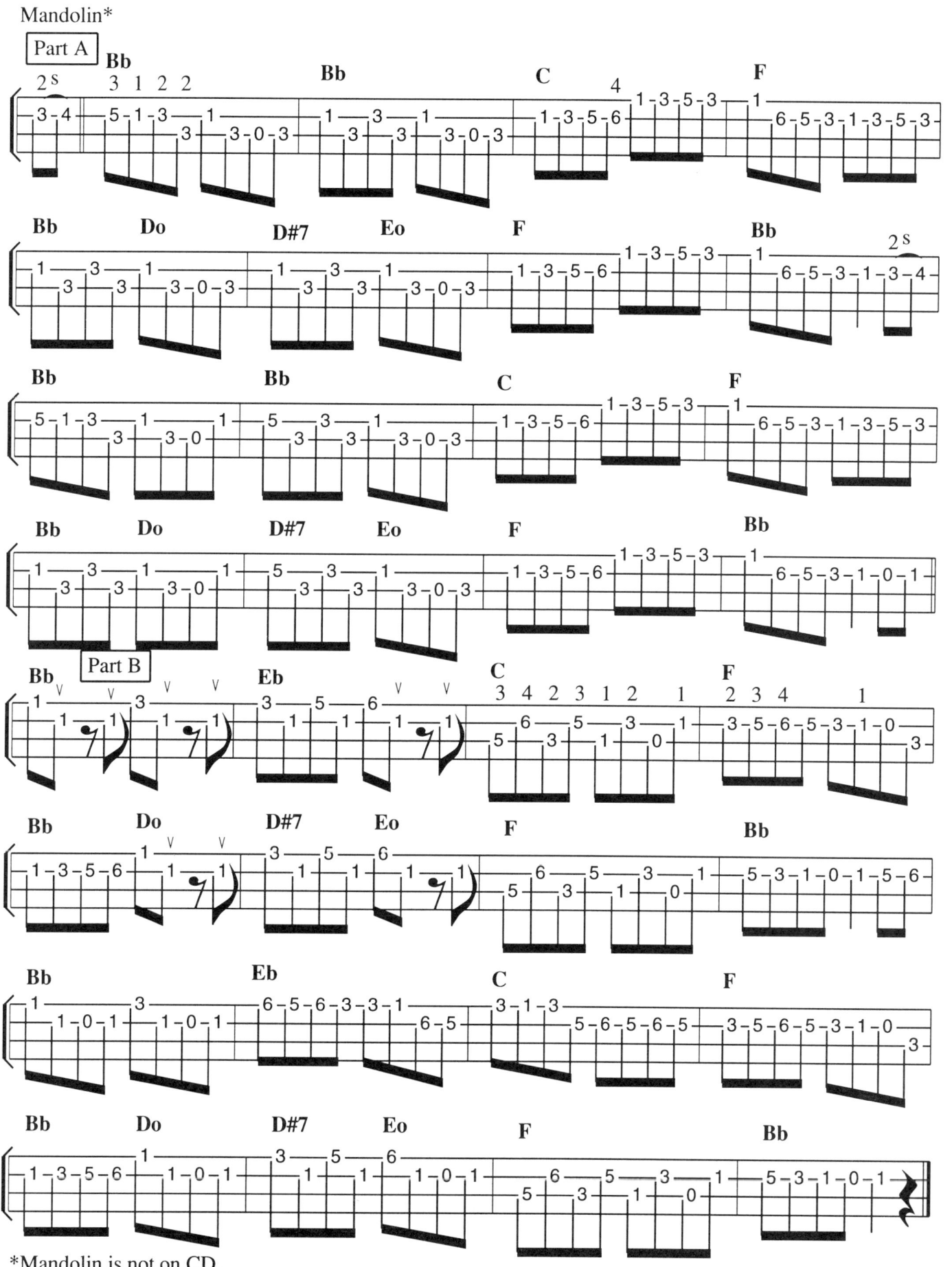

*Mandolin is not on CD.

Disc 3
Track 4

Saint Anne's Reel

Mandolin (melody)

Irish

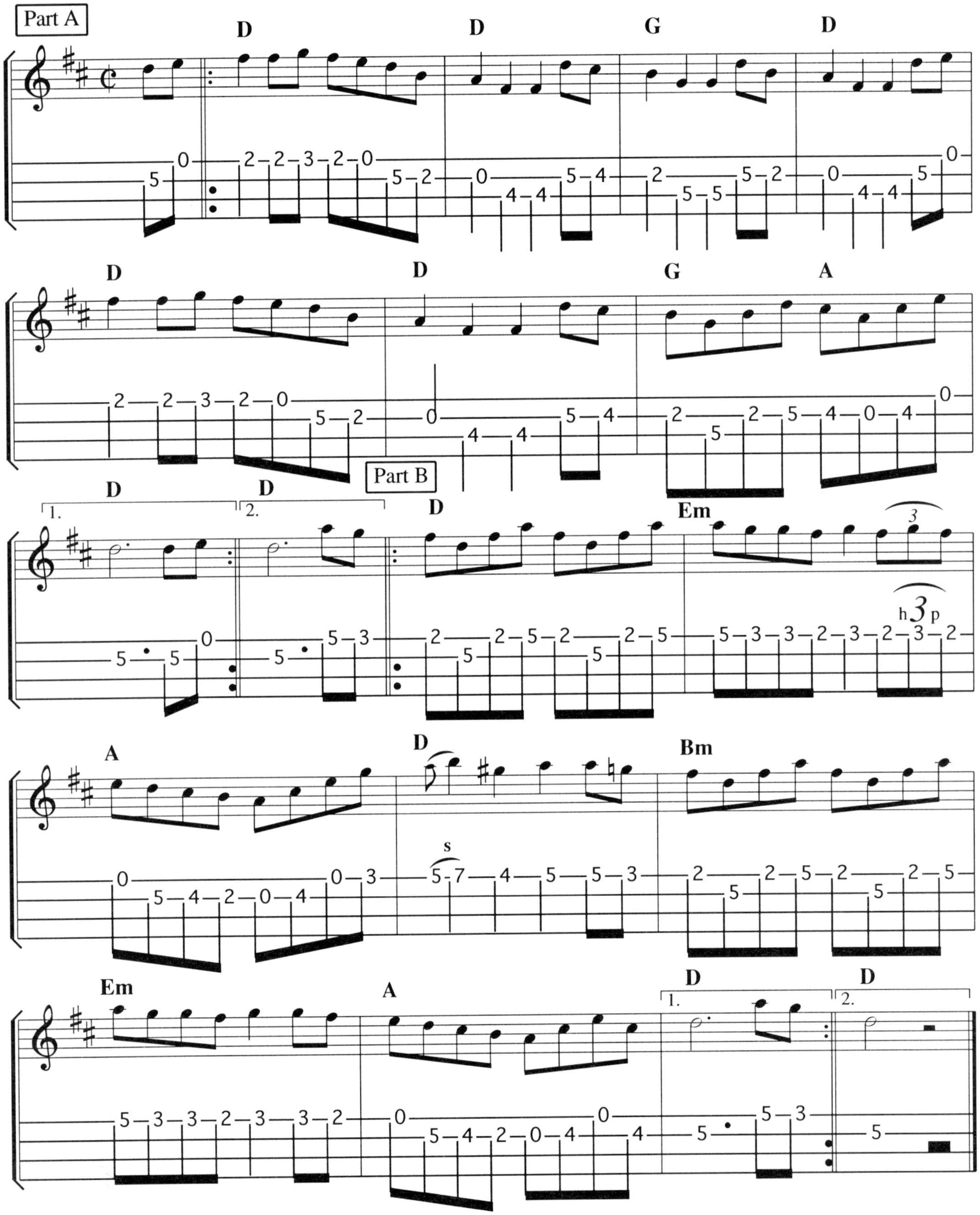

Saint Anne's Reel

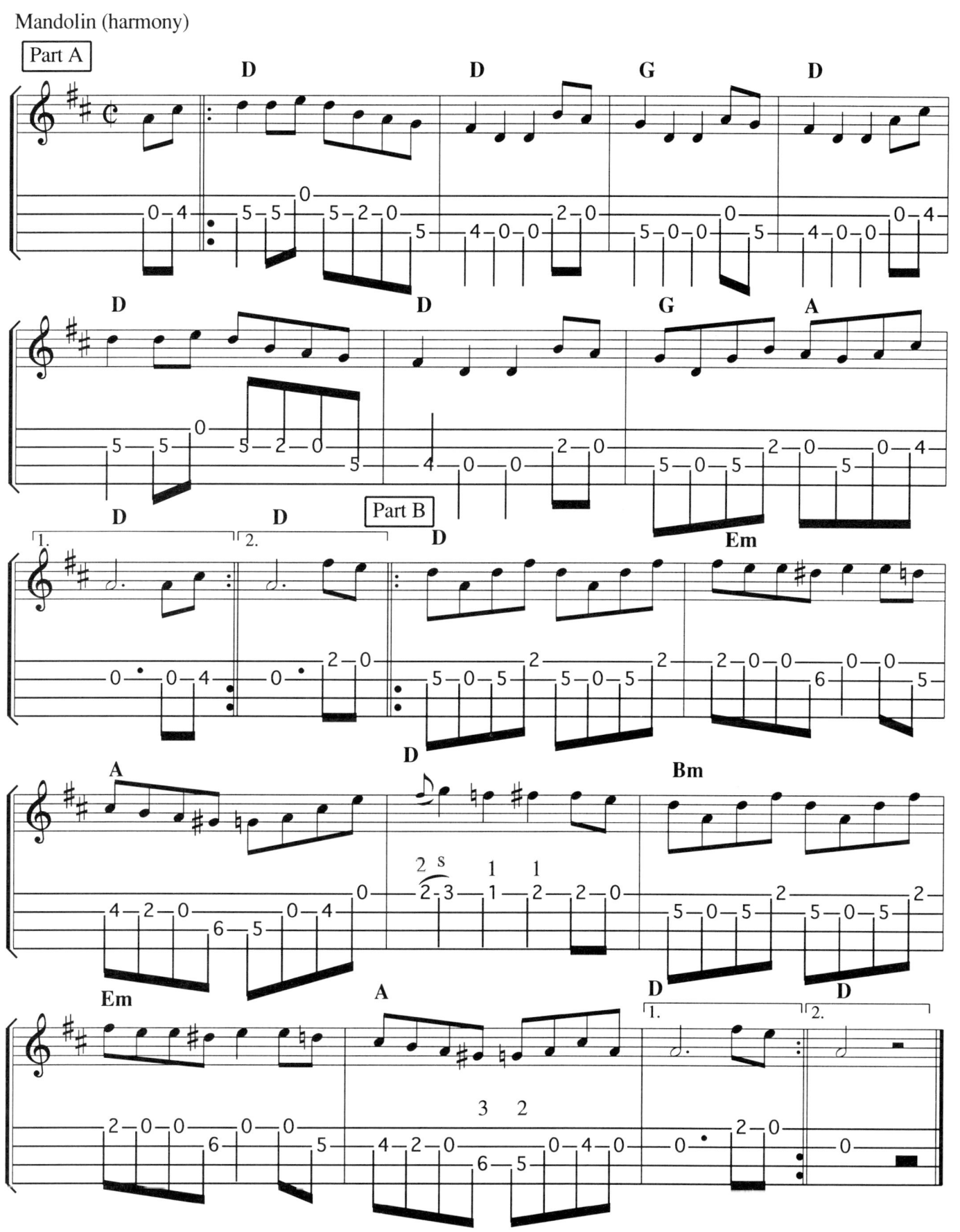

Sally Ann

Mandolin 1 (melody)*

North American

Part B

Part B

*Mandolin 1 melody is not on CD.

*Can be played with capo 2 for key of A.

Sally Ann

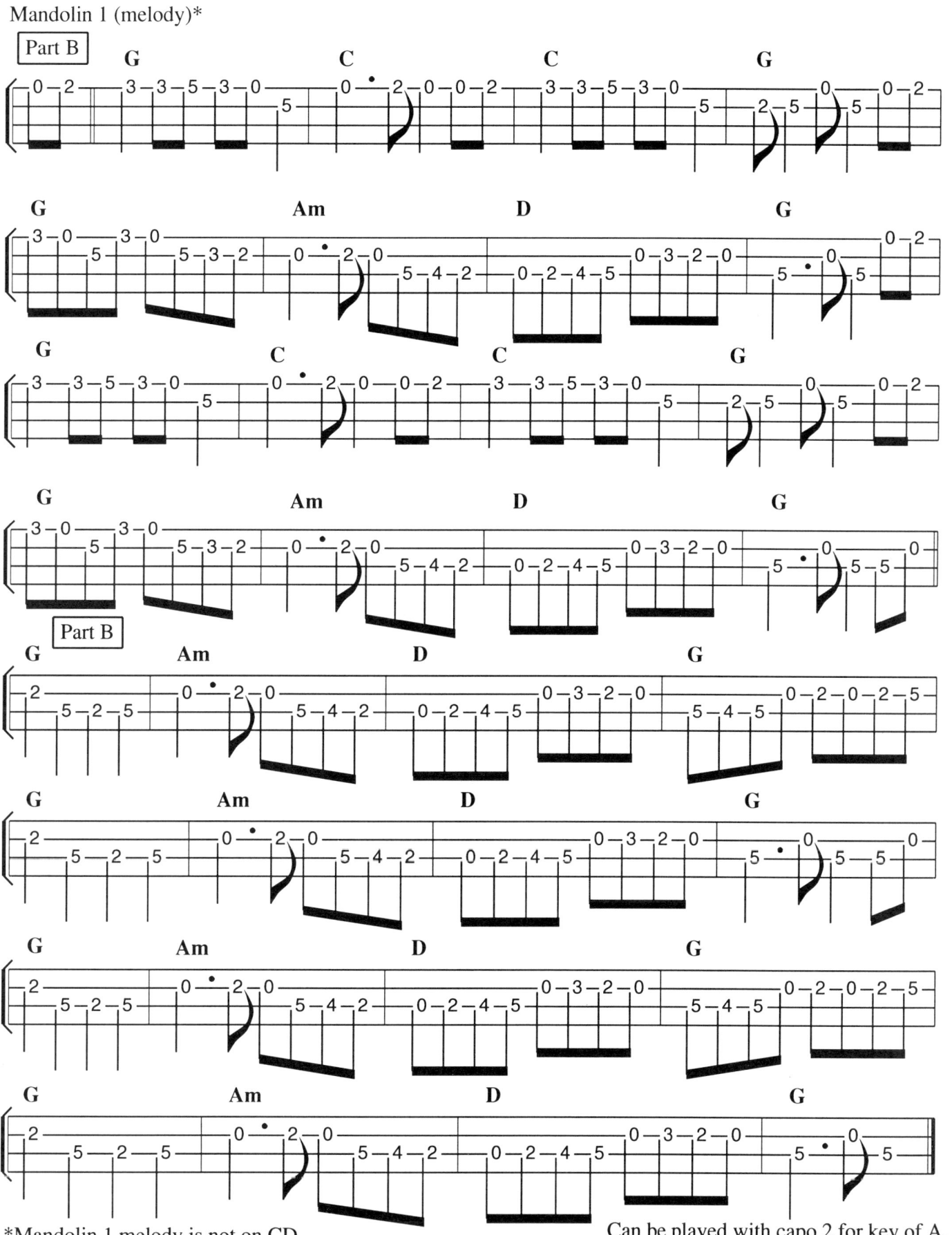

*Mandolin 1 melody is not on CD.   Can be played with capo 2 for key of A.

Sally Ann

Mandolin 1 (harmony)*

*Mandolin 1 harmony is not on CD.   *Can be played with capo 2 for key of A.

Sally Ann

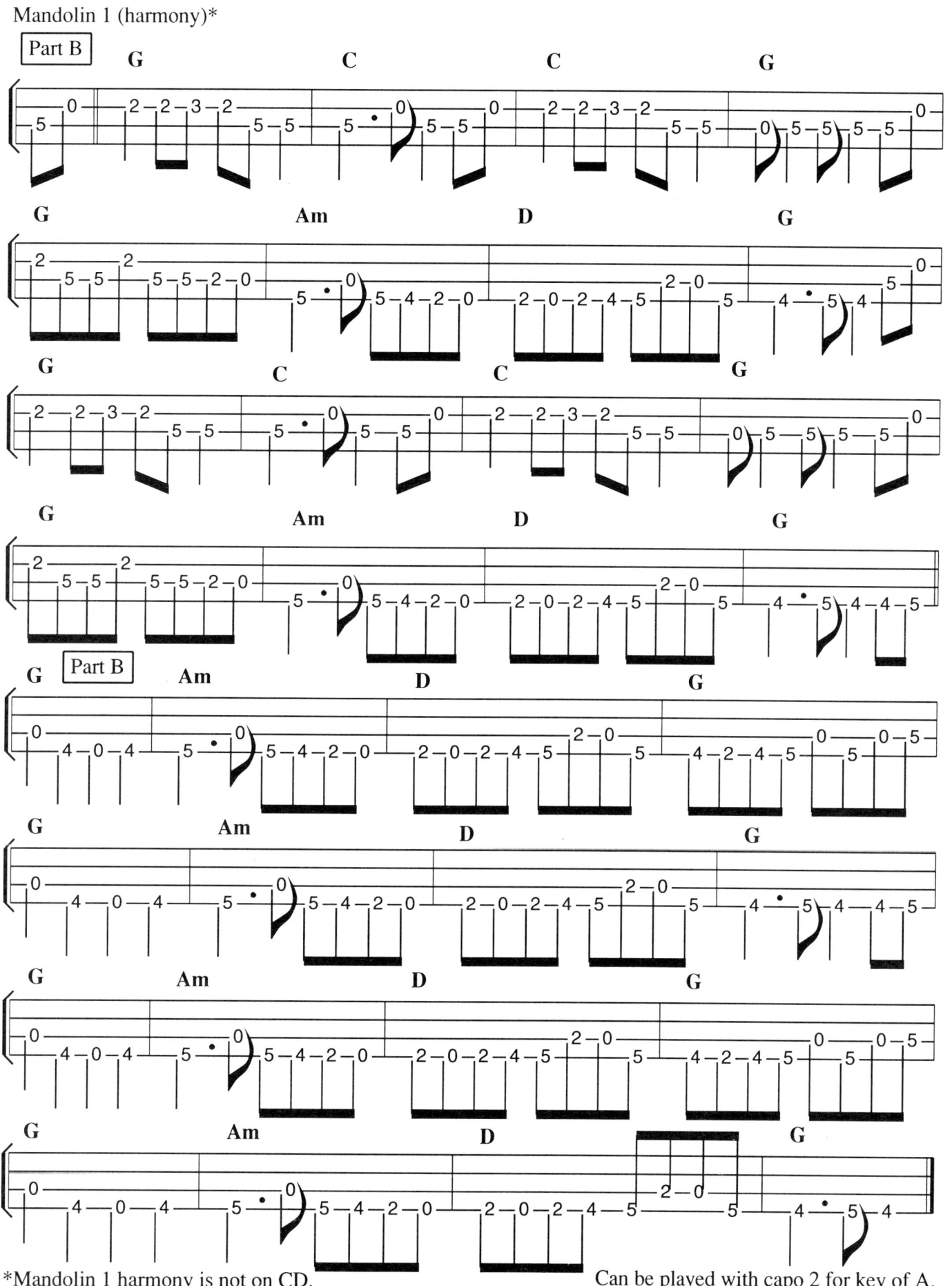

*Mandolin 1 harmony is not on CD.   Can be played with capo 2 for key of A.

Sally Ann

Sally Ann

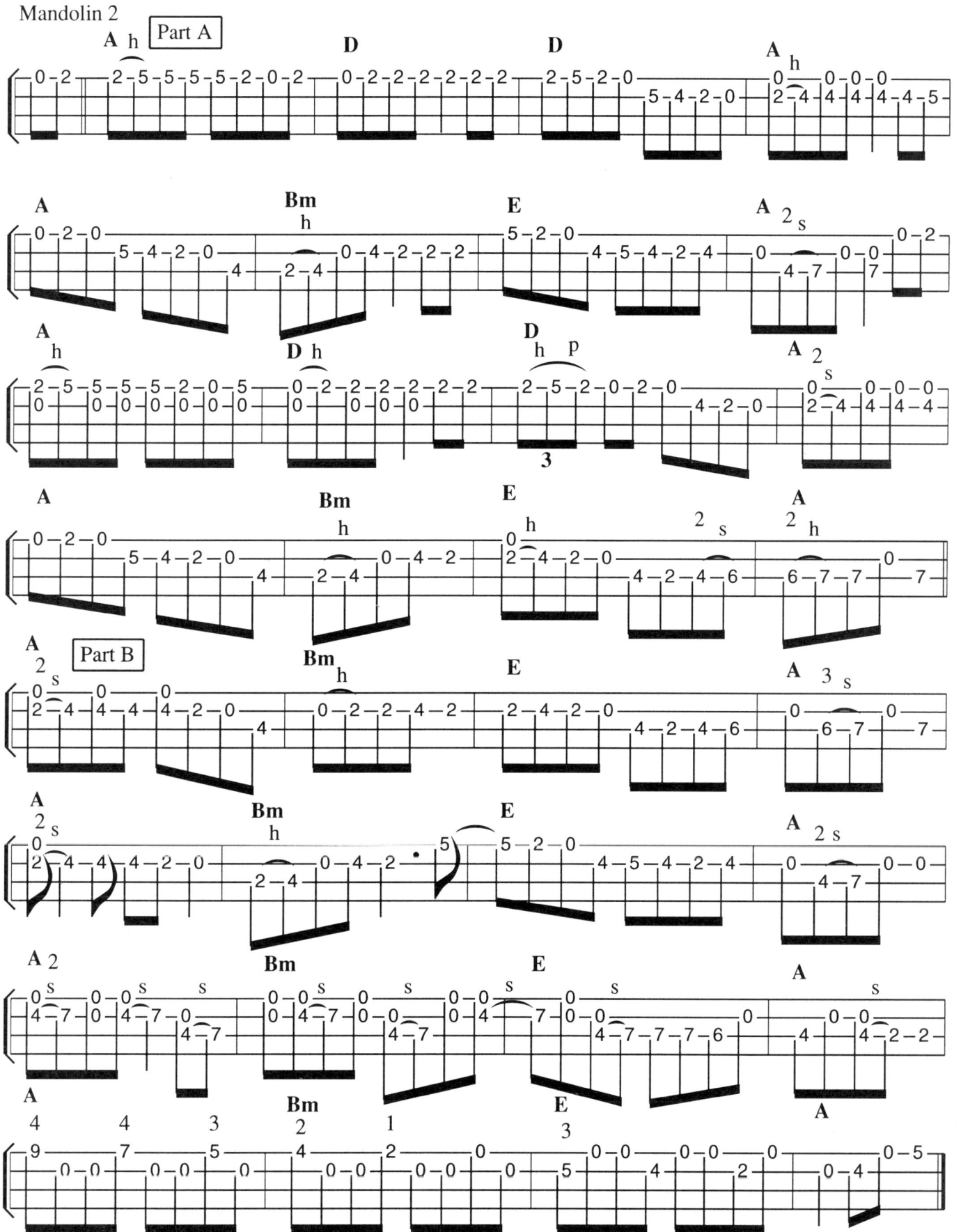

Sally Goodin'

Mandolin 1

North American

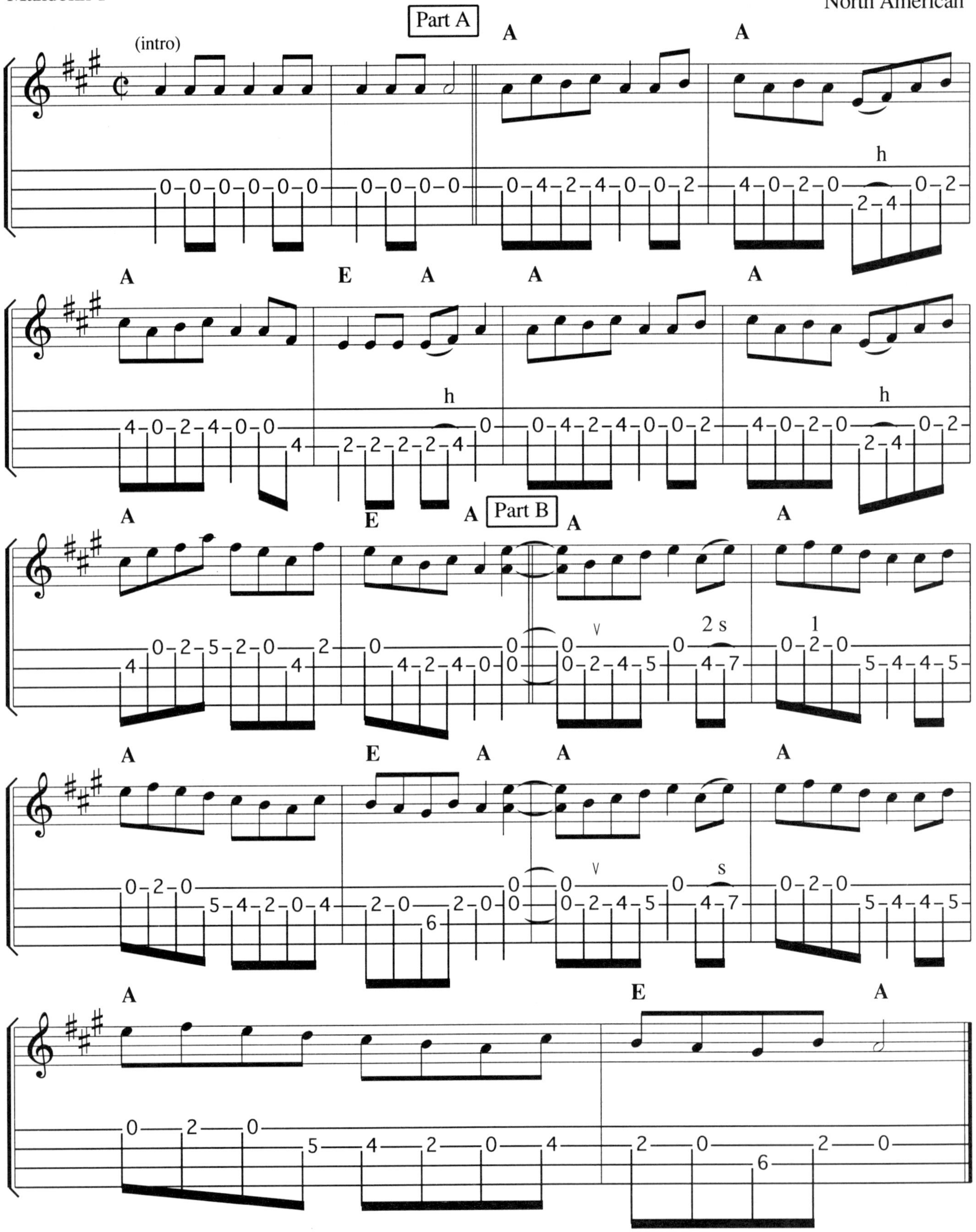

Sally Goodin'

Mandolin 2

Disc 3
Track 7

Sally Johnson

Mandolin

North American

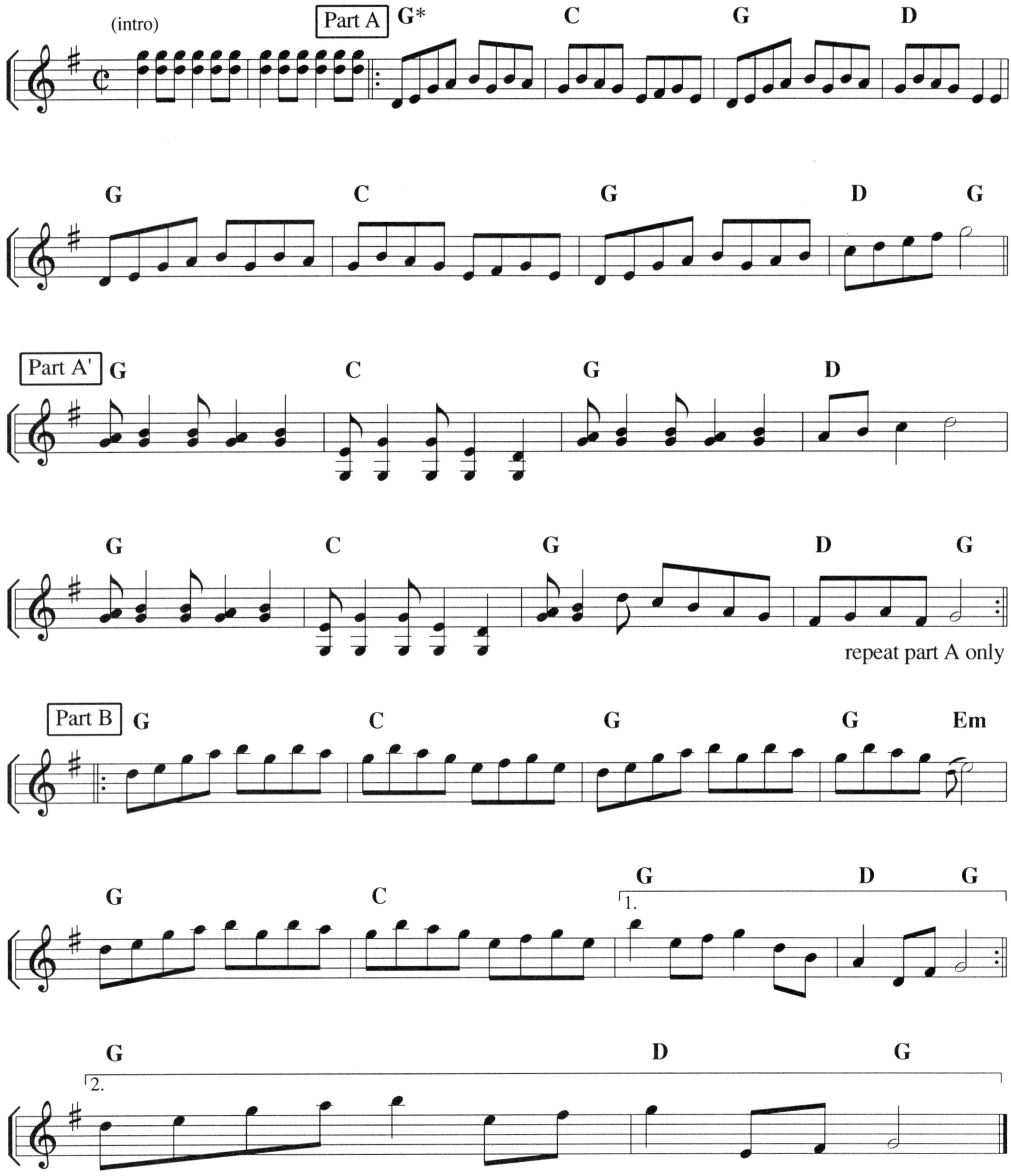

See appendix for Texas-style chord sequences.

Sally Johnson

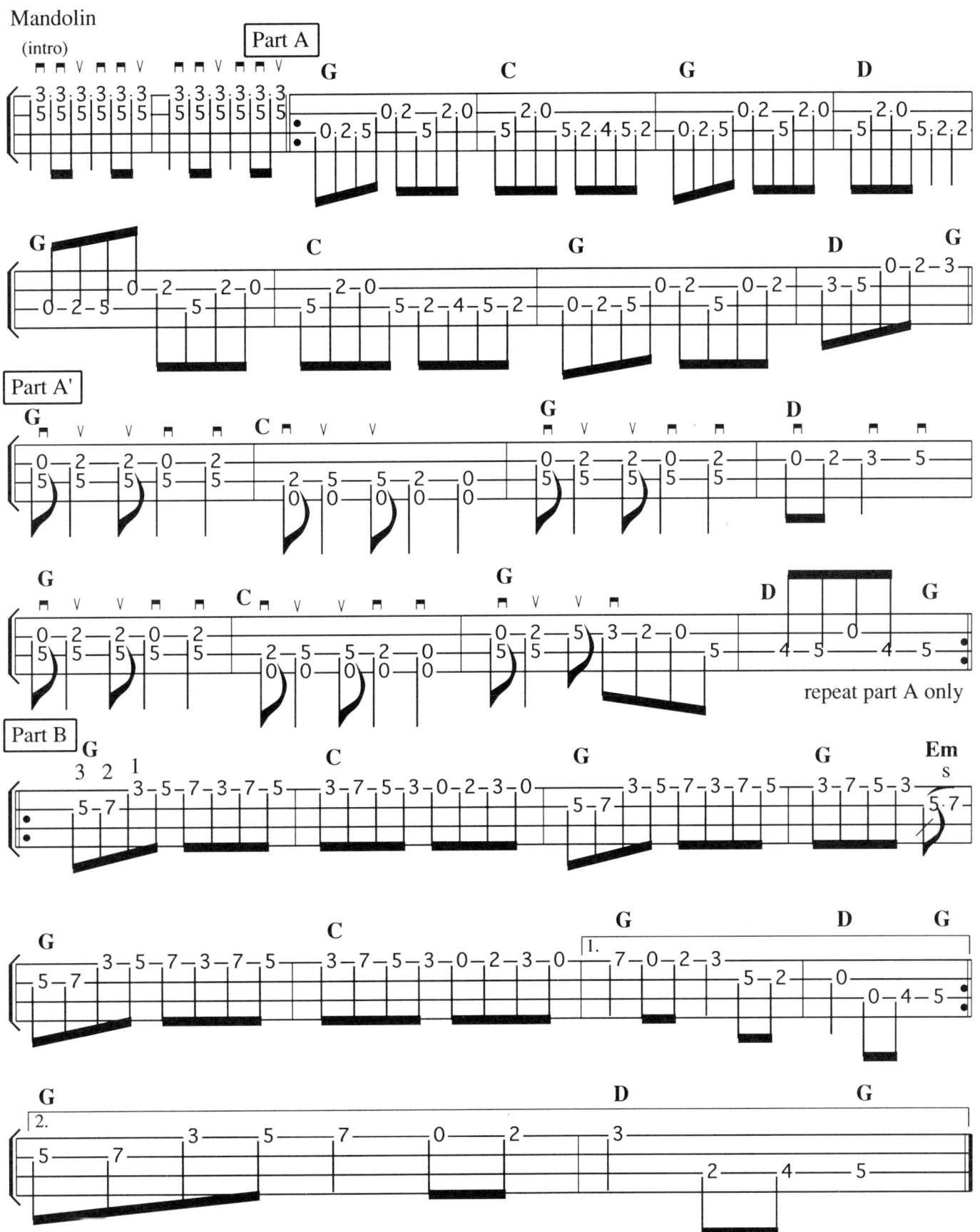

Disc 3
Track 8

Salt Creek

Mandolin (melody)

North American

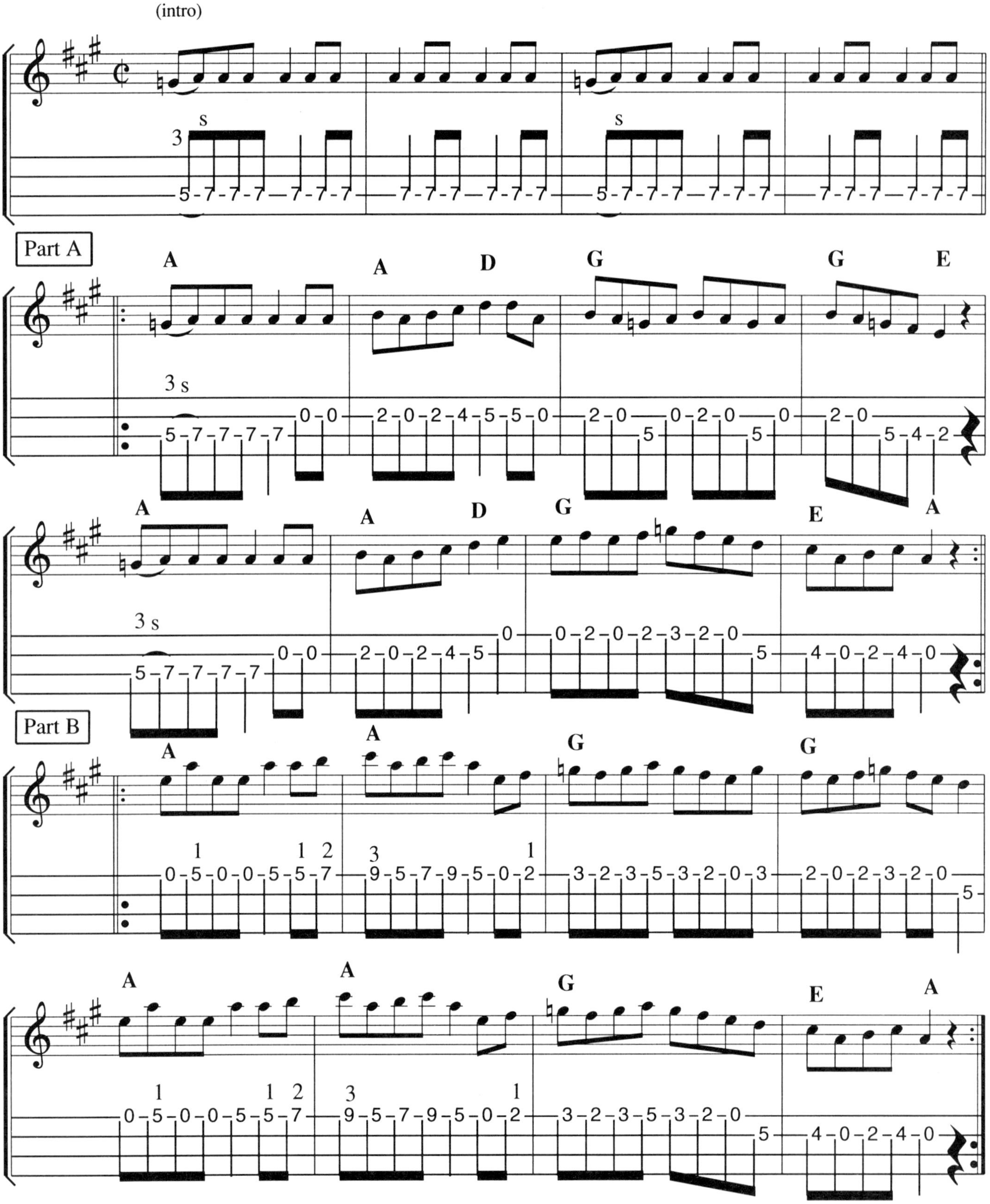

Salt Creek

Mandolin (harmony)

Salt Creek

Mandolin Ending (melody)

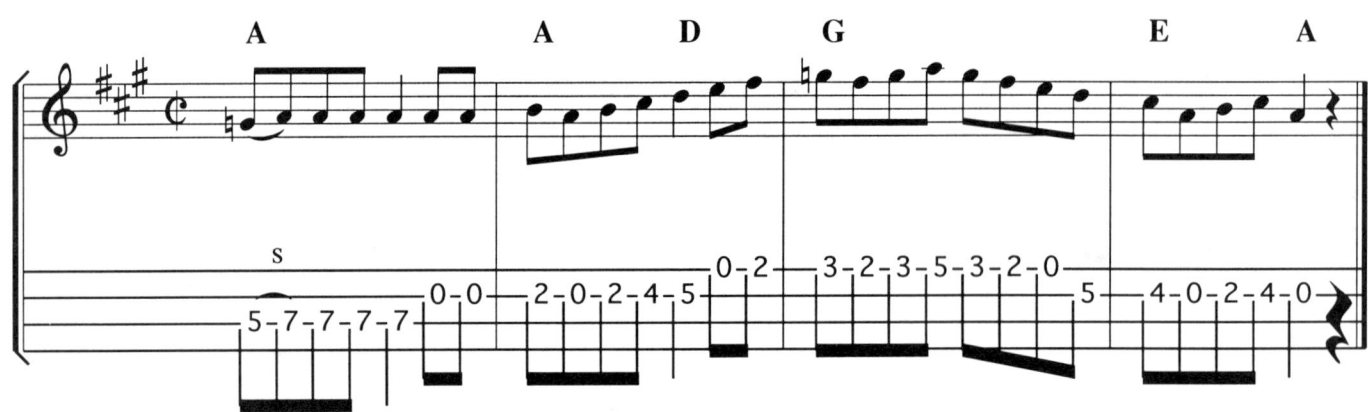

Mandolin Ending (harmony)

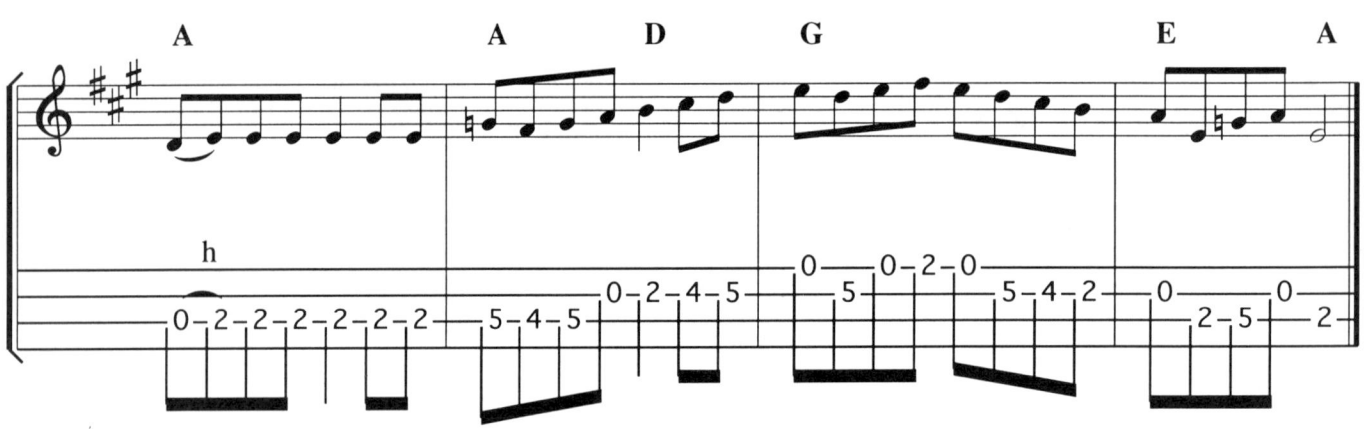

Soldier's Joy

Disc 3
Track 9

Mandolin (melody)

Part A

North American

Soldier's Joy

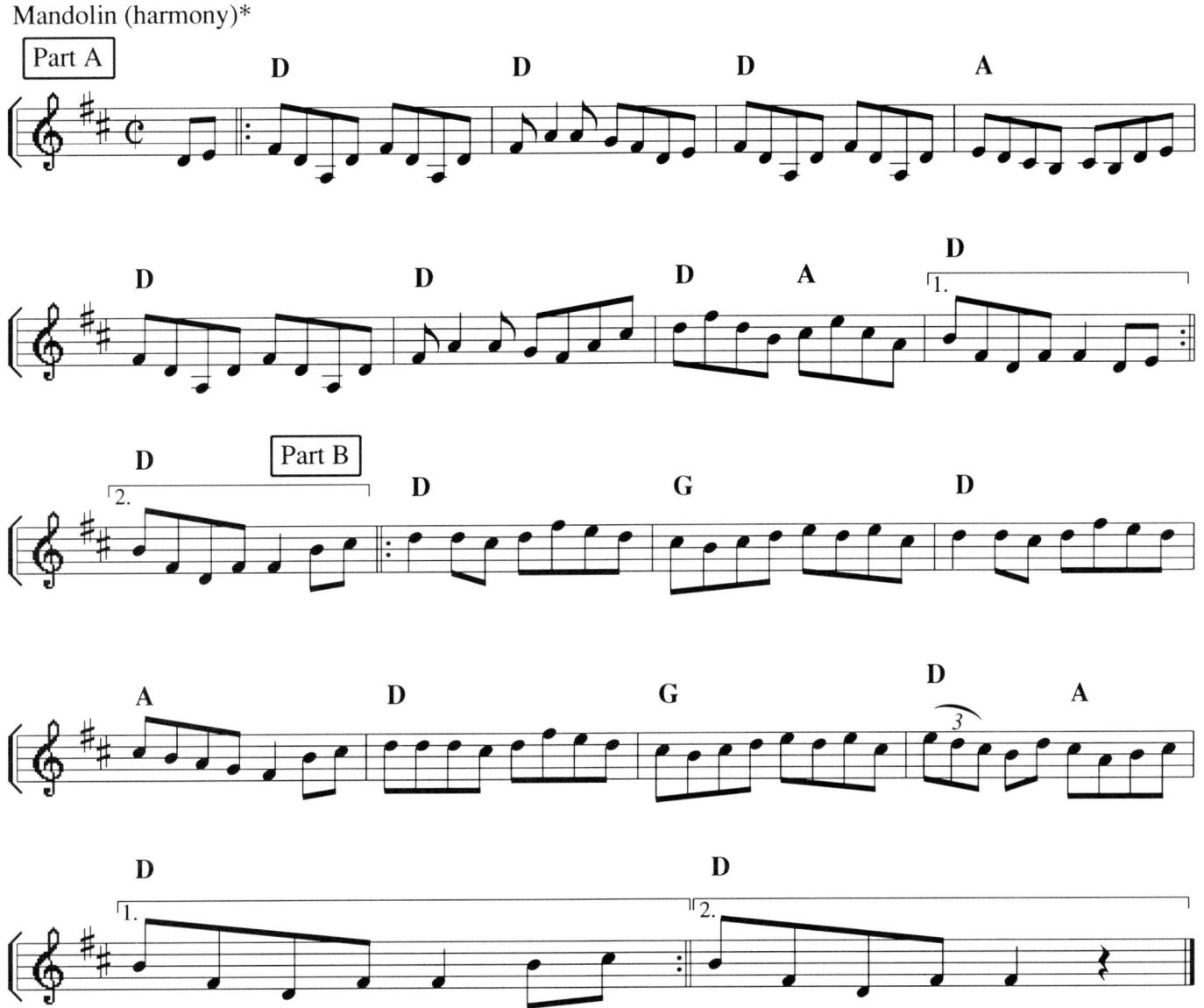

*Mandolin harmony is not on CD.

Soldier's Joy

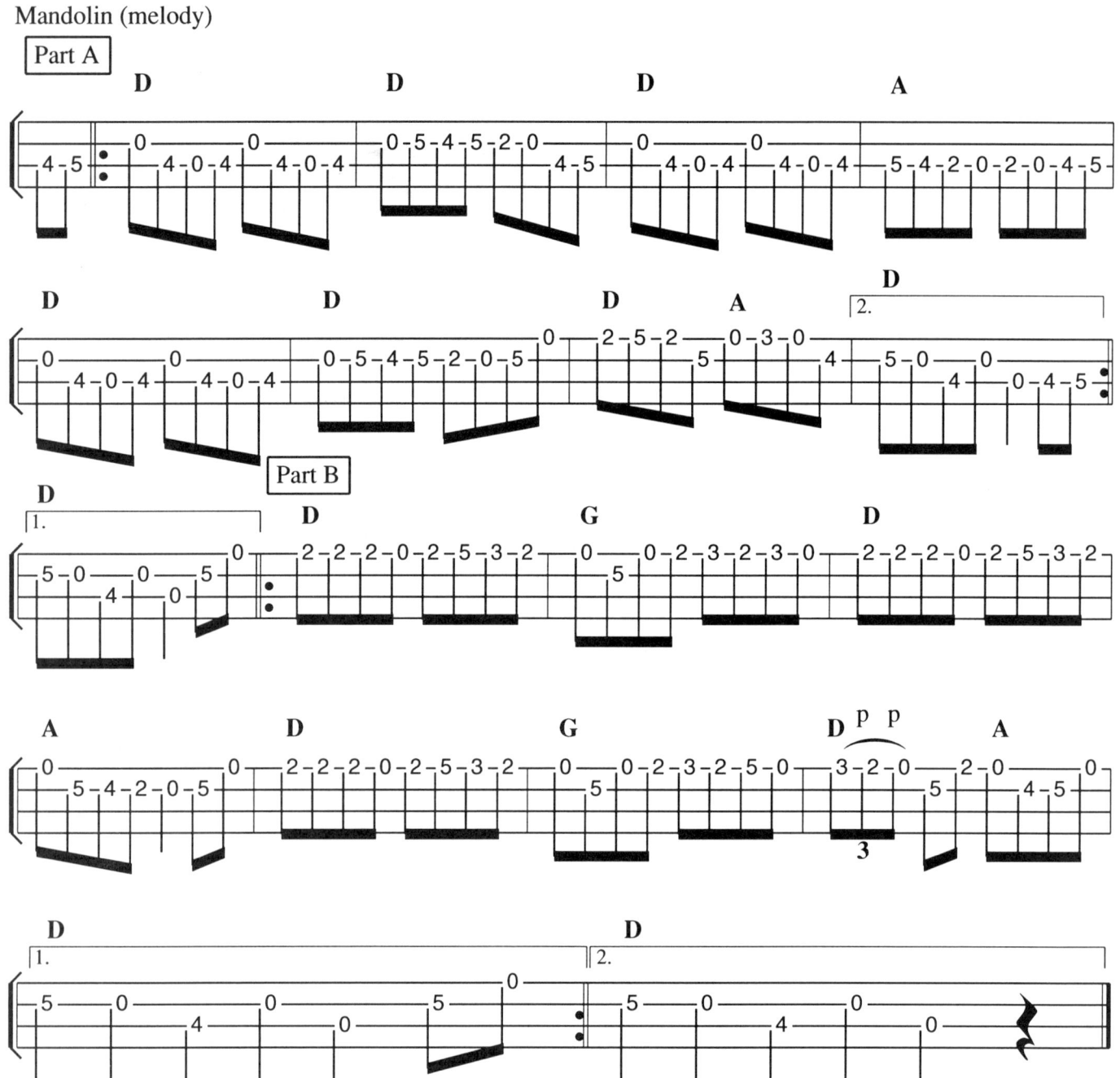

Soldier's Joy

Mandolin (harmony)*

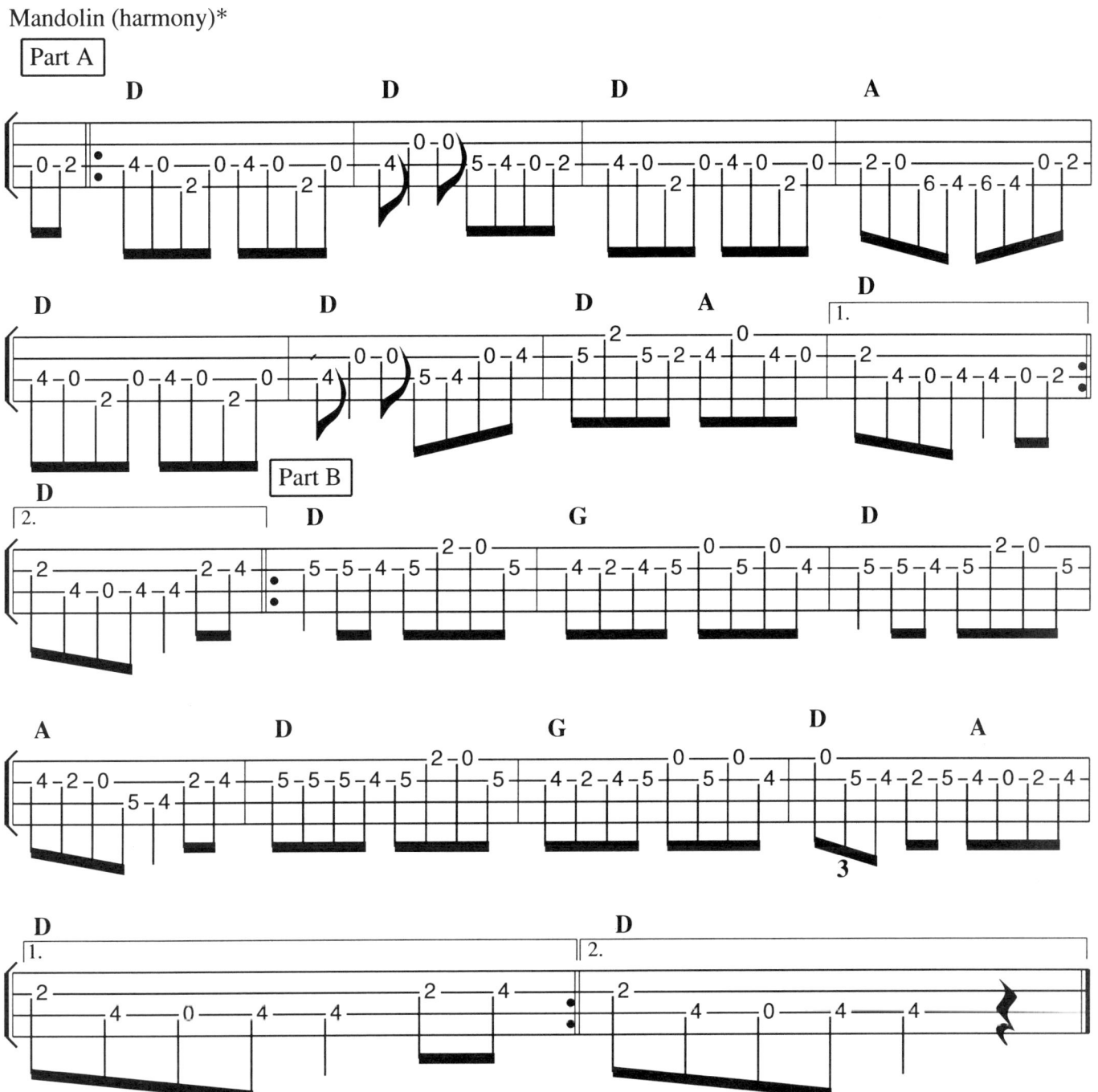

*Mandolin harmony is not on CD.

Swallowtail Jig

Mandolin

Irish

Temperance Reel

Disc 3
Track 11

Mandolin (melody)

North American

Part A

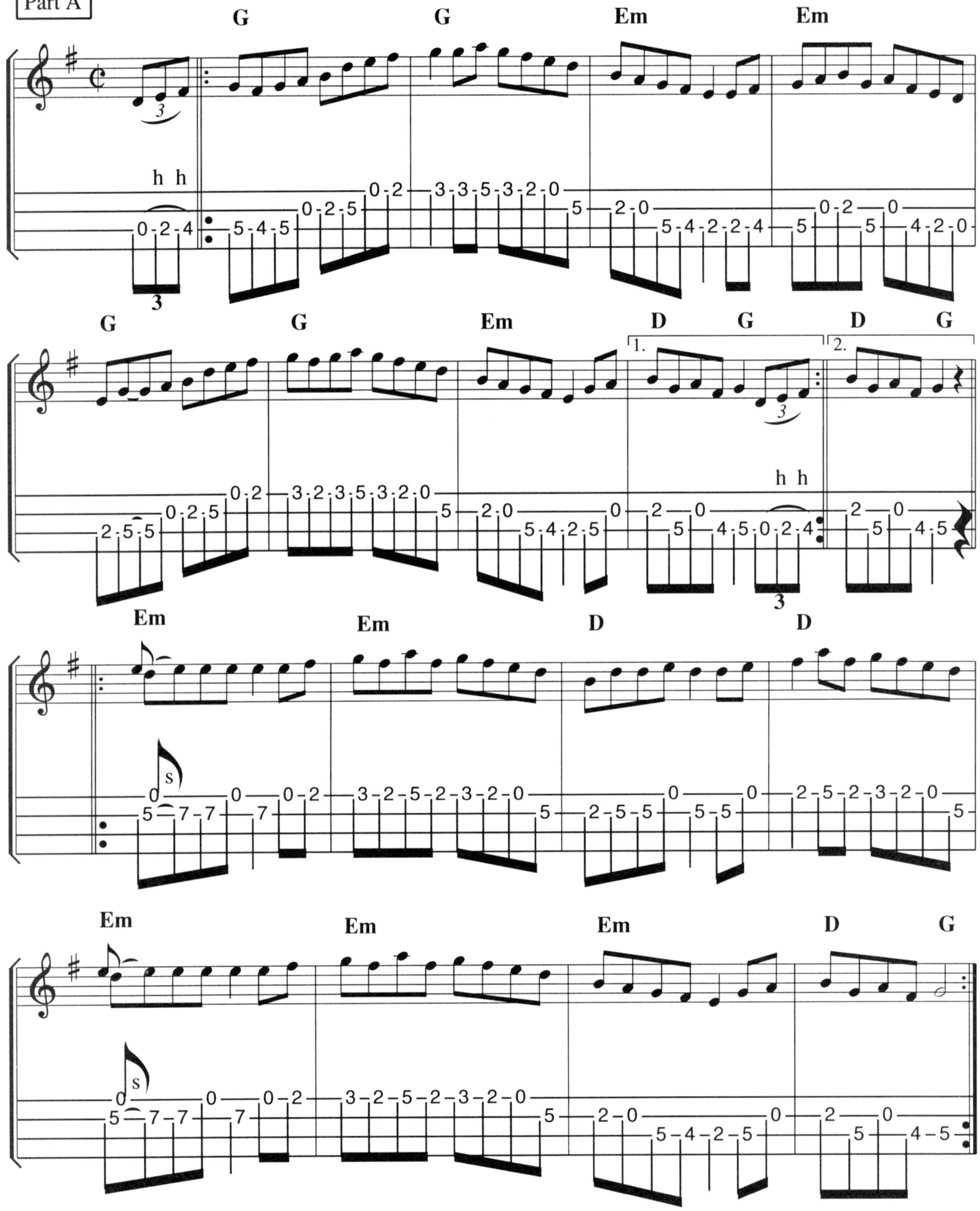

Temperance Reel

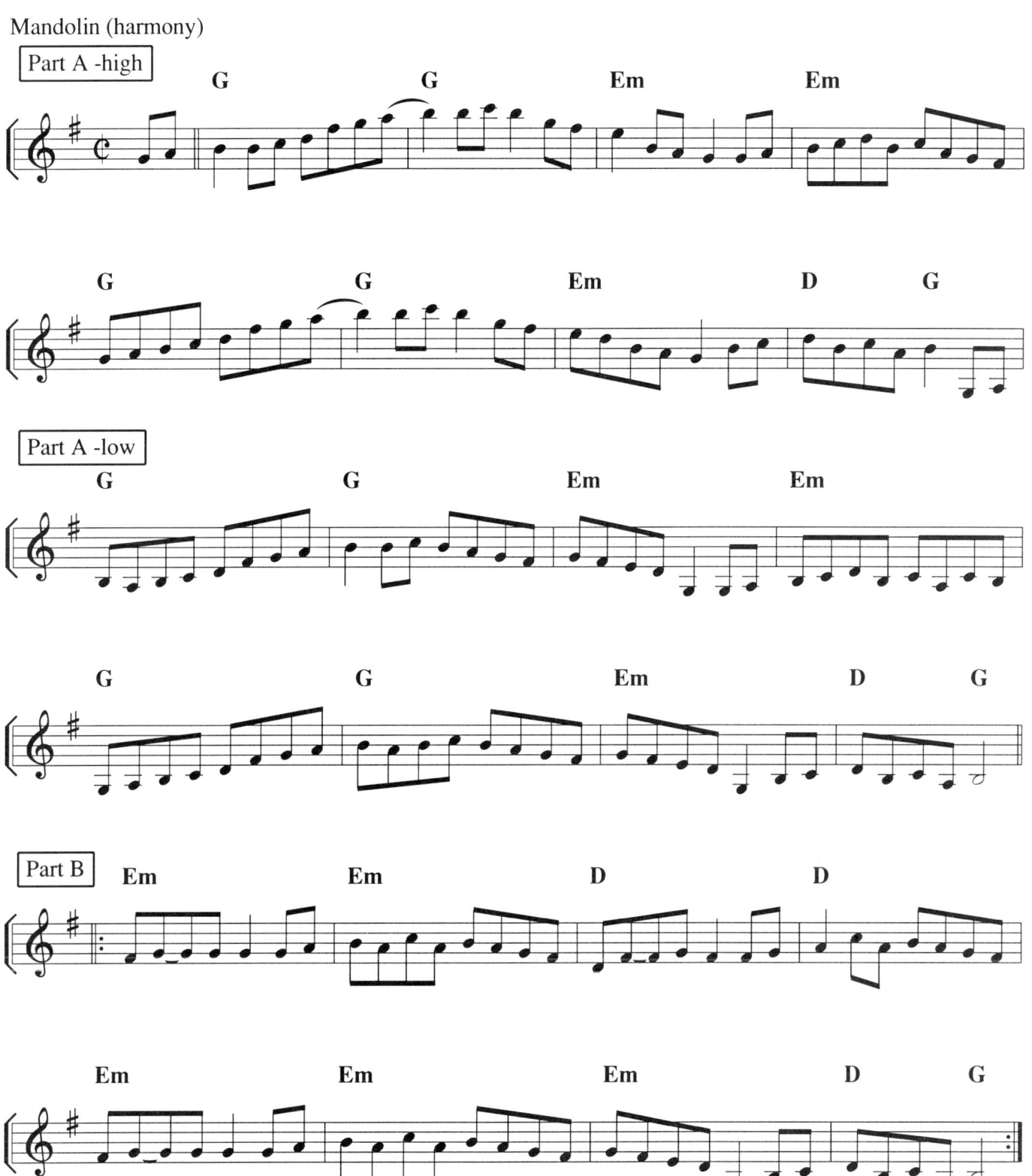

Temperance Reel

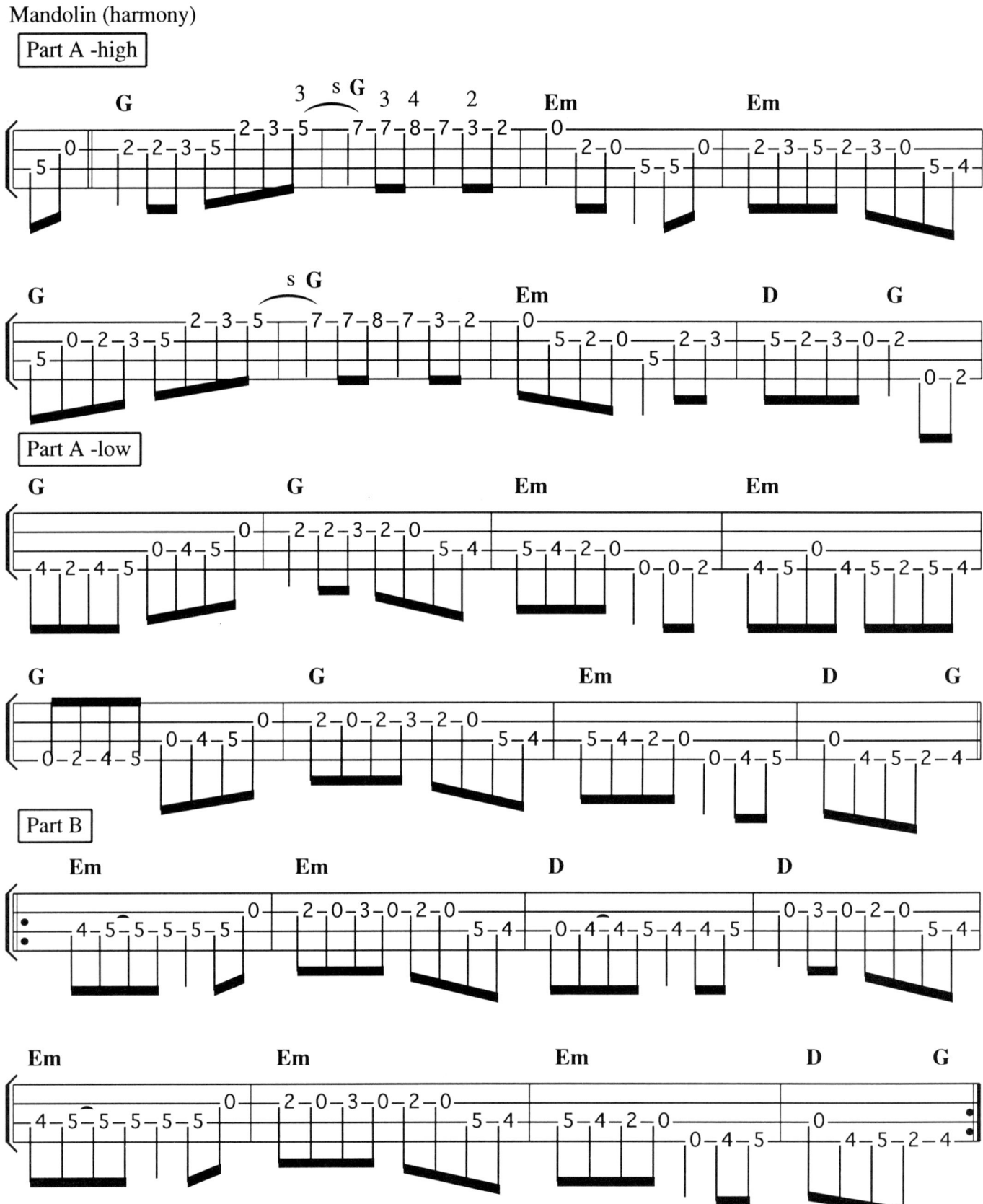

Tom and Jerry

Mandolin 1

North American

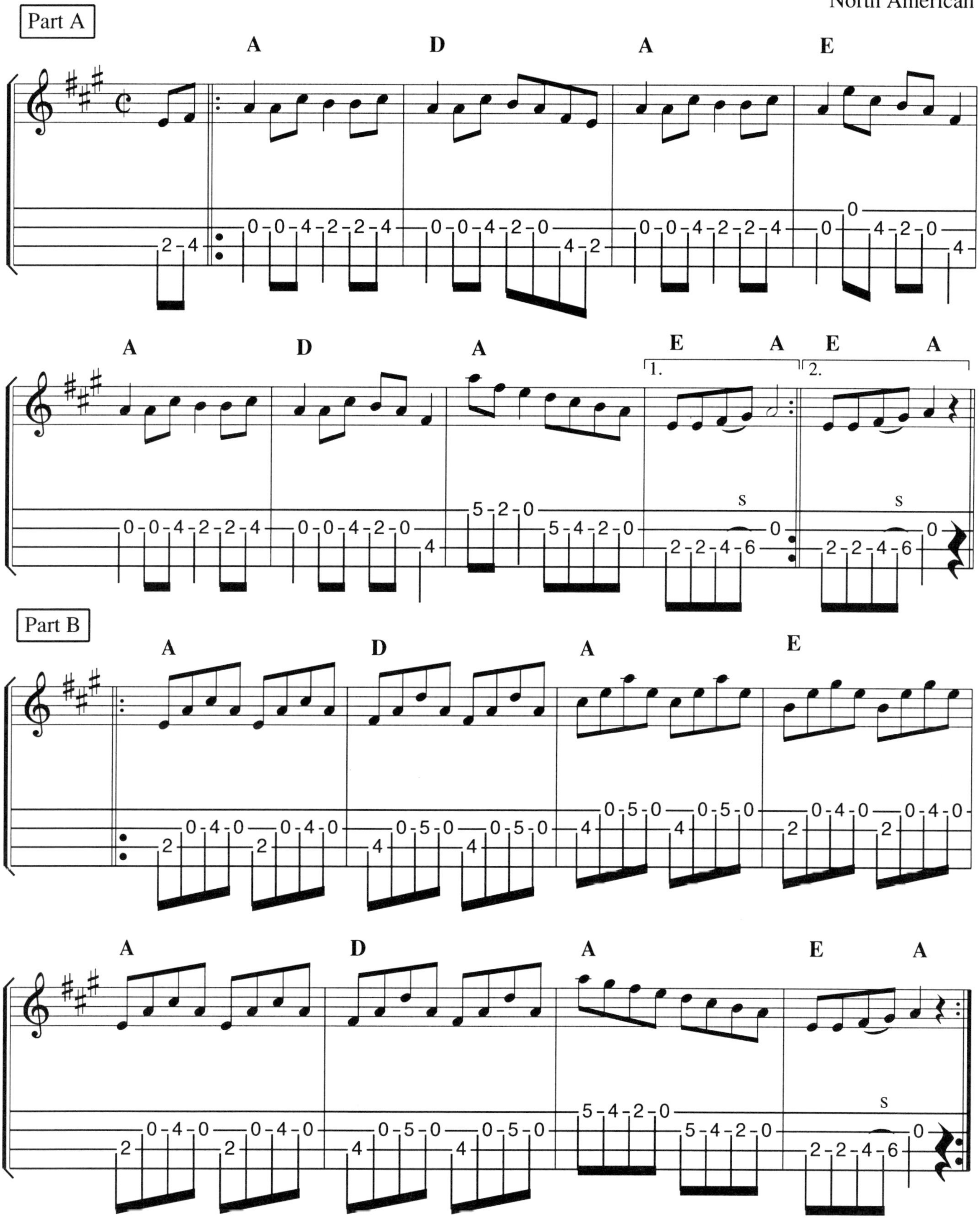

Part A

Part B

Tom and Jerry

138

Tom and Jerry

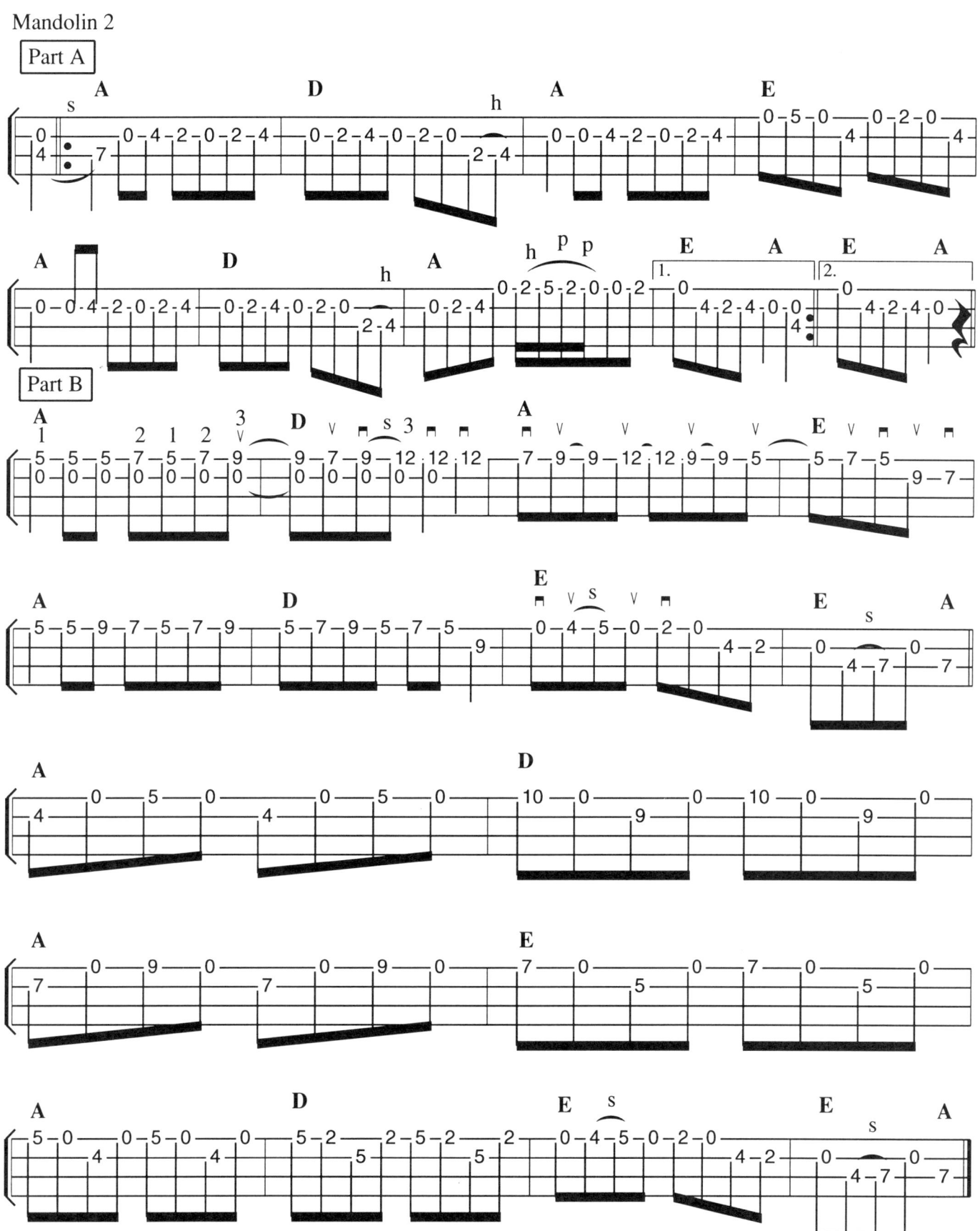

Disc 3
Track 13

Turkey in the Straw

Mandolin 1* (G)

North American

Part A

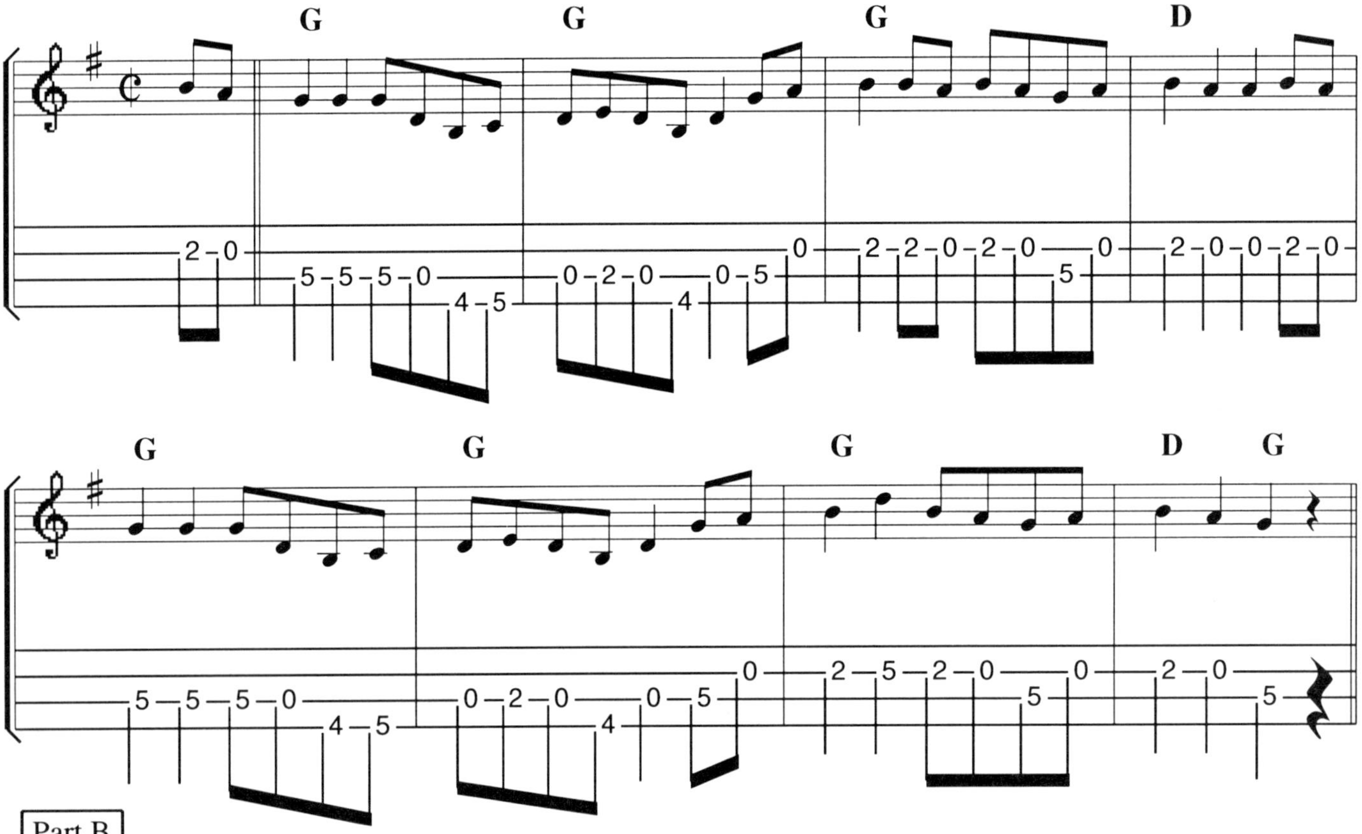

Part B

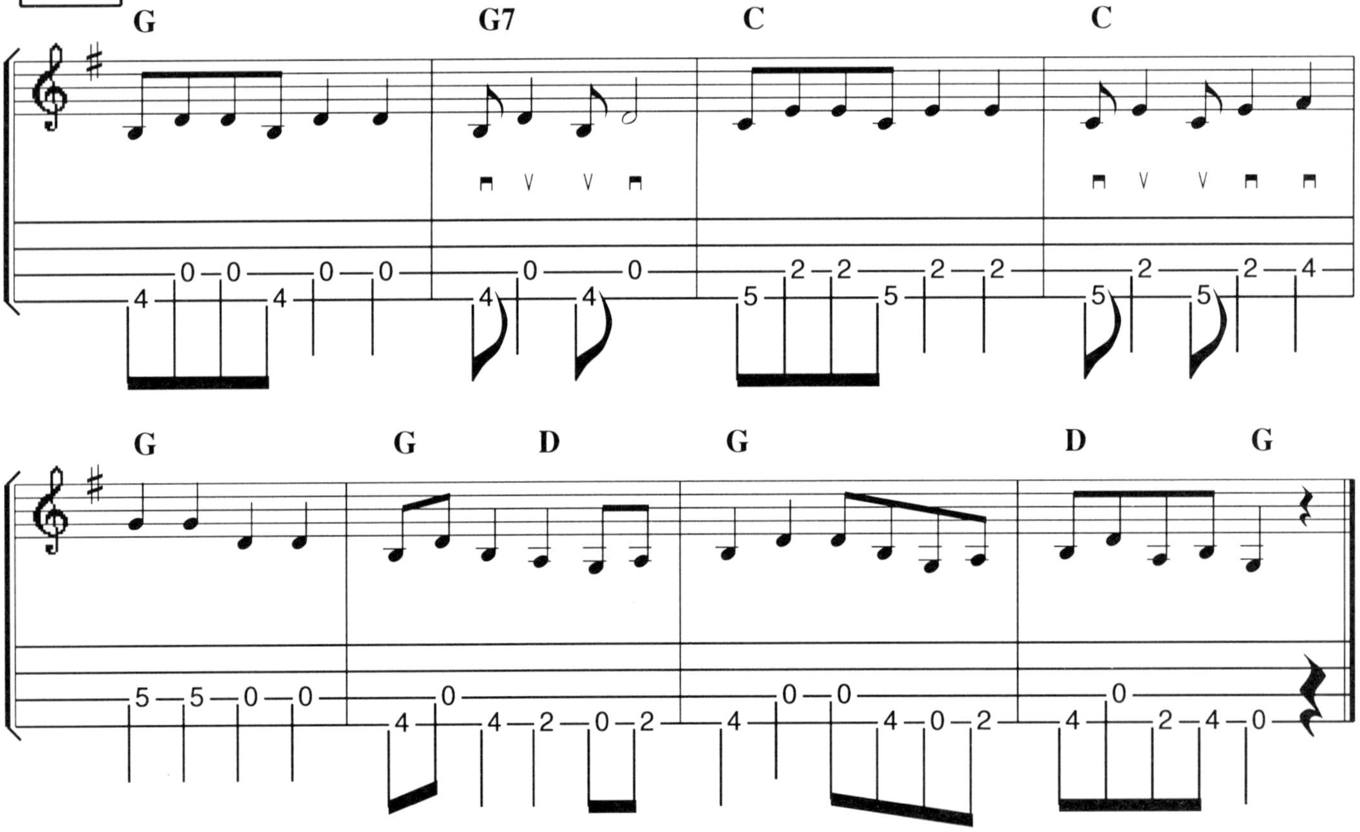

*Mandolin 1 in G is not on CD.

Turkey in the Straw

Mandolin 2 (G)

Turkey in the Straw

Turkey in the Straw

Mandolin 2* (C)

*Mandolin 2 in C is not on CD.

This page has been left blank to avoid awkward page turns.

Uncle Joe

Mandolin   Scotland

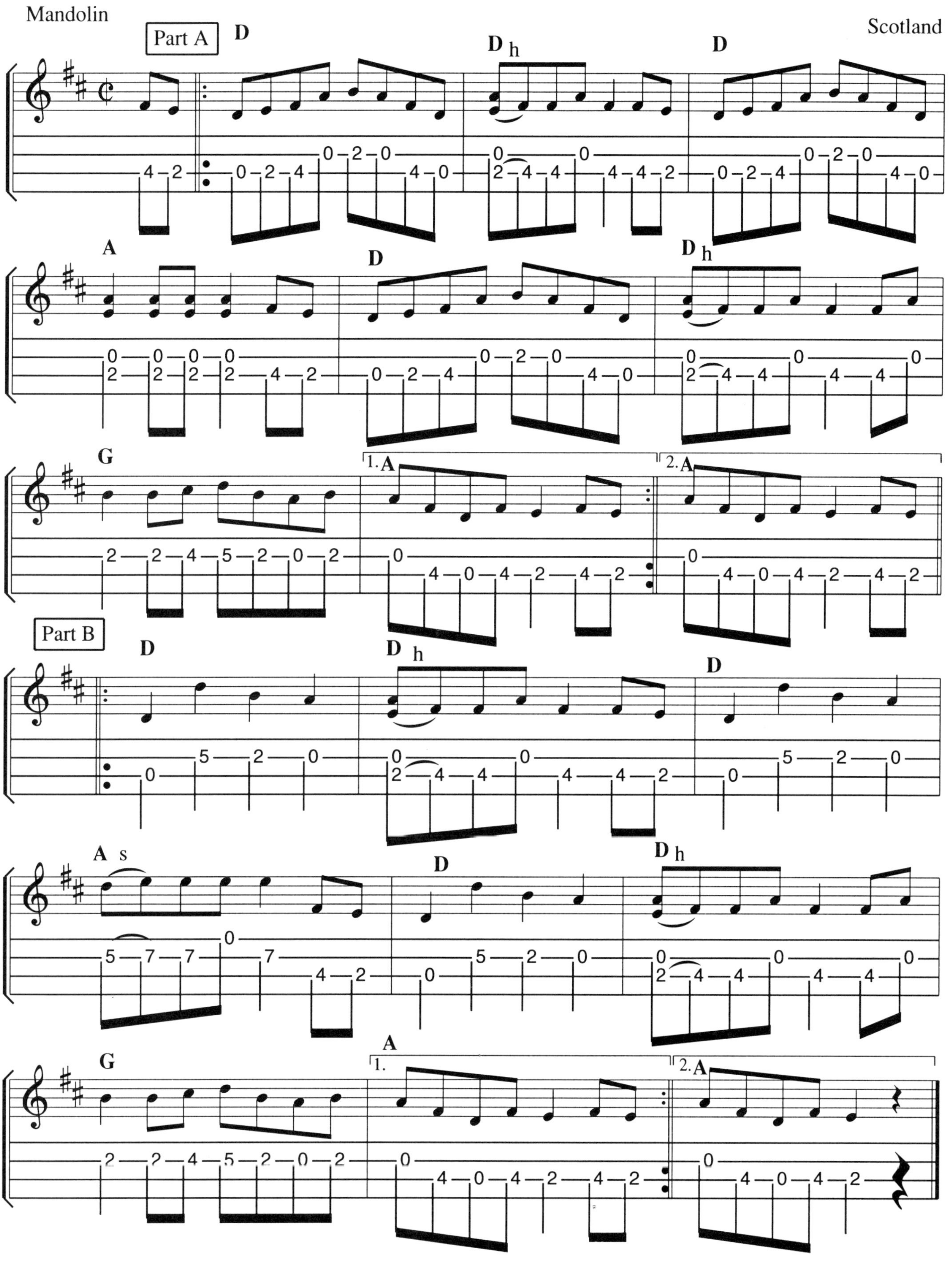

Disc 3
Track 15

Under the Double Eagle

Mandolin

North American

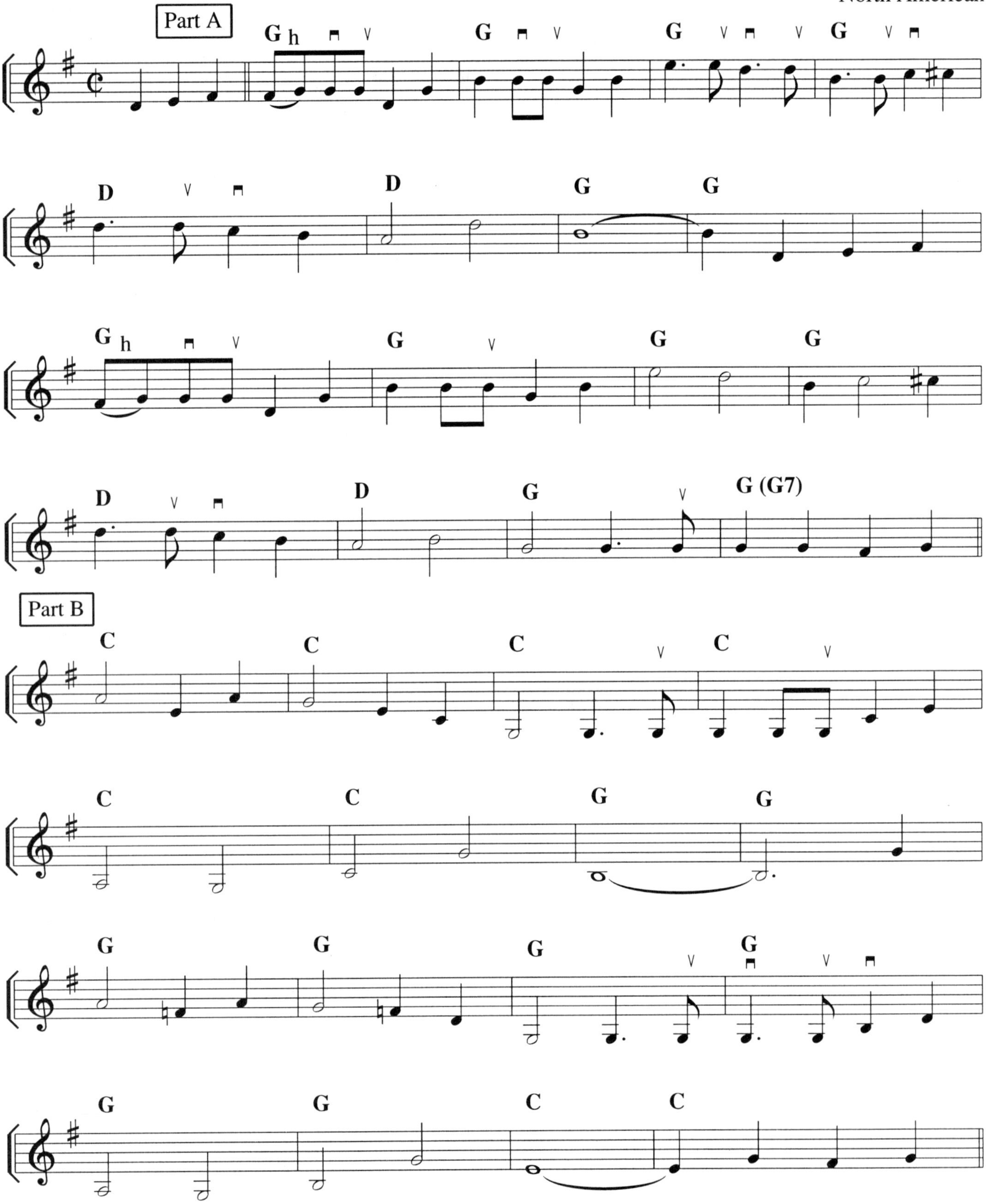

Under the Double Eagle

Mandolin (cont.)

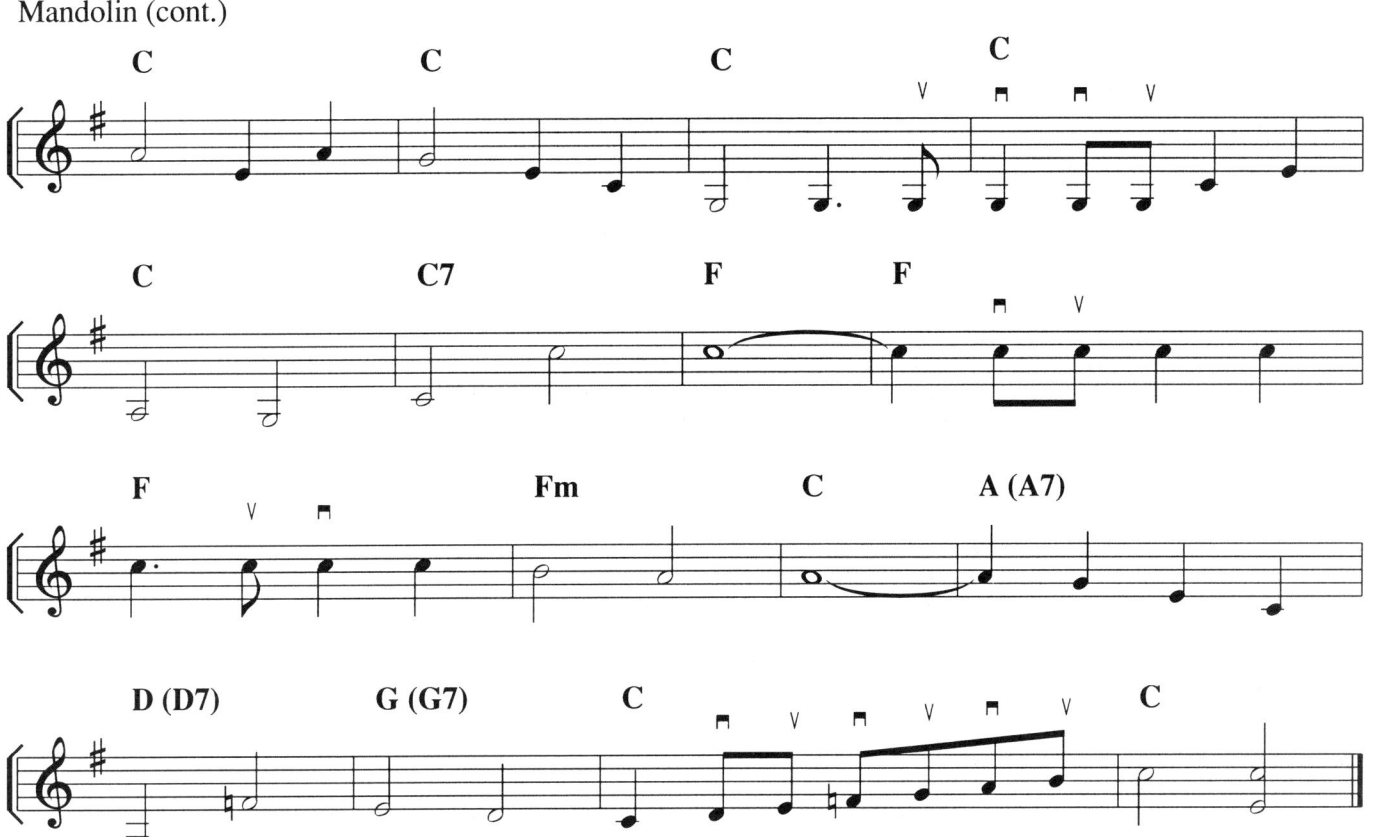

Under the Double Eagle

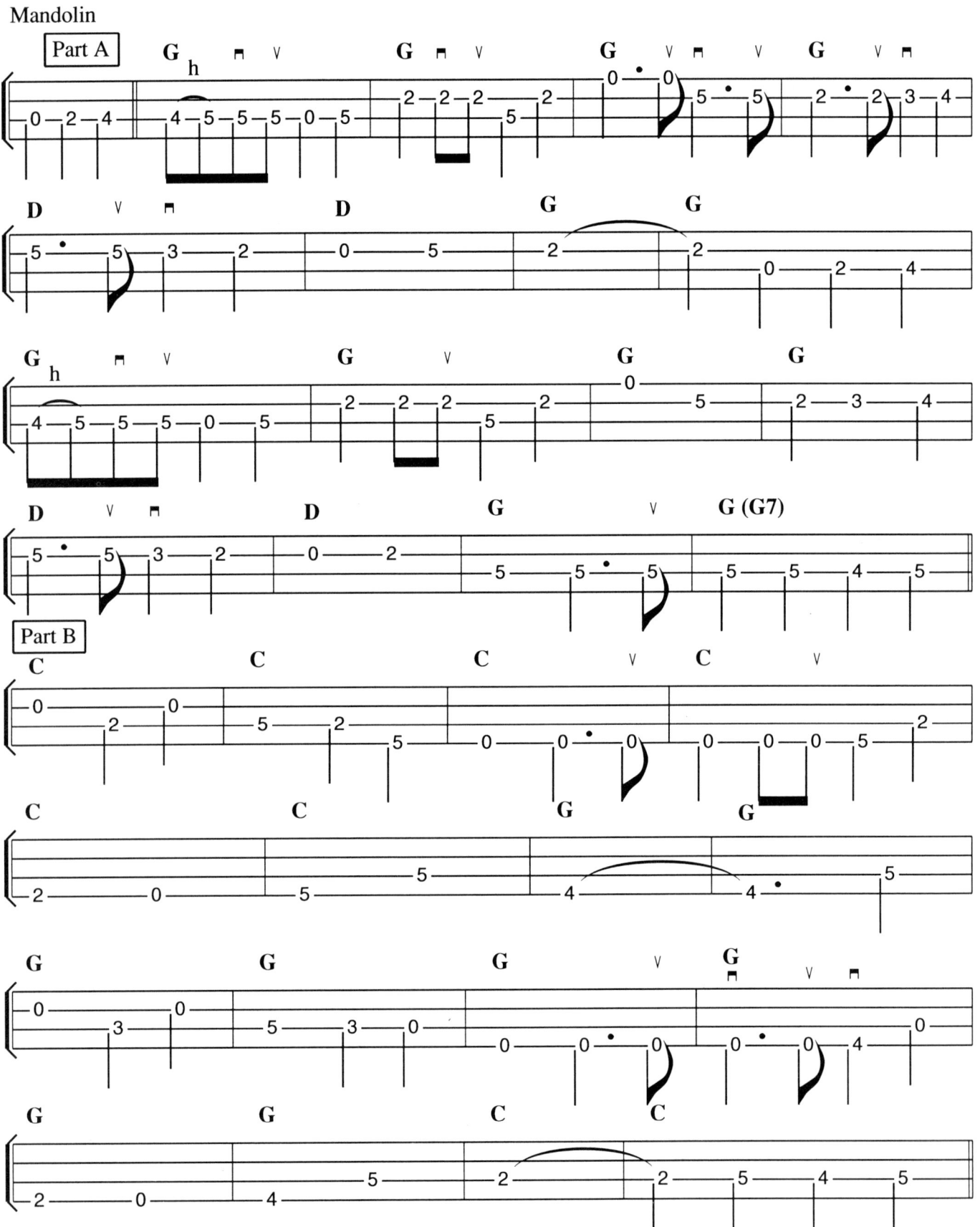

Under the Double Eagle

Mandolin (cont.)

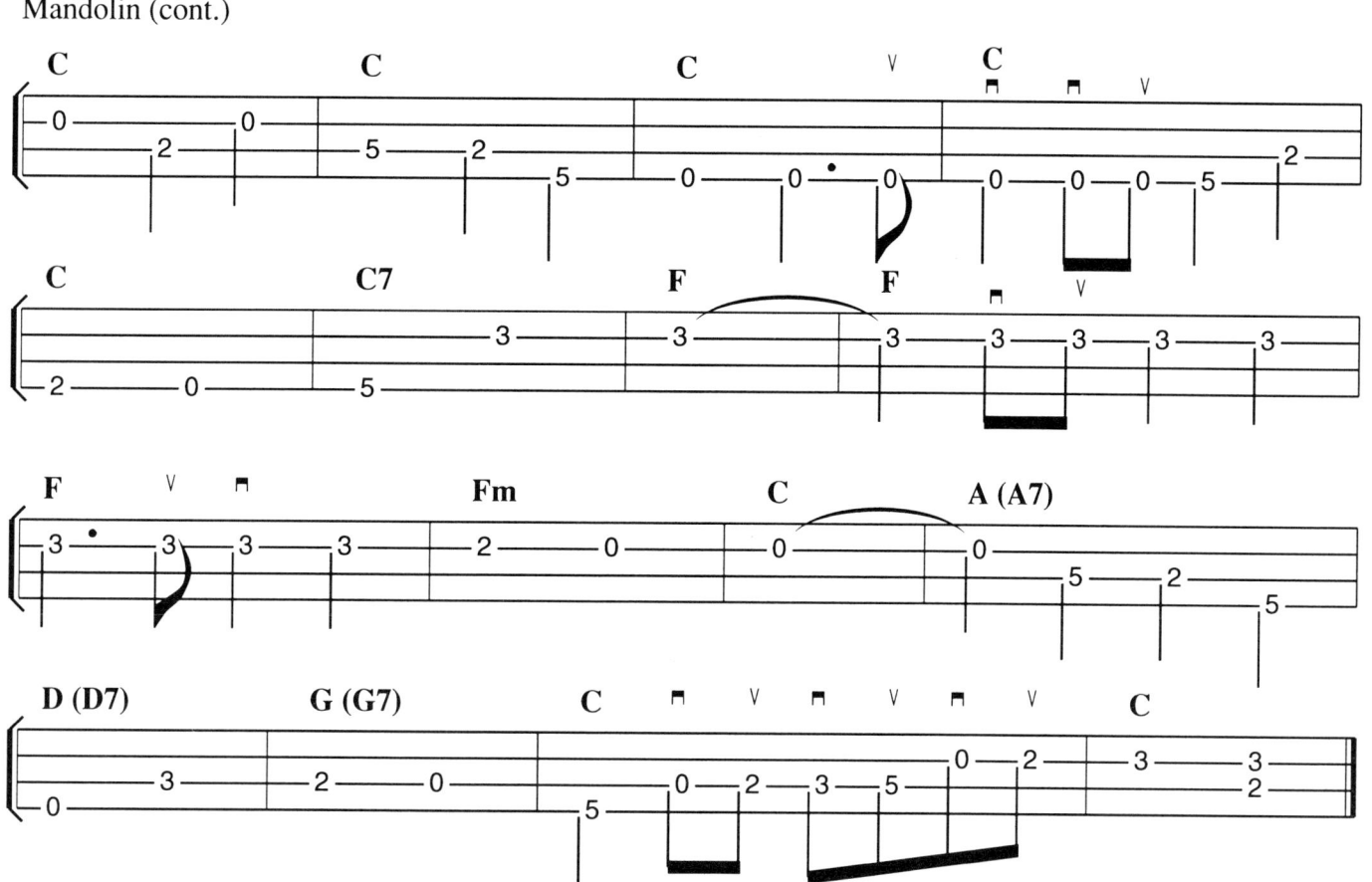

Disc 3
Track 16

Whiskey Before Breakfast

Mandolin 1 (melody)

Scottish

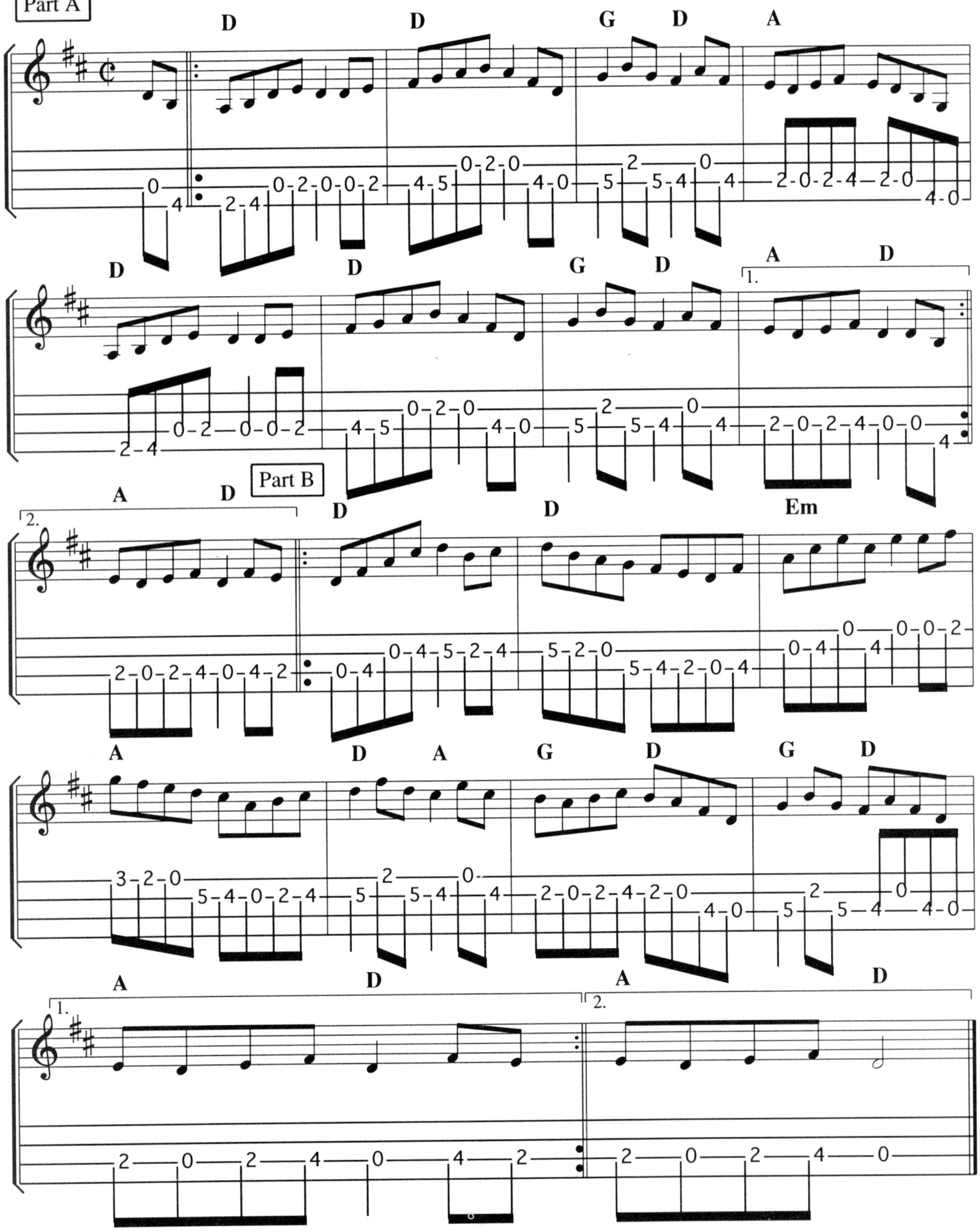

Whiskey Before Breakfast

Mandolin 1 (harmony)

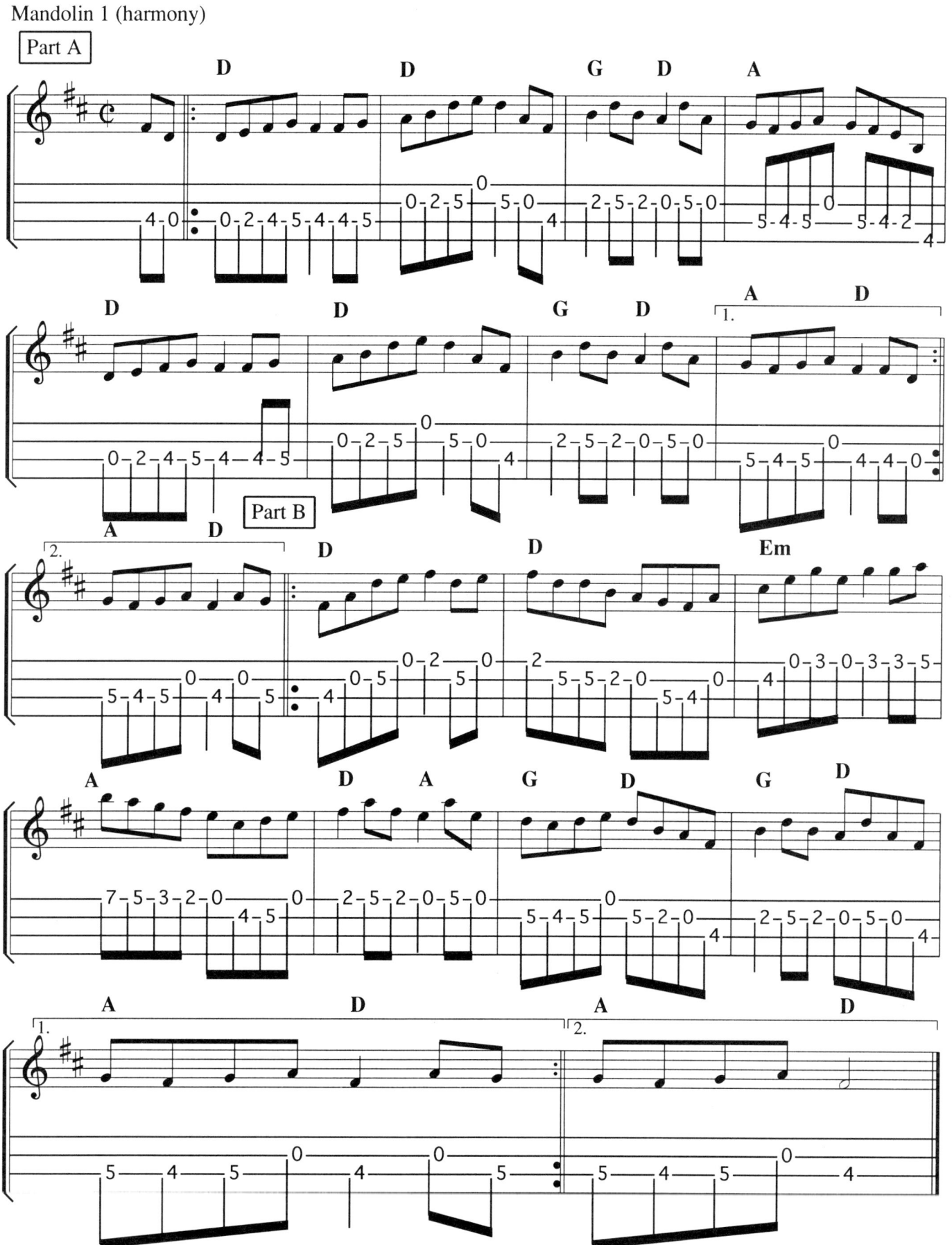

Whiskey Before Breakfast

Whiskey Before Breakfast

Mandolin 2 (intro)

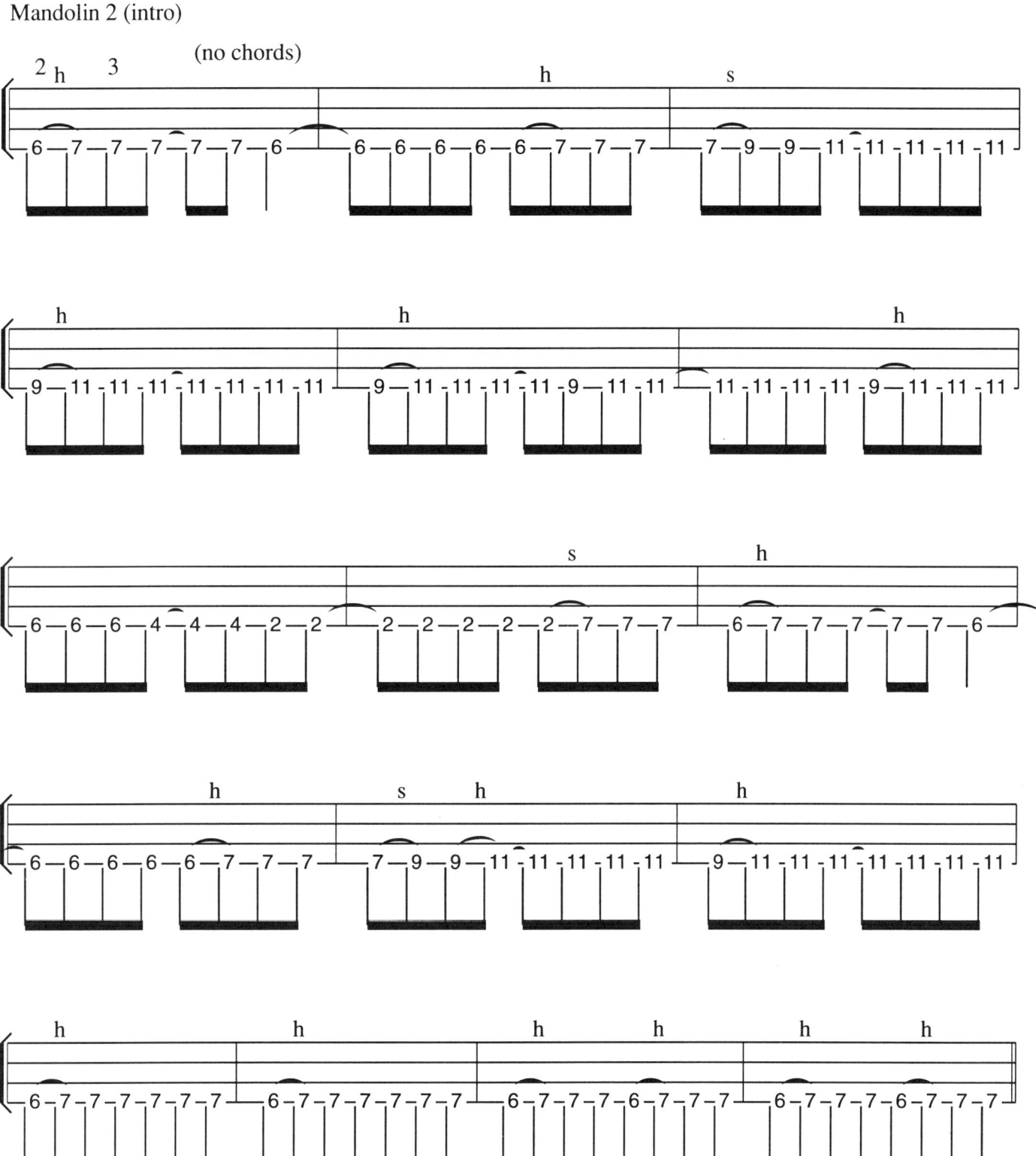

Whiskey Before Breakfast

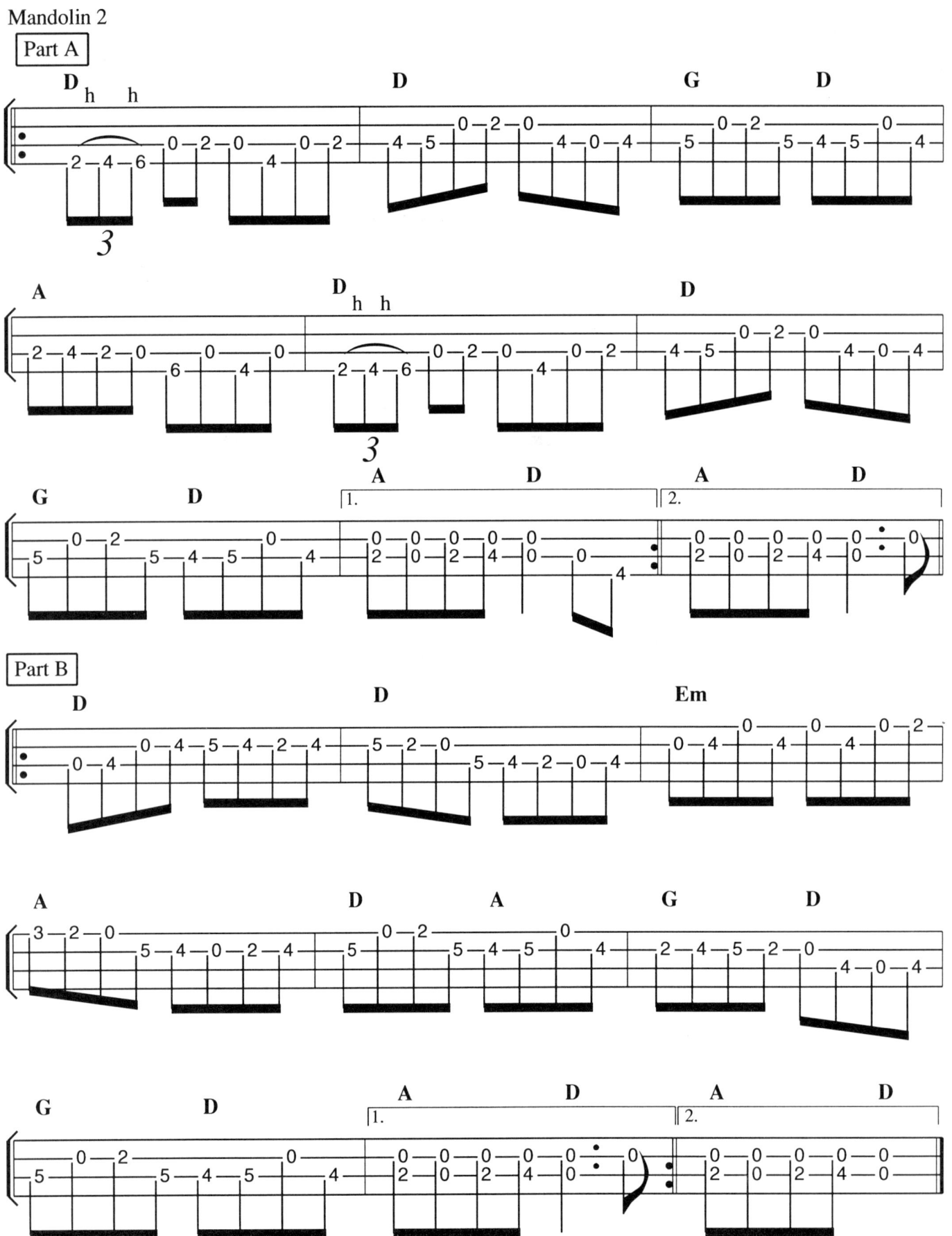

Appendix

Picking

In order to pick the mandolin with speed, it is absolutely necessary to pick correctly. Picking should always go in a down/up motion. The down beats (or on beats) within every measure should always be picked down with the up-beats (or off beats) always being picked up. There are only 2 times when this down-up pattern does not apply: 1) with jigs that use eighth notes in sets of six and 2) with crosspicking patterns (see exercise 10).

The symbol for picking down (toward the ground) is: ⊓

The symbol for picking up (toward the sky) is: V

Holding the pick

It is important that you hold the pick in a way that is comfortable to you. Some people choose to hold the pick between their thumb and their index (pointer) finger with the index finger curled up like a cinnamon roll. Other people choose to place the pick between the thumb and both the index and middle fingers with neither finger rolled up. Some people prefer to place the pick between the thumb and curled up index finger, only with the whole hand rolled up into a fist. Try different ways until you feel comfortable with "your" way of holding the pick.

IMPORTANT NOTE: 5 tunes in this book show detailed picking for every note on every string. These tunes are: *Bonaparte's Retreat 1* and *2*, *Cripple Creek 1* and *2*, *Devil's Dream* (melody and harmony), *Mississippi Sawyer* melody and *Old Joe Clark 1* and *2*. It would be a good idea to learn these simpler variations before moving on to more difficult versions. The remaining tunes show the picking direction for only the trickiest picking sections. The following pages show exercises that are intended to prepare the picking hand for the tunes in this book. Be Sure to work these exercises thoroughly.

Chords and Rhythm

Chords are a very vital part of mandolin playing. When you aren't playing notes, you will likely play chords in a particular rhythm. It is usually necessary to emphasize the offbeat of every beat. Many mandolin players focus on the offbeat by striking the chord with power. Some mandolin players also strum chords similar to the way a guitar player does. In other words, they pick the lowest string lightly on the on beat, then pick across every string boldly on the offbeat. This creates a "pick-strum" pattern. You should learn to play both ways in order to prepare yourself for differing music styles.

Most of the tunes in this book are played in cut time. Cut time means that there are 2 beats in every measure. Each of these beats is equivalent to 1 pick-strum. Therefore, each measure, which contains 2 beats, has 2 pick-strums (and 2 off beats).

Moving from chord to chord

The most difficult part of playing chords is getting the fingering hand to move from one chord to the next chord rapidly. Since chords are made up of several notes played at once, it becomes necessary to use more than one finger to play a chord. Making several fingers move quickly from one position to a completely new position requires practice. The exercise that will best help this ability to develop is one that forces the fingers to move quickly from chord to chord. The following exercise steps will prove very helpful:

Step 1:   Learn the open version of the following 5 chords (A, D, G, C, E).

Step 2:   Place the fingers on the first chord "A."

Step 3:   With someone's help, or with a clock in front of you, see how many times you can play all 5 chords in the space one 1 minute. You can pick-strum each chord, or to move even faster, simply strum each chord once.

Step 4:   Count your results. If you were able to play all 5 chords 6 times plus 3 chords of a 7th time, you got a score of 6.3. If you were able to play all 5 chords 8 times plus 1 chord of a 9th time, you got a score of 8.1. The goal is to get a 12.0 because at 12.0 you are changing chords once every second!

The next step is to attempt this exercise using a variety of chords that include open, full, bar, minor, major, diminished and augmented. You can also practice chords in 'like' groups simply by choosing 5 bar chords or 5 full chords (etc.) to use in your exercise. If you always practice simple and difficult chords you will become efficient at all chords and chord changes.

Chords Diagrams and Sequences

The following pages contain chord charts of some (not all) of the most used and most practical chords for the mandolin. Get to know these chords well and you will be ready for the chord sequences that follow.

Left hand symbols

s = **Slide** -Sliding a finger from a note to a higher note; or sliding from a note to a lower note. The sliding finger should maintain full pressure on the string throughout the slide motion in order for the notes to be loud.

h = **Hammer-on** -Like when a hammer hits a nail, a finger hits a note and makes it ring without being plucked by the pick. The note that is hammered should be as loud as any plucked note.

p = **Pull-off** -This is more like flipping the string with a finger on the fingering hand (as opposed to the picking hand). The note that is pulled-off (or flipped) should be as loud as any plucked note.

b = **Bend** -This is done by bending the string at a particular note (push the string upward and then bring it back into place). If possible, use the ring finger, assisted by the middle and index fingers, to better control the bend. This practice places less strain on the ring finger—especially on acoustic guitars.

Picking Exercises

(Try these exercises on all strings)

Mandolin

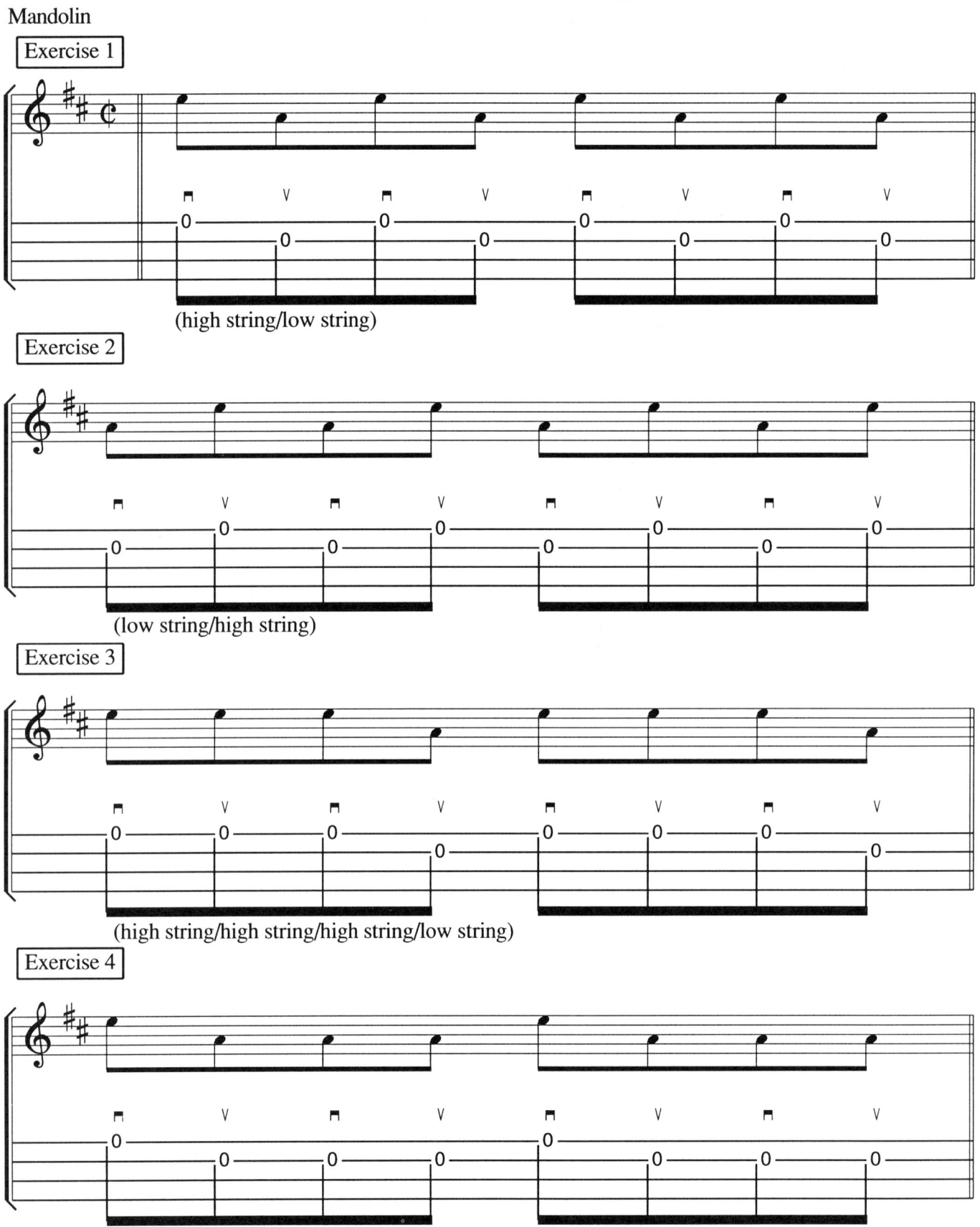

Picking Exercises (cont.)

Mandolin

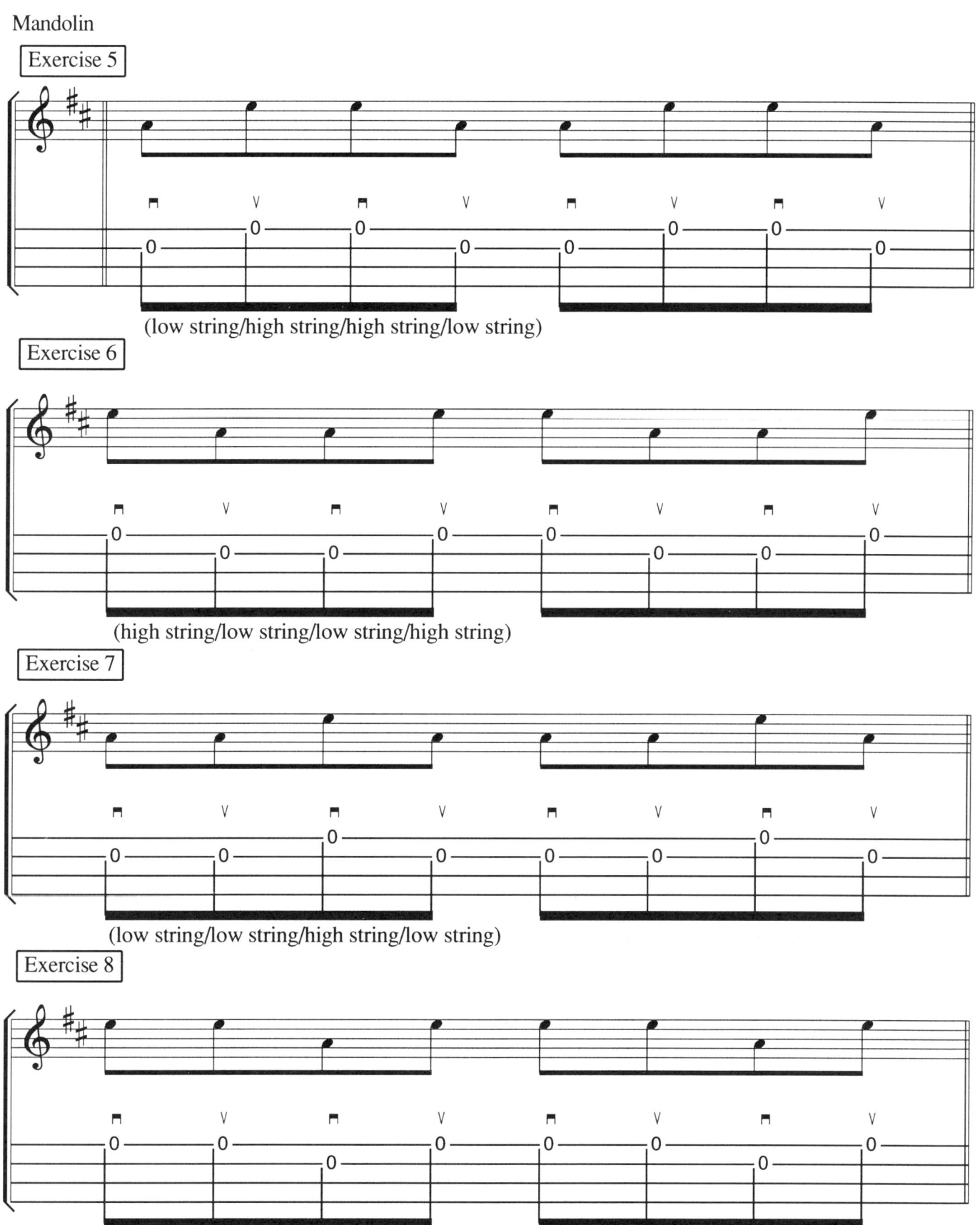

Picking Exercises (cont.)

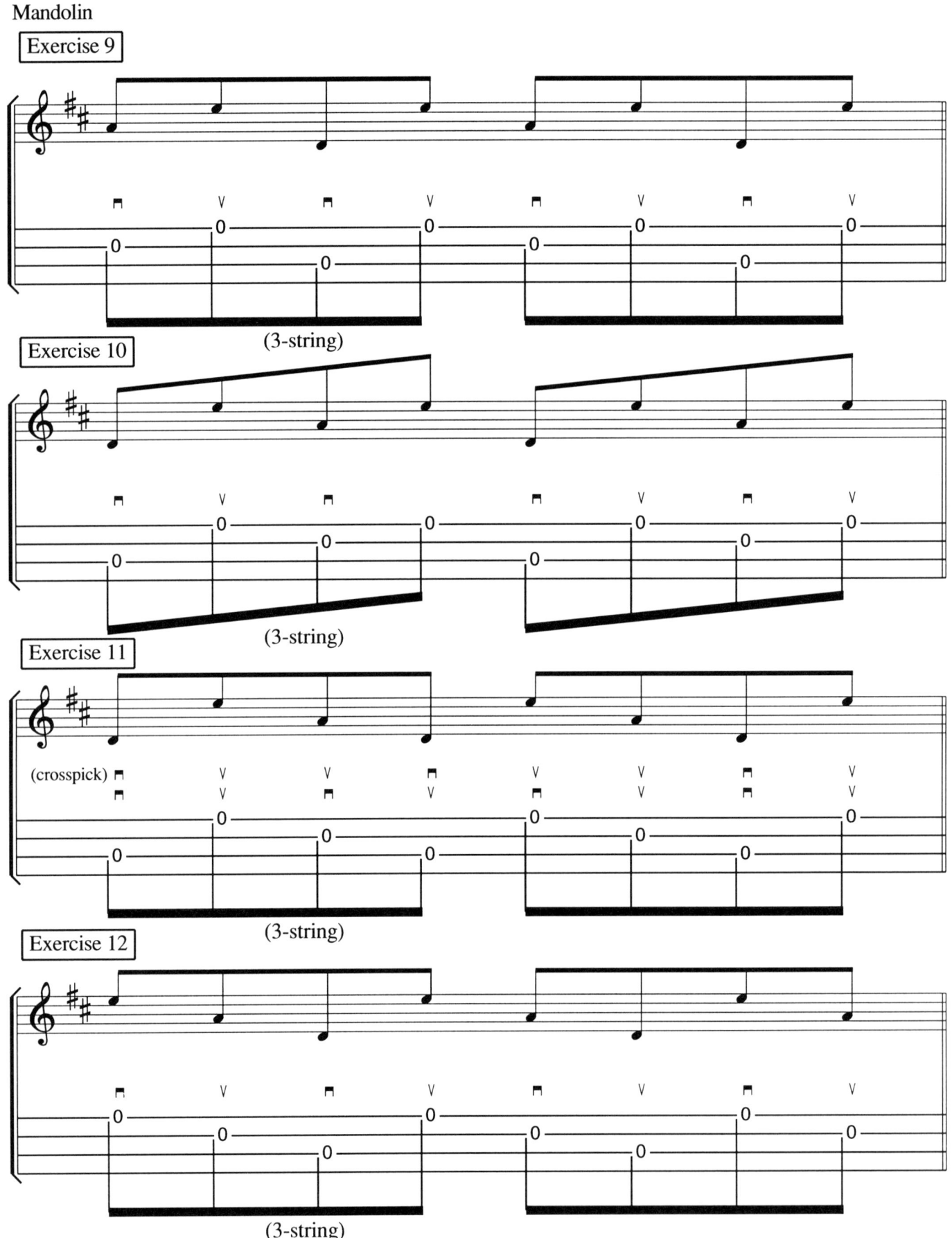

How to Read Mandolin Tablature

(and music and measure symbols)

1. **Each line on a tablature staff represent each set of strings of the mandolin.**

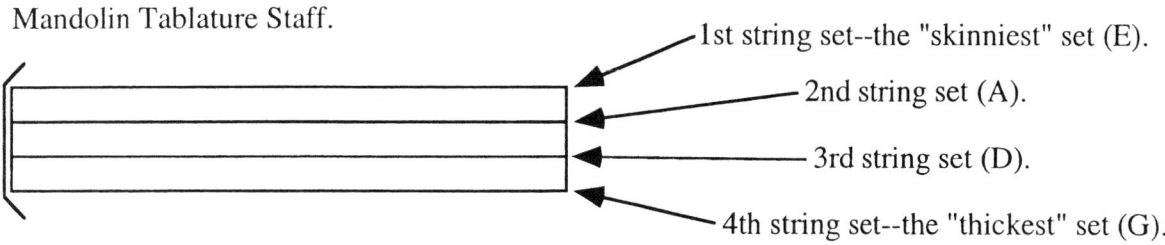

2. **Types of measure lines.**

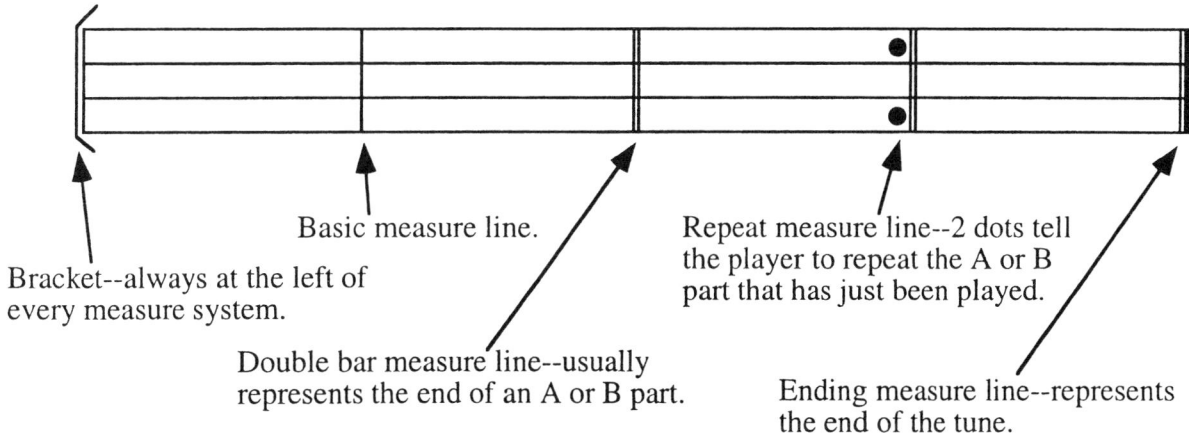

3. **Tablature staff numbers represent <u>fret</u> to be fingered.**

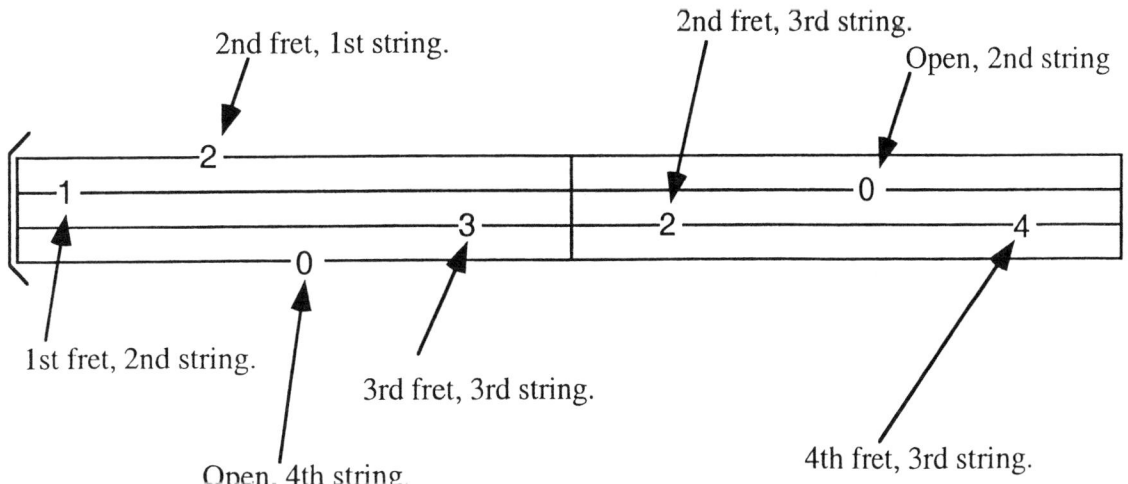

4. Stems, beams and note values.

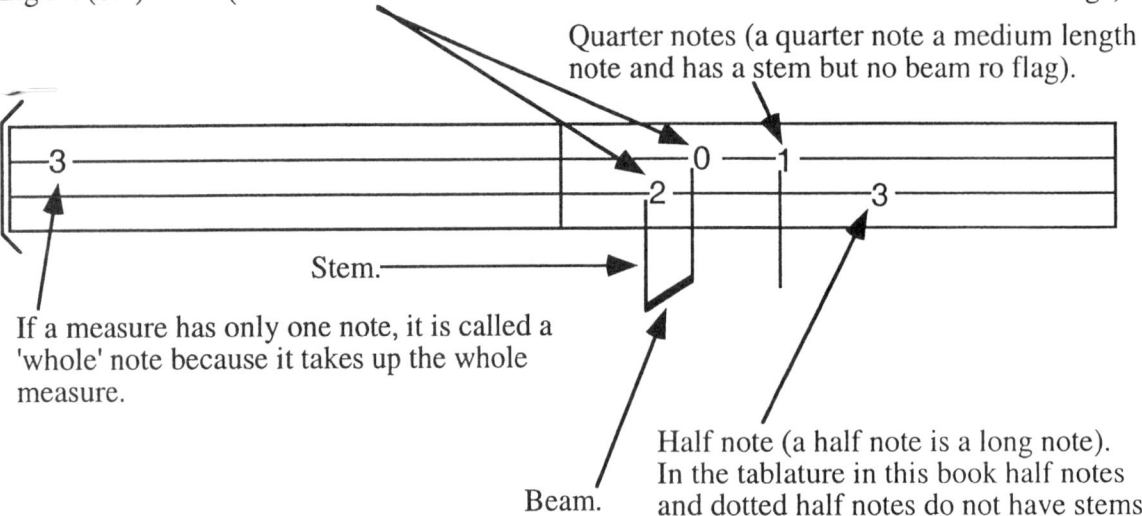

5. Rests (rests tell you to stop playing for a brief time).

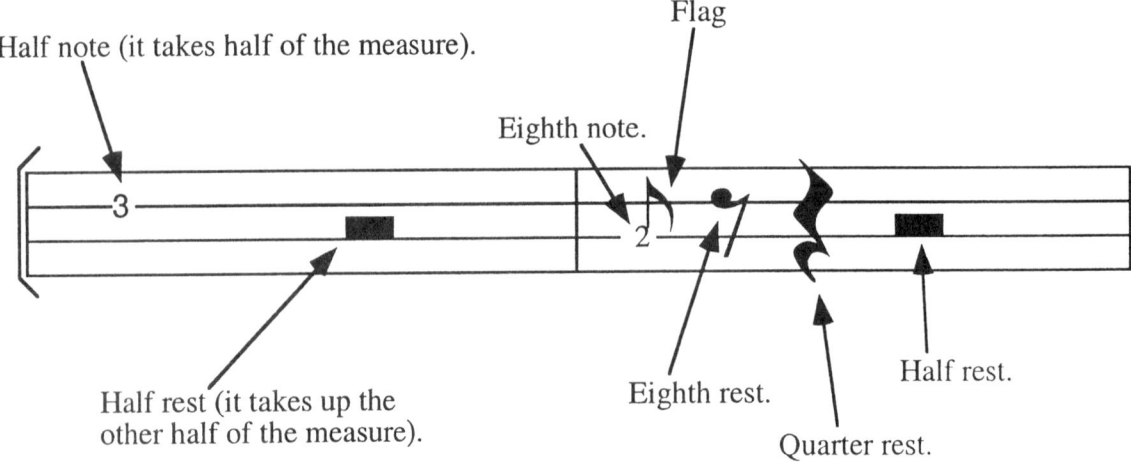

6. Numbers above notes represent which finger is to play the note below.

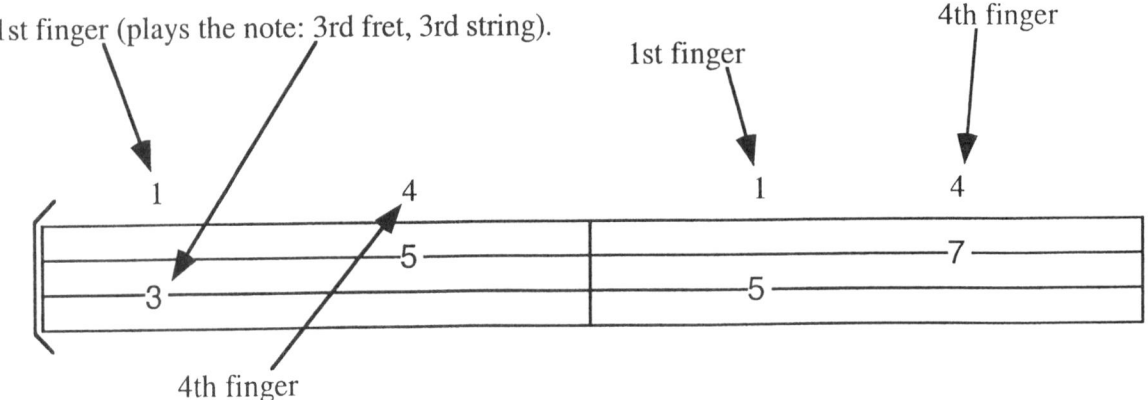

Open Chords

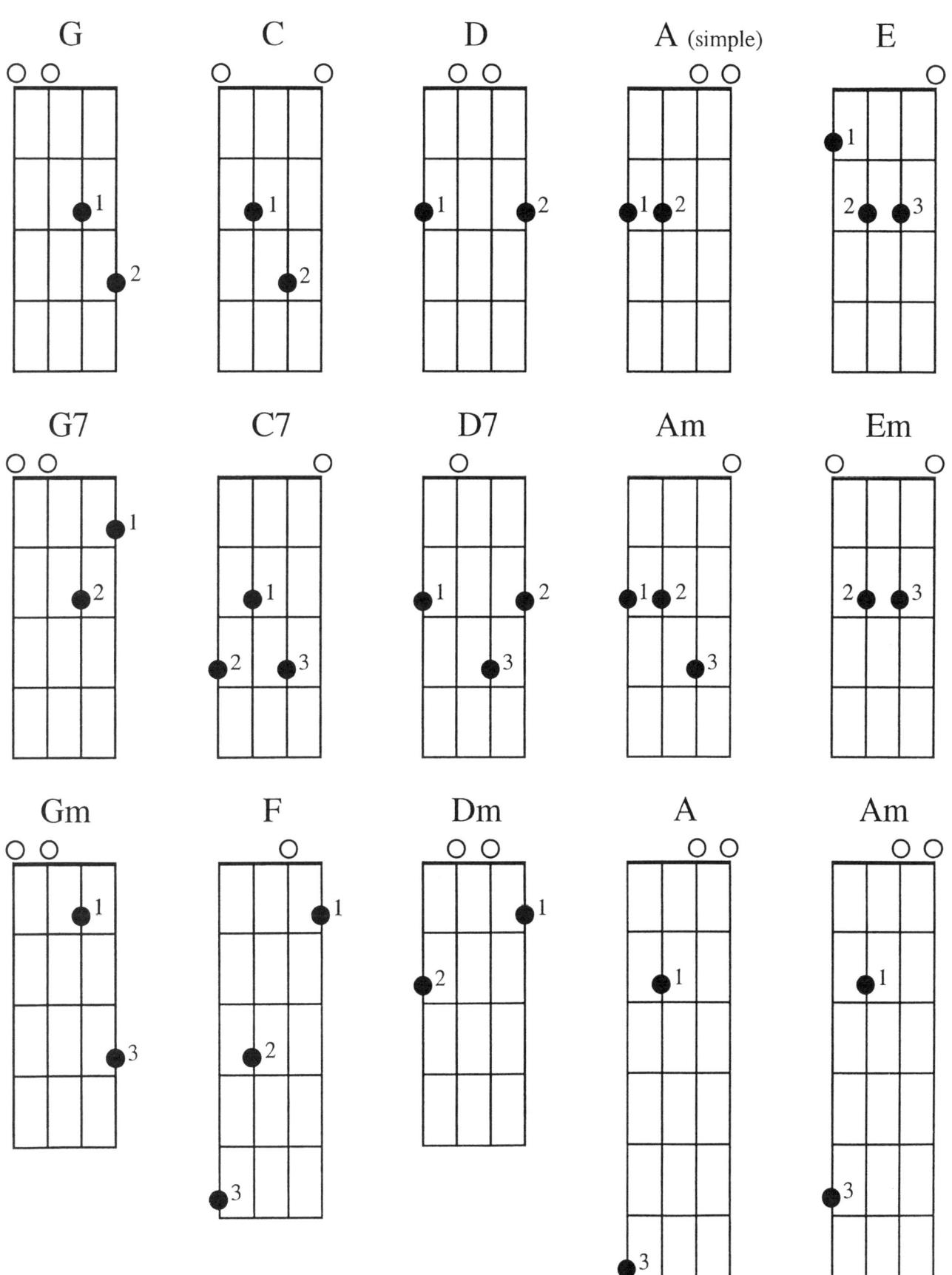

Full Chords (4-finger/3-finger)

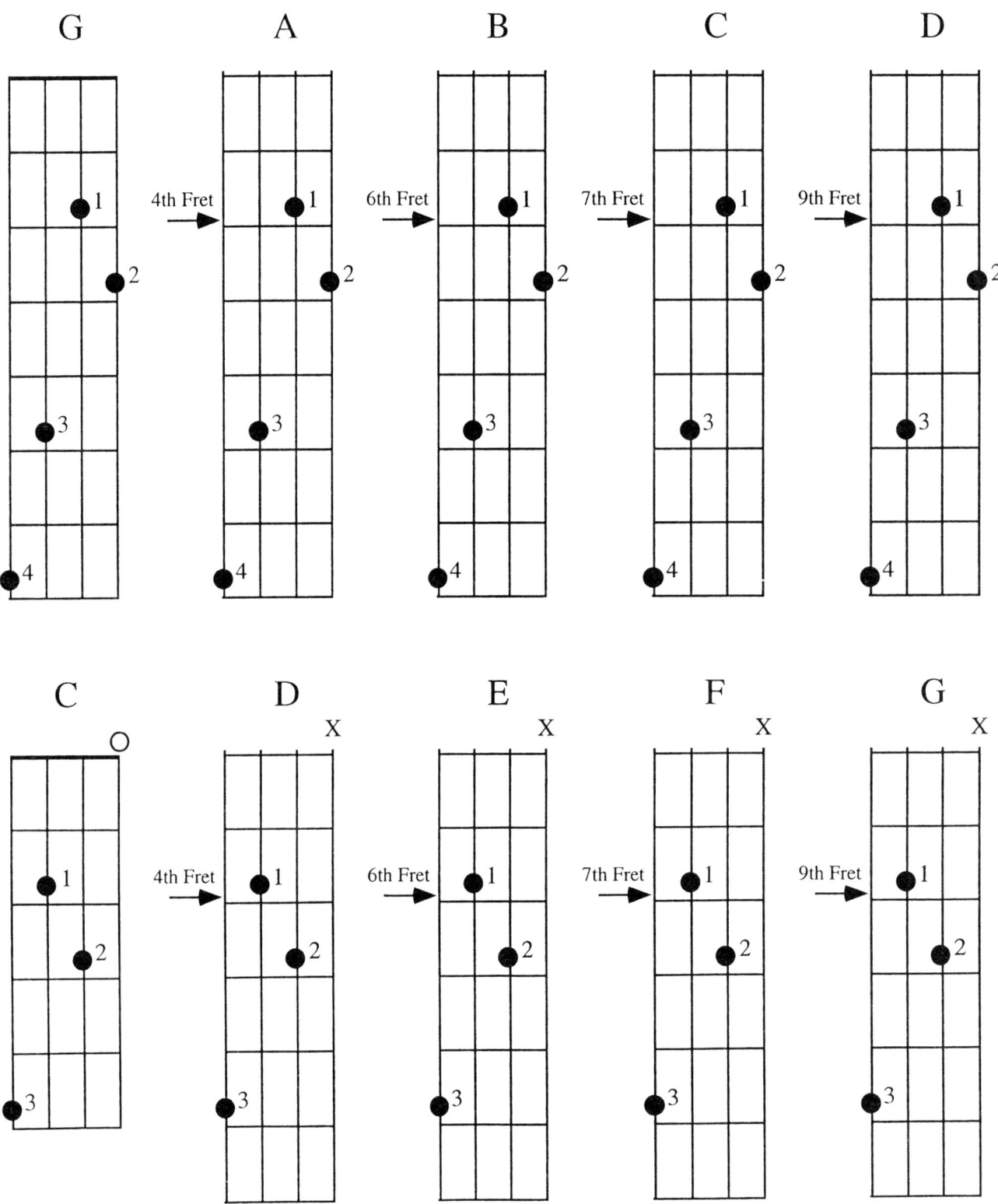

x = mute (do not allow string to vibrate or "ring").

Bar Chords

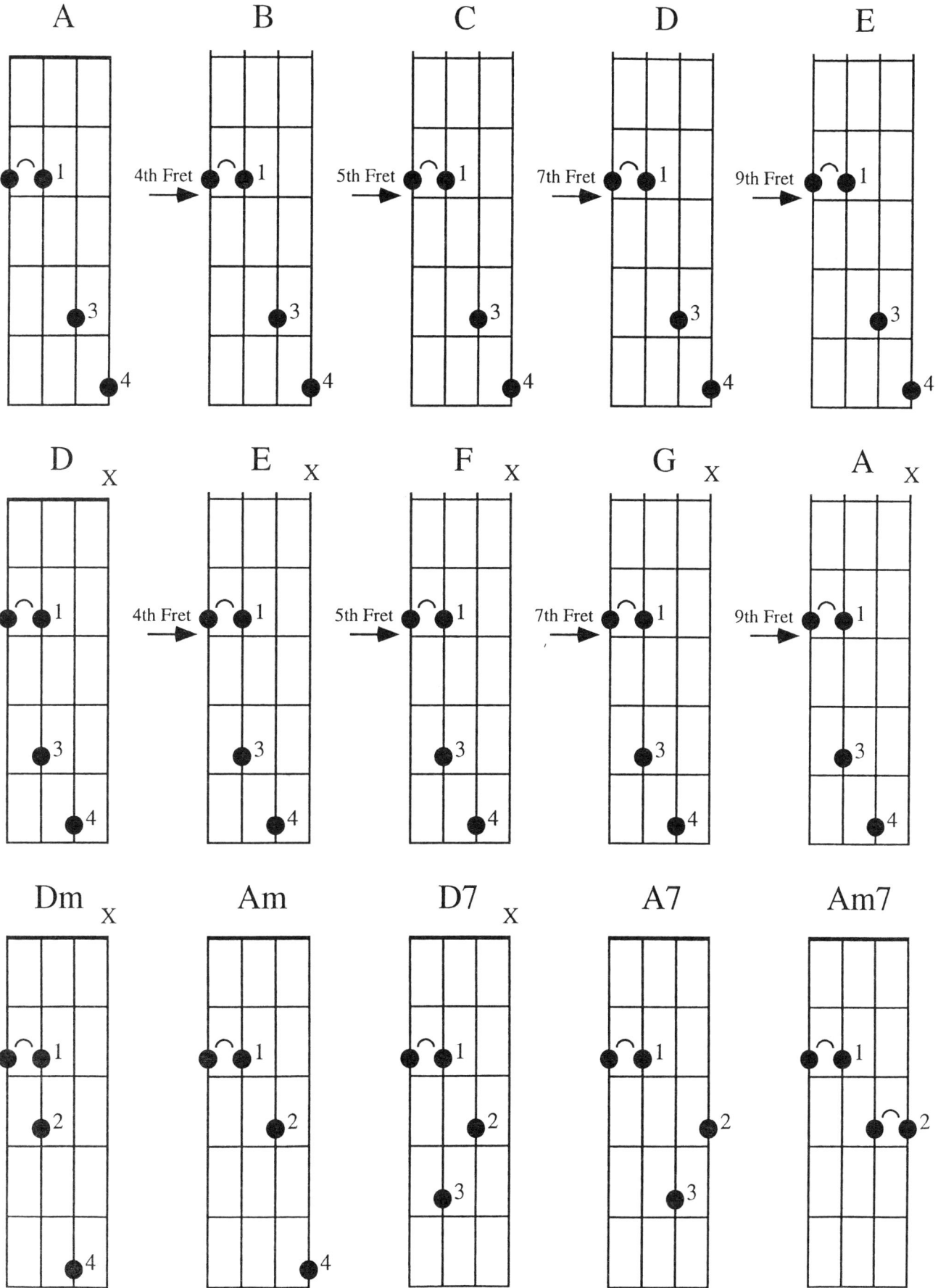

Bar Chords (cont.)

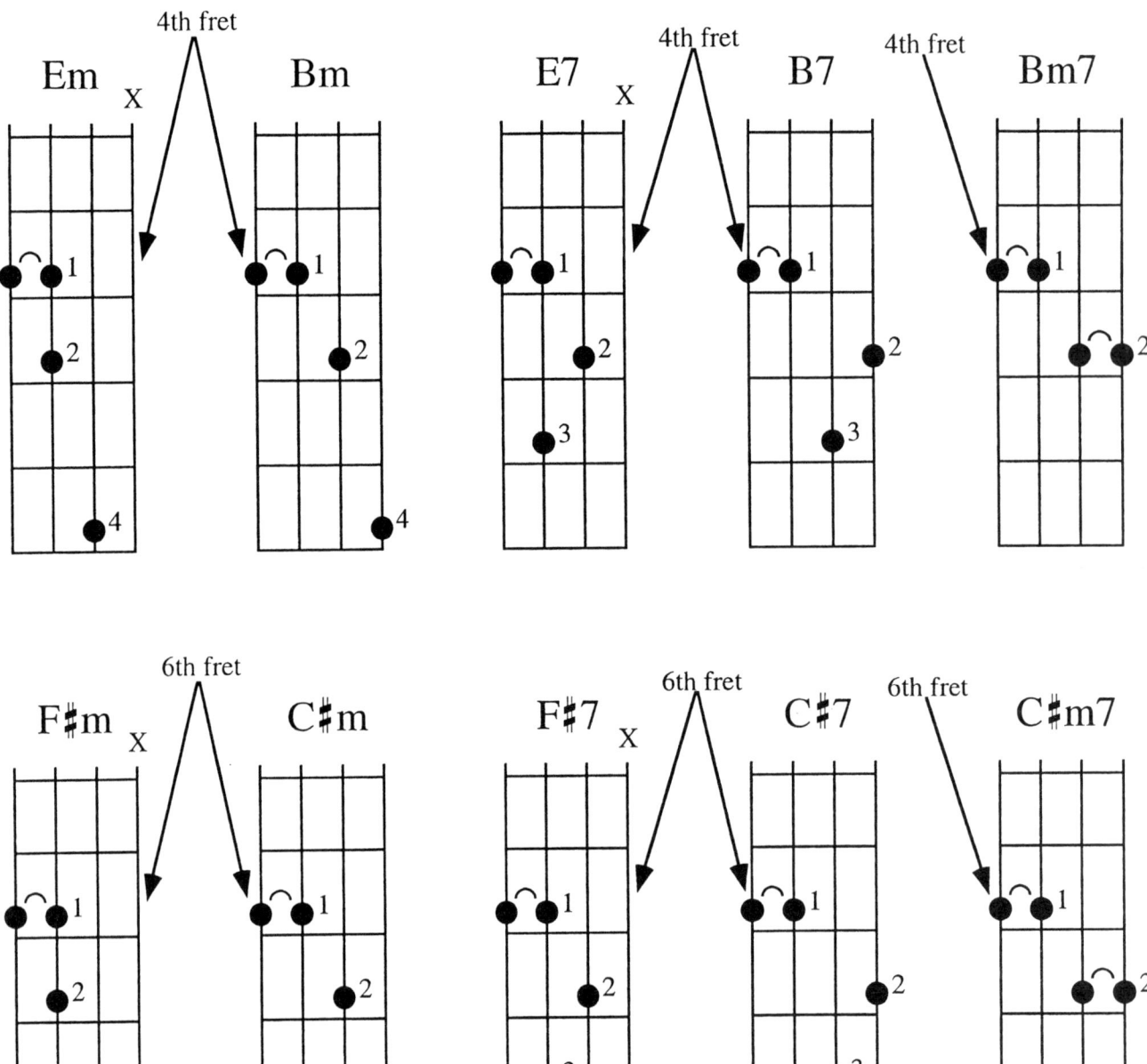

For chords not found in these pages, play the chord nearest to the chord you are seeking and move up or down one fret. For example, Fm is not found in these pages, therefore, an F♯m can be played one fret lower and it becomes an Fm. For a Cm, play the C♯m one fret lower or play the Bm one fret higher. (The Cm chord is barred on the 5th fret).

Bar Chords (sharp/flat)

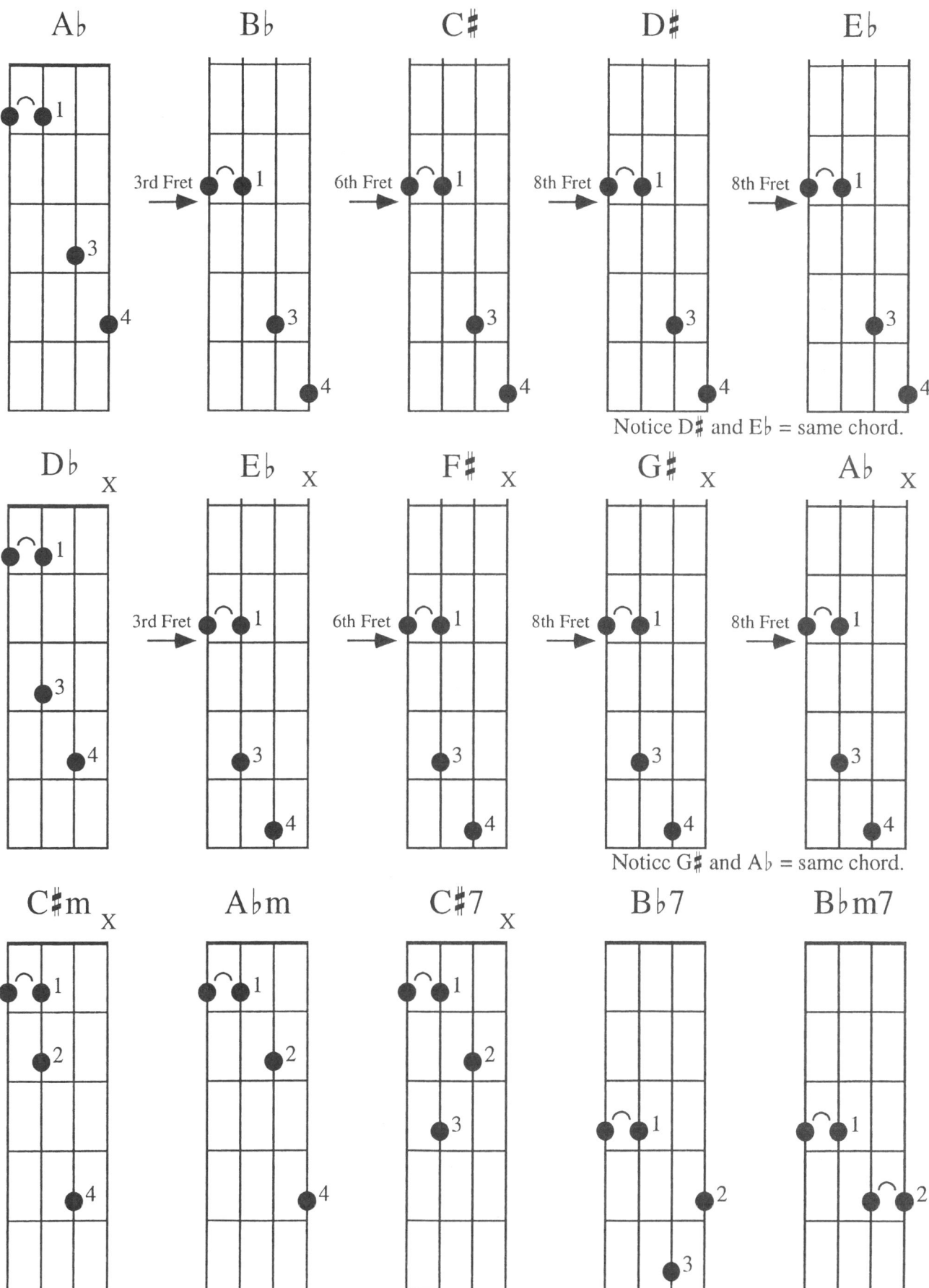

Diminished/Augmented Chords

Diminished 7

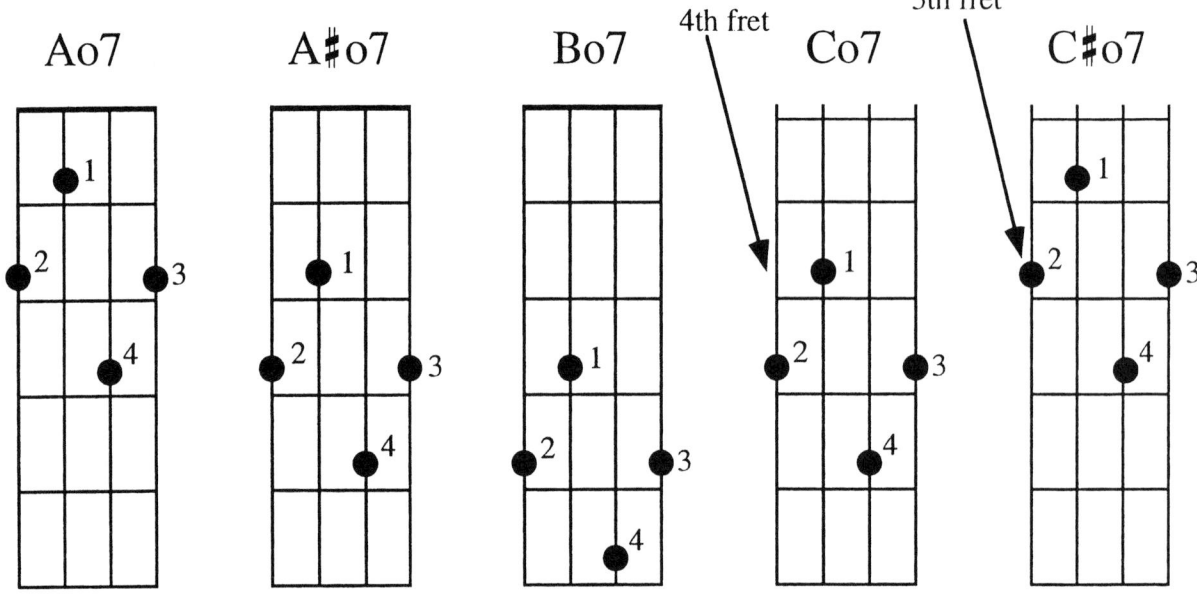

Augmented

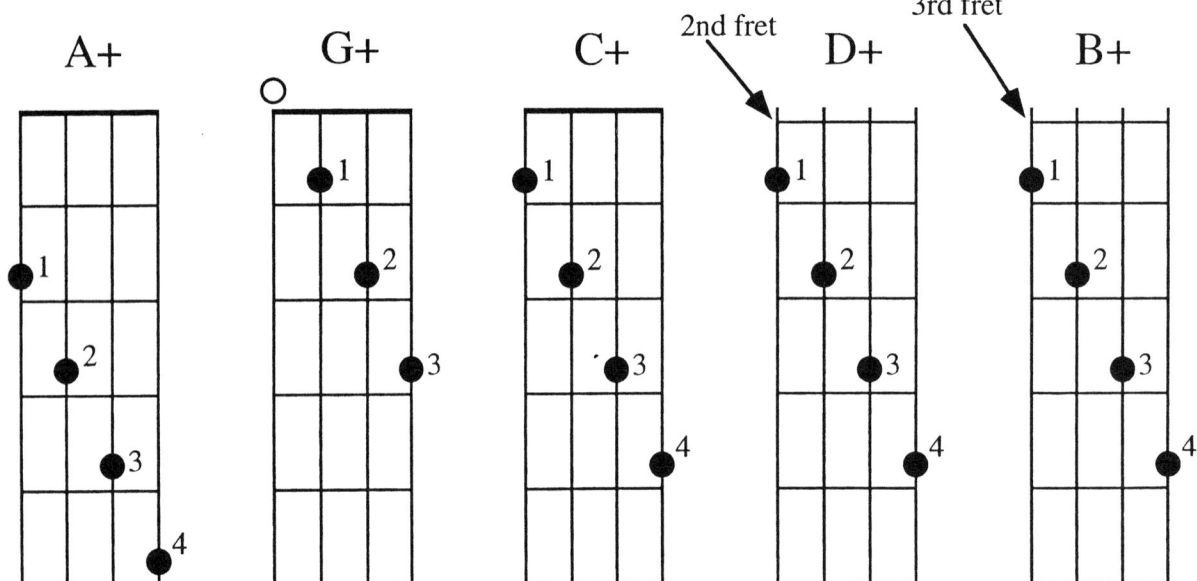

Each diminished 7 chord is actually multiple dim. 7 chords:
Ao7 = D#o7, Ebo7, Co7, F#o7, Gbo7. **A#o7** = Eo7, Bbo7, C#o7, Dbo7, Go7.
Bo7 = Fo7, Do7, G#o7, Abo7. (Every note of a dim. 7 chord counts as the root note for a new dim. 7 chord.)

Unique to the mandolin, the above formation of the aug. chord is actually multiple aug. chords:
A+ = F+, C#+, Db+. **G+** = D#+, Eb+, B+. **C+** = G#+, Ab+, E+, C+. **D+** = A#+, Bb+, F#+, Gb+, D+. **B+** = G+, D#+, Eb+.
(Like the dim. 7 chord, every note of an aug. chord counts as the root note for a new aug. chord.)

(Diminished 7 general rule = 4-note chord: **root, minor 3rd, flat 5th, flat dominant 7th**.)

(Augmented general rule = 3-note chord: **root, major 3rd, sharp 5th**.)

Angus Campbell

Chords
Part A
|: A | A | D A | E |
| A | A | D A | E A :|

Part B
|: A | A | E | E |
| A | A | D A | E A :|

(capo 2)
Part A
|: G | G | C G | D |
| G | G | C G | D G :|

Part B
|: G | G | D | D |
| G | G | C G | D G :|

Arkansas Traveler

Chords
Part A (key of D)
|: D Bm | A D | A | A | D Bm | A D | D G | A D :|

Part B
|: D G | D A | D A | Bm A | D G | D A | D G | A D :|

Fiddle, Mandolin & Bass
Part A (key of C)
|: C Am | G C | G | G | C Am | G C | C F | G C :|

Part B
|: C F | C G | C G | Am G | C F | C G | C F | G C :|

Guitar will use these chords
Part A (key of G – Banjo solo)
|: G Em | D G | D | D | G Em | D G | G C | D G :|

Part B
|: G C | G D | G D | Em D | G C | G D | G C | D G :|

Aura Lee

Chords
4/4
Part A
|: A | D | E7 | A :|

Part B
| A C#7 | F#m |
| D Dm | A |
| A C#o Bm F#m |
| B7 | Bm7 E7 | A |

The Battle Cry of Freedom

Chords
Key of F
Part A
| F | F | B♭ | B♭ | F | F | F | C |
| F | F | B♭ | B♭ | F | F | C | F |

Part B
| F | B♭ | F | F | F | B♭ | F | C |
| F | F | B♭ | B♭ | F | F | C | F |

(capo 5) for Key of F (C position)
Part A
| C | C | F | F | C | C | C | G | C | C | F | F | C | C | G | C |

Part B
| C | F | C | C | C | F | C | G | C | C | F | F | C | C | G | C |

Key of G
Part A
| G | G | C | C | G | G | G | D |
| G | G | C | C | G | G | D | G |

Part B
| G | C | G | G | G | C | G | D |
| G | G | C | C | G | G | D | G |

Beaumont Rag

Chords
Key of F
Parts A & B

: C7	C7	F	F
C7	C7	F	F
C7	C7	F	F7
B♭	F D7	G7 C7	F :

Key of C
Parts A & B

: G7	G7	C	C
G7	G7	C	C
G7	G7	C	C7
F	C A7	D7 G7	C :

Billy in the Lowground

Chords
Part A

|: C | C | Am | Am |
| C | C | Am | G C :|

Part B

|: C | C | Am | F |
| C | C | Am | G C :|

Blackberry Blossom

Chords
Part A

|: G D | C G | C G | A D |
| G D | C G | C G | D G :|

Part B

|: Em | Em | Em | B7 |
| Em | Em | C G | D G :|

Bonaparte's Retreat

Chords
Part A

|: D | D | D | D :|

Part B (melody 1 -simple)

| D | D | A | A |
| D | D | A | D |

Part B (melody 2 -fancy)

|: D | A | D | A D :|

Carthage Waltz

Chords
Part A

G	D	C	G
Am	Bm	Am7	D
G	*D D G	Am7	D

Part B

*G C C	G	*G D D	G
G	C	G	Em
Am	G	D	G

*1 strum per chord (all other chords: pick/strum/strum)

Cherokee Shuffle

Chords
Part A

|: A | A | A | F#m |
| D | A | D E | A :|

Part B

|: D | A | D | A | D | A |
| A | F#m | D E | A :|

(capo 2)
Part A

|: G | G | G | Em |
| C | G | C D | G :|

Part B

|: C | G | C | G | C | G |
| G | Em | C D | G :|

Cluck Old Hen

Chords
Part A
|: A | A D | A | E A :|
Part B
|: A | A G | A | E A :|
(capo 2)
Part A
|: G | G C | G | D G :|
Part B
|: G | G F | G | D G :|

Cotton-eyed Joe

Chords
Key of A
Part A
|: A | A D | A | E A :|
Part B
|: A | A | A | E A :|
Key of G (or Capo 2 for key of A)
Part A
|: G | G C | G | D G :|
Part B
|: G | G | G | D G :|
Key of D
Part A
|: D | D G | D | A D :|
Part B
|: D | D | D | A D :|

Cotton Patch Rag

Chords
Parts A & E
| C | C7 | F F/E | F/E♭ D | G | G | C | G |
| C | C7 | F F/E | F/E♭ D | G | G | G | C |
Part B (can be used as Parts A and B for Guitar, Mandolin & Banjo)
| C | C7 | F | F | G | G | C | G |
| C | C7 | F | F | G | G | G | C |
Part C
| Am | Am | Dm | Dm | G | G | C | G |
| Am | Am | Dm | Dm | G | G | G | C |
Part D
| A7 | A7 | D7 | D7 | G | G | C | G |
| A7 | A7 | D7 | D7 | G | G | G | C |
Part F
| C | C | B | B | Dm | Dm | C | G |
| C | C | B | B | Dm | Dm | G | C |

Cripple Creek

Chords
Part A
|: A | D A | A | E A :|
Part B
|: A | A | A | E A :|
(capo 2)
Part A
|: G | C G | G | D G :|
Part B
|: G | G | G | D G :|

Devil's Dream

Chords
Part A & B (key of D)
|: D | D | Em | Em |
| D | D | G D | A D :|

Fiddle parts
Parts A & B (key of G)
|: G | G | Am | Am |
| G | G | C G | D G :|

Guitar and 1st Mandolin part
Parts A & B (key of A)
|: A | A | Bm | Bm |
| A | A | D A | E A :|

2nd Mandolin part
For chords on Banjo, use key of G chords
(w/capo 2 for key of A)

Down Yonder

Chords
G	G	G	G
C	C	C	C
G	G	G	G
G	G	G	G
A	A	A	A
D (tacet)	(cont.)	D (tacet)	(cont.)
G	G	G	G
C	C	C	C
G	G	G	G
A	D	G	G

Eighth of January

Chords
Key of D
Part A
|: D | G | A | D :|
Part B
|: D | D | D | A D :|
(capo 2)
Part A
|: C | F | G | C :|
Part B
|: C | C | C | G C :|

Chords (Texas-style)
Key of D
Part A
|: D | G | A | D :|
Part B
D F#o	G G#o	D	A D
D F#o	G G#o
A Bo	C#o D
(capo 2)
Part A
|: C | F | G | C :|
Part B
| C Eo | F F#o | C | G |
| C Eo | F F#o | G Ao | Bo C |

Forked Deer

Chords
Part A
|: D | G A | D | A |
| D | G A | D G | A D :|

Part B
|: A | A | A | D |
| A | A | D G | A D :|

(capo 2)
Part A
|: C | F G | C | G |
| C | F G | C F | G C :|

Part B
|: G | G | G | C |
| G | G | C F | G C :|

Gardenia Waltz

Chords
3/4
Key of G (1st part)
G	Bm	Em	G	G	Bm	Am7	D
Am	AmM7	Am7	Am6
D	D+	G	D
G	Bm	Em	G	G	G7	C	Am
C	Cm	G	E7	Am7	D	G	G

Key of D (2nd part)
D	Bm	F#m	Bm	D	D#o
Em7	A7	Em	C	D	A7	A
A/C#	D	A
D	Bm	F#m	Bm	D	D7	G
Em	G	Gm	D	B7	Em7	A7
D	D

Grandfather's Clock

Chords
Part A
| G | D | G | C | G | D | G | D | | G | D | G | C | G | D | G | G |

Part B
G	G	C	G
G	Em	Am7	D
G	D	G	C	G	D	G	G

Part C (Banjo)
|: G | C G | G (tacet) | (tacet cont.) :|
| G | D | G | C | G | D | G | G |

Green Willis

Chords
Part A
:D | D | A | E A |
| D | D | A | D :|

Part B
|: D | D | Em | A |
| D | D G | A | D :|

(capo 2)
Part A
|: C | C | G | D G |
| C | C | G | C :|

Part B
|: C | C | Dm | G |
| C | C F | G | C :|

Indian's Farewell Waltz

Chords
Part A

Dm	Gm	Gm	A
C	C	Dm	A
Dm	C	Dm	Gm
Dm	A	Dm	Dm

Part B

| F | C | F | Gm |
| Dm | C | Dm | Dm |

(capo 5)
Part A

Am	Dm	Dm	E
G	G	Am	E
Am	G	Am	Dm
Am	E	Am	Am

Part B

| C | G | C | Dm |
| Am | G | Am | Am |

Irish Washerwoman

Chords (6/8)
Part A

|: G | G | D | D |
| G | G | C D | G :|

Part B

: G	G	D	D
C G	C G
C D	G :

La Bastringue

Chords
Part A

: D	A D	A	D
D	A D
G	A D :

Part B (repeat 1st line 2 times)

|: D | C | D | A D :|
| D | C | D G | A D |

Leather Britches

Chords
Part A

|: G | G | G | D |
| G | G | D | D G :|

Part B

|: G | C | G | D |
| G | C | D | D G :|

Texas-style
Parts A & B

: G Bo	C7 C#o
G Bo	D
G Bo	C7 C#o
D Eo	F#o G :

Liberty

Chords
Part A
|: D | D | G | G |
| D | D | A | D :|
Part B
|: D | D | D | A |
| D | D | A | D :|
(capo 2)
Part A
|: C | C | F | F |
| C | C | G | C :|
Part B
|: C | C | C | G |
| C | C | G | C :|

Martin's Waltz

Chords
3/4
Part A
D	F#7	G	E7
A7	A7	D	A7
D	F#7	G	E7
A7	A7	D	D
Part B
A	C#m	F#m	A
E7	E7	A	E7
A	C#m	F#m	A
E7	E7	A	A7	(Return to Part A)

Mason's Apron

Chords
Parts A & B
|: A | A | Bm | Bm |
| A | A | D | E A :|
(capo 2)
Parts A & B
|: G | G | Am | Am |
| G | G | C | D G :|

Mississippi Hornpipe

Chords
Part A
|: G | C | G | D |
| G | C | D | G :|
Part B
: G D	Em Bm
C G	Am D
G D	Em Bm
C G	D G :

Mississippi Sawyer

Chords
Part A
|: D | D | G | G |
| D | D | A | D :|
Part B
|: D | D | A | A |
| D | D | A | D :|

Old Dan Tucker

Chords
Part A
|: C | C | C | G C :|
Part B
|: C | F | G | C :|

Old Joe Clark

Chords
Parts A & B
|: A | A | A | G |
| A | A | A G | A :|
(capo 2)
Parts A & B
|: G | G | G | F |
| G | G | G F | G :|

President Garfield's Hornpipe

Chords
Part A
|: B♭ | B♭ | F | F |
| B♭ | B♭ | F | B♭ :|
Part B
|: E♭ | B♭ | F | B♭ |
| E♭ | B♭ | F | B♭ :|
(capo 3)
Part A
|: G | G | D | D |
| G | G | D | G :|
Part B
|: C | G | D | G |
| C | G | D | G :|

Pretty Peg

Chords
Part A
| D | D A | Bm | A |
| Bm A | G A | G | A |
Part B
D D/C♯	D/B A	D	D A
D D/C♯	D/B A
Bm G	A D
(capo 2)
Part A
| C | C G | Am | G | Am G | F G | F | G |
Part B
| C C/B | Am G | C | C G |
| C C/B | Am G | Am F | G C |

Red-haired Boy

Chords
Part A
|: A | A D | A | G |
| A | A D | A | E A :|
Part B
|: G | D | A | G |
| A | A D | A | E A :|
(capo 2)
Part A
|: G | G C | G | F |
| G | G C | G | D G :|
Part B
|: F | C | G | F |
| G | G C | G | D G :|

Red Wing

Chords
Part A

G	G	C	G
D	G	A	D
G	G	C	G
D	G	A D	G

Part B

C	C	G	G
D	D	G	G7
C	C	G	G
D	D	G	G

College Hornpipe

Chords
Part A

|: B♭ | B♭ | C | F |
| B♭ Do | D♯7 Eo | F | B♭ :|

Part B

|: B♭ | E♭ | C | F |
| B♭ Do | D♯7 Eo | F | B♭ :|

(capo 3)
Part A

|: G | G | A | D |
| G Bo | C7 C♯o | D | G :|

Part B

|: G | C | A | D |
| G Bo | C7 C♯o | D | G :|

Sailor's Hornpipe

Chords
Part A

G	G	A	D
G Em	C Am
G D	G

Part B

G	C	A	D
G Em	C Am
G D	G

Saint Anne's Reel

Chords
Part A

|: D | D | G | D |
| D | D | G A | D :|

Part B

|: D | Em | A | D |
| Bm | Em | A | D :|

(capo 2)
Part A

|: C | C | F | C |
| C | C | F G | C :|

Part B

|: C | Dm | G | C |
| Am | Dm | G | C :|

Sally Ann

Chords
Part A
|: A | D | D | A |
| A | Bm | E | A :|

Part B (repeat 3 times)
|: A | Bm | E | A :|

(capo 2)
Part A
|: G | C | C | G |
| G | Am | D | G :|

Part B (repeat 3 times)
|: G | Am | D | G :|

Sally Goodin'

Chords
Parts A & B
|: A | A | A | E A | A | A | A | E A :|

(capo 2)
Parts A & B
|: G | G | G | D G | G | G | G | D G :|

Texas-style
Parts A & B
: A C#o	D7 D#o
A C#o	E
A C#o	D7 D#o
E F#o	G#o A :

(capo 2)
Parts A & B
|: G Bo | C7 C#o | G Bo | D |
| G Bo | C7 C#o | D Eo | F#o G :|

Sally Johnson

Chords
A part
|: G | G | G | D |
| G | G | D | D G :|

B part
|: G | C | G | G Em |
| G | C | D | D G :|

Texas-style
Part A
|: G Bo | C7 C#o | G Bo | B♭o Ao |
| G Bo | C7 C#o | D Eo | F#o G :|

Part B
|: G Bo | C7 C#o | G Bo | G Em |
| G Bo | C7 C#o | D Eo | F#o G :|

Salt Creek

Chords
Part A
|: A | A D | G | G E |
| A | A D | G | E A :|

Part B
|: A | A | G | G |
| A | A | G | E A :|

(capo 2)
Part A
|: G | G C | F | F D |
| G | G C | F | D G :|

Part B
|: G | G | F | F | G | G | F | D G :|

Soldier's Joy

Chords
Part A
|: D | D | D | A |
| D | D | DA | D :|
Part B
|: D | G | D | A |
| D | G | DA | D :|

(capo 2)
Part A
|: C | C | C | G | C | C | CG | C :|
Part B
|: C | F | C | G | C | F | CG | C :|

Swallowtail Jig

Chords
Part A
|: Em | Em | D | D |
| Em | Em | D | Em :|
Part B
: Em	Em
Em	Em D
Em	Em	D	Em :

Temperance Reel

Chords
Part A
|: G | G | Em | Em |
| G | G | Em | D G :|
Part B
: Em	Em	D	D
Em	Em
Em	D G :

Tom & Jerry

Chords
Parts A & B (simple)
|: A | A | A | E | A | A | A | EA :|
Parts A & B (w/D-chord)
|: A | D | A | E | A | D | A | EA :|
Parts A & B (w/E-chord 3rd and 7th measures)
|: A | D | E | E | A | D | E | EA :|
Texas-style
Part A & B
|: A C#o | D7 D#o | A C#o | Co Bo |
| A C#o | D7 D#o | E F#o | G#o A :|

(capo 2)
Parts A & B (simple)
|: G | G | G | D | G | G | G | DG :|
Parts A & B (w/C-chord)
|: G | C | G | D | G | C | G | DG :|
Parts A & B (w/D-chord 3rd and 7th measures)
|: G | C | D | D | G | C | D | DG :|
Texas-style
Part A & B
|: G Bo | C7 C#o | G Bo | B♭o Ao |
| G Bo | C7 C#o | D Eo | F#o G :|

Turkey in the Straw

Chords
Key of G
Part A
|: G | G | G | D |
| G | G | G | D G :|
Part B
|: G | G7 | C | C (C#o)* |
| G | G D | G | D G :|
Key of C
Part A
|: C | C | C | G |
| C | C | C | G C :|
Part B
|: C | C7 | F | F (F#o) |
| C | C G | C | G C :|

*chords in parentheses are optional for the measure (these chords can be heard on CD).

Uncle Joe

Parts A and B
|: D | D | D | A | D | D | G | A :|

Under the Double Eagle

Chords
(Guitar solo)
Part A
|: C | C | C | C | G | G | C | C :|
Part B
C	C	C	C	C	C	G	G
G	G	G	G	G	G	C	C
C	C	C	C	C	C7	F	F
F	G#	C	A7	D7	G7	C* C#	D

(Mandolin solo)
Part A
|: G | G | G | G | D | D | G | G :|
Part B
C	C	C	C	C	C	G	G
G	G	G	G	G	G	C	C
C	C	C	C	C	C7	F	F
F	Fm	C	A7	D7	G7	C	C

*If you decide not to change to key of G, end on C chord.

Whiskey Before Breakfast

Chords
Part A
|: D | D | G D | A |
| D | D | G D | A D :|
Part B
|: D | D | Em | A |
| D A | G D | G D | A D :|

(capo 2)
Part A
|: C | C | F C | G |
| C | C | F C | G C :|
Part B
|: C | C | Dm | G |
| C G | F C | F C | G C :|